Sherlock Holmes On the Air

By M J ELLIOTT

Paperback ISBN 9781780921037
ePub ISBN 9781780921044
PDF ISBN 9781780921051

Published in the UK by MX Publishing
335 Princess Park Manor, Royal Drive, London, N11 3GX
www.mxpublishing.com

Cover layout and construction by
www.staunch.com

For my three best girls: Gill, Megan and Martha Rose
And my best boy: Joe

Contents

Acknowledgements

This book would not have been possible without the warm, wonderful, talented people at Imagination Theater: Jim and Pat French, Lawrence Albert, John Patrick Lowrie, Sable Jak, Lee Pasch, Rick May, Dennis Bateman and John Armstrong, among many others. You could do a lot worse than visit www.jimfrenchproductions.com and listen to their most recent shows.

I'd also like to thank Bert Coules, who gave me several pieces of invaluable advice before I set out on this adventures, and David Stuart Davies who, as editor of the much-missed SHERLOCK Magazine, gave me my first break. We all need someone who believes in us.

About the Author

Matthew J Elliott is a writer and radio dramatist living in the United Kingdom.

For the radio, he has scripted episodes of *The Further Adventures of Sherlock Holmes*, *The Classic Adventures of Sherlock Holmes*, *The Twilight Zone*, *Raffles the Gentleman Thief*, *The Father Brown Mysteries*, *Kincaid the Strangeseeker*, *The Adventures of Harry Nile*, *The Perry Mason Radio Dramas*, *Vincent Price Presents*, *Wrath of the Titans*, *Jeeves and Wooster*, *Masters of Mystery* and the Audie Award-nominated *New Adventures of Mickey Spillane's Mike Hammer*. He is the creator of *The Hilary Caine Mysteries*, which first aired in 2005. His stage play *An Evening With Jeeves & Wooster* was performed at the Palace Theatre, Grapevine, Texas in 2007

He has contributed Holmes pastiches to the collections *Curious Incidents 2*, *The Game's Afoot* and *Gaslight Grimoire*. His story *Art in the Blood* can be found in *The Mammoth Book of Best British Crime 8*. Matthew is the editor of *The Whisperer in Darkness*, *The Horror in the Museum* and *The Haunter of the Dark* by H P Lovecraft, *The Right Hand of Doom* and *The Haunter of the Ring* by Robert E Howard, and *A Charlie Chan Omnibus* by Earl Derr Biggers. His articles, fiction and reviews have appeared in the magazines *SHERLOCK*, *Total DVD* and *Scarlet Street*. Once a year, he acts as host of the Sherlock Holmes Society of London's Film Evening.

On the lighter side, Matthew works with the makers of cult sci-fi comedy *Mystery Science Theater 3000* on their RiffTrax website, writing and recording humorous commentaries for hit movies, including, of course, Guy Richie's *Sherlock Holmes*.

Introduction: The Power of the Imagination

For two decades, Sherlock Holmes ruled the airwaves in the United States. Beginning in 1931, the character – and, of course, his faithful friend, Dr John H Watson – were regular guest in American homes via the wireless, with Basil Rathbone and Nigel Bruce taking the lead roles from 1940 to 1946.

With the coming of television however, radio drama more of less died out in the States, and new Holmesian audio material became extremely scarce. The exception to the rule seemed to be the *CBS Radio Mystery Theater* of the 1970s which featured a handful of adaptation of stories from the Canon, most of them featuring *Invasion of the Bodysnatchers* star Kevin McCarthy as Holmes. But the rest was silence.

Until 1998 that is, when the Seattle-based Jim French Productions recorded the first episode of *The Further Adventures of Sherlock Holmes* (not to be confused with the BBC radio series of the same name, which did not air until 2002). *Further Adventures* is one of several rotating drama series produced by French and his associates; new episodes are produced at the rate of roughly one a month. The man behind the series is, naturally, writer/producer Jim French, whose experience in radio dates back to 1943 when he served as announcer and pianist for KPAS in Pasadena. French's credits include scripts for *Dick Powell Theater* and *Suspense*. In the 1980s he began writing and directing a series of weekly dramas for radio station KIRO in Seattle. On 17 March 1996, French's plays were syndicated under the name "Imagination Theater" and American radio drama began its rebirth.

The series came about almost b accident when French's business partner versatile actor/director Lawrence Albert, came across an unfinished Holmes script amongst his colleague's papers. As a Holmes enthusiast Albert was understandably excited by the discovery. "I said to Jim, 'You gotta finish this thing!'" Obtaining the necessary permissions from the Conan Doyle estate did not prove to be a problem, and *The Poet of Death*, the first of many *Further Adventures of Sherlock Holmes* was broadcast on May 17, 1998. For the first time since 1950, when actors Ben Wright and Eric Snowden had taken their last bows, Holmes and Watson had a home on American radio. The new Master Detective was John Gilbert whose delivery put one in mind of the legendary Peter Cushing in the same role. Lawrence Albert, who was struck by the actor's physical resemblance to Holmes suggester Gilbert to Jim French. "Jim said 'What about Watson?'" Albert recollects. "Of course I said 'Me,'" But the actor had a very clear idea of the sort of Watson he wished to be: "Two of the greatest insults to literary characters are the portrayal of Tarzan onscreen and the depiction of Watson as a boob". For his depiction of the good doctor, Albert drew inspiration from his two favourite Watsons, Michael Williams in BBC Radio's complete Canon series and Richard Johnson in the

1991 film *The Crucifier of Blood*. "Johnson to me, looked like Watson as I see him. I'm probably closer to Williams in some respects, but then I bring my own turn to it. Watson has become such a part of me that I can become the character without any trouble at all. I wanted Watson to be real. I wanted people to experience who he really is."

With Lee Paasch and Rick May providing sterling support as Mrs Hudson and Inspector Lestrade respectively, Gilbert and Albert appeared together in eighteen episodes, notable among them *The Adventure of the Painted Leaf*, in which Holmes is retained by H G Wells to recover the stolen manuscript of *The Time Machine*, and two stories featuring the criminally insane Dr John Bennington, French's Moriarty-like recurring villain. Following the recording of *The Adventure of the Missing Link*, however, John Gilbert decided to retire from the role of Sherlock Holmes, and Jim French was faced with the problem of finding a new actor to replace him. To switch lead actors in mid-run is a hazardous but not necessarily fatal business. True, the Tom Conway/Nigel Bruce partnership during the 1946/7 radio season could not hope to match the natural chemistry between Bruce and his former Holmes, Basil Rathbone. But when Edward Hardwicke replaced David Burke as Watson to Jeremy Brett's Sherlock, the Granada television series enjoyed the same if not greater success. The casting of John Patrick Lowrie as Imagination Theater's second Sherlock Holmes was a natural decision. Lowrie, a towering presence both vocally and physically, served as the announcer on the first twenty episodes as well as providing a variety of additional voices. The easy on-air relationship between Lowrie and Albert ensured that the changeover between Holmeses was a smooth one. "Much of our relationship is similar in real life" Albert notes. "I like to approach Sherlock historically and unreconstructed", explains Lowrie. "He is very definitely a product of his times. Sherlock is the embodiment of the late nineteenth century idea that man's intellect might be capable of conquering nature and solving all of mankind's woes. This was before World War 1 taught Europeans that they might not be as smart as they thought they were and before the environmental problems of the twentieth century thought us that conquering nature might not be that great an idea. At the time Doyle was writing, Europe was a very confident, optimistic and chauvinistic place. Sherlock exudes all of those qualities. It's always tricky for a writer other than Doyle to explore Holmes emotional being and I've been very lucky to work with writers who have been very successful in doing so without creating a kinder, gentler, fuzzy, squishy Holmes. Doyle created a wonderfully complex character. Holmes cares deeply about people and yet has very little patience with them. He is passionate about the just and fair treatment of women and yet has almost no understanding of them and doesn't trust them. He likes human beings a great deal and wants them to succeed, he's generous almost to a fault with his time and is money and yet he is reclusive to the point of being misanthropic. I think I have the most fun with him when writers put him in situation that challenge his

4

intellectual detachment and force him to feel. He must always, however at the end of his musings, remain Holmes: the puzzle solver, the hermit, the Moses who guides others to the promised land but must himself remain always at Baker Street."

And this is the point where *I* come in. My name is Matthew J Elliott, and I'm a writer, based in the United Kingdom. I'd been contributing articles and stories for David Stuart Davies' SHERLOCK Magazine for some years before I stumbled across the Imagination Theater website. In an unusually cocky mood, I sent Jim French a copy of my first published Holmes pastiche, *The Adventure of the Mendicant's Face*, and enquired whether I might be of use to them as a scriptwriter. This despite the fact that I'd never written a script in my life. I was fortunate, firstly that Jim French saw some potential in my story, and also that he supplied me with a couple of his own sample scripts, which I studied in detail and did my best to emulate, incorporating commercial breaks and using the appropriate abbreviations - "FX" for sound effects, and "BG" for background conversation. Fortunately, my script was received enthusiastically, and was aired on September 28, 2003. At the time of writing this introduction, eight years have passed, and I've written close on 60 Sherlock Holmes scripts, and around 120 others for various radio production companies in the United States – all thanks to Jim French and Imagination Theater.

This book is a collection of some of my favourite scripts for *The Further Adventures of Sherlock Holmes*. I've added detailed introductions, explaining the inspiration for each episode (note that each introduction contains spoilers), continuity references and anything I've learned about the process of writing for radio over the years. I should add that I'm *still* learning; each new assignment presents its own challenges, and new lessons to learn. Hopefully, if you've ever thought of writing your own radio script, you might find some of what you read in these pages useful. I also hope that this book will raise awareness of radio's only continuing Sherlock Holmes drama series. It's high time the word got out.

The Further Adventures of Sherlock Holmes - The Amateur Mendicant Society (Original Airdate September 28, 2003)

I decided to play it safe with my first script, basing it upon my earlier short story, *The Adventure of the Mendicant's Face*. At the time, it seemed important that print and radio version should have different titles. If there was a good reason for this, I've long since forgotten what it was, but it evidently worked both ways – when I adapted my second radio script, *The Living Weapon*, for the 2008 short story anthology *The Game's Afoot*, I changed the title to *The Adventure of the Forgetful Assassin*. Over the years, I've dramatised a few of my other stories – *The Adventure of the Extraordinary Lodger* became *The Blackmailer of Lancaster Gate* (which aired in the January of 2004), and *The Adventure of the Mocking Huntsman* was recorded some months later as *The Covetous Huntsman*. One other Holmes story, *The Adventure of the Patient Adversary* formed the basis of *Patience is a Vice*, an episode of Imagination Theater's 1950s private eye series, *The Adventures of Harry Nile*.

Adapting my own story proved a useful experience, which taught me a great deal about adapting the works of other writers. A dramatist has an obligation to the story – he or she must present it in the most interesting fashion possible for the listener. This means something different depending upon the source material – sometimes, certain elements must be emphasized, others toned down or even omitted. Anyone who thinks it's simply a question of removing all the "He said"s and "She said"s is doing the story – and the listener – no favours at all.

The first adjustment to the original story was the removal of Mrs Hudson, simply because I felt her contribution to the story was too small to warrant her inclusion. If one can tell the tale with the fewest characters possible, one should certainly do so. The policeman in the original was Inspector Peter Jones (from *The Red-Headed League*), solely because I wanted to make a point about him being the brother of Inspector Athelney Jones from *The Sign of Four*. I imagine Conan Doyle intended both characters to be the same person, and either forgot his first name or assumed that no-one would notice or care. I wasn't sure at this point whether the producers of *The Further Adventures* had a preference regarding the obligatory police presence, and as Lestrade is the pastiche writer's copper of choice, I made the obvious selection. Thus, poor old Peter Jones had to wait until 2011 to make his radio début in *The Mystery of Edelweiss* Lodge, also included in this volume. I had also written Lestrade into my second script, *The Living Weapon*, but actor Rick May was unavailable, and his lines were given to Inspector Gregson.

You'll notice that there is an awful lot of narration in this episode, and I think this is down to my timidity and inexperience. Don't get me wrong, I like a bit of narration in any Holmes radio drama, but I've learned that, in the main, it's best to let the dialogue tell the story. Nowadays, I tend to use Watson's voice-over only at the beginning of an episode. If you hear any narration later on, it probably means there wasn't enough time to tell the story in the time allotted.

For many years, I tended to avoid basing my scripts on the many hints dropped throughout the Canon concerning Holmes' many other cases (or so I thought until I reviewed *The Ripper Inheritance*), but this one is very clearly based on a reference in *The Five Orange Pips*. In fact, you get two for the price of once in this episode – the will of the late Lord Hammerford ties this to "the Hammerford Will Case" mentioned in *The Illustrious Client*. With *The Adventure of the Perfect Match* in 2009, I decided that I should try to connect all my scripts to those "missing" tales, just as Greene and Boucher had done with their shows in the mid-1940s (remember when you could write "mid-'40s" without having to specify a decade? God, I feel old).

Looking back over the script, it's clear to me that I must have been reading both *Wuthering Heights* and something by P G Wodehouse when I wrote it – the name Edwin Hinton sounds rather like Egar Linton, and there's also a Hindley in the mix. No doubt the nerve specialist Sir Edgar Glossop was intended to be the father of Sir Roderick Glossop, the bane of Bertie Wooster's life in Wodehouse's Jeeves stories. Howard Craven, however, was meant to suggest the term "craven coward". As for Holmes' client, Crawford Gilchrist, he shares his name with a tax official I knew during my years working for the Inland Revenue. In writing radio mysteries, it's important that the listener should remember each suspect and be able to differentiate, so I prefer to select names that are memorable without being bizarre, although I admit that the appearance of a "Jago Meridian" in the first episode of *The Hilary Caine Mysteries* raised a few eyebrows.

CAST:

ANNOUNCER (DENNIS BATEMAN)

HOLMES (JOHN PATRICK LOWRIE)

WATSON (LAWRENCE ALBERT)

INSPECTOR LESTRADE (RICK MAY)

CRAWFORD GILCHRIST (DENNIS BATEMAN)

HINDLEY LEWIS (JOHN ARMSTRONG)

HOWARD CRAVEN (LAWRENCE ALBERT)

EDWIN HINTON (TONY DOUPE)

DIRECTED BY JIM FRENCH

FX:	OPENING SEQUENCE, BIG BEN
ANNOUNCER:	*The Further Adventures of Sherlock Holmes*, featuring John Patrick Lowrie as Holmes, and Lawrence Albert as Dr Watson.
MUSIC	*DANSE MACABRE* UP AND UNDER
WATSON:	My name is Dr John H Watson, and I was privileged to share the adventures of Sherlock Holmes. I have witnessed many dramatic intrusions into our bachelor lodgings on Baker Street over the years, but surely none as alarming as that of Mr Crawford Gilchrist. It was a spring evening in 1887, and Holmes was reviewing his files while I attempted to put pen to paper and write an account of our first adventure together. Without warning, the door burst open, and we were confronted by a wild-eyed, bedraggled young man.
MUSIC:	OUT
FX:	THE SITTING ROOM DOOR IS THROWN OPEN. WATSON JUMPS UP FROM HIS CHAIR
GILCHRIST:	Mr Holmes! Mr Holmes!
WATSON:	My God! Stand back, Holmes!
GILCHRIST:	Mr Holmes, I must see you! Hindley Lewis plans to kill me!
HOLMES:	It's quite all right, Watson. Young man, please take a seat before you collapse from exhaustion. I have no notion of who Hindley Lewis is, any more than I know who you are, save for the obvious fact that you are a medical man who has taken to posing as a vagrant. Doctor, a drink for our guest, I think.
WATSON:	I don't know what Mrs Hudson's going to say about this.
HOLMES:	Oh, the devil with Mrs Hudson! Please take a seat, sir.
FX:	HE SITS. WATSON TINKERS WITH A DECANTER
GILCHRIST:	Mr Holmes… How did you guess?

HOLMES:	Guessing is an appalling habit. The dirt on your face has not accumulated over a period of time, but has instead been smeared on by hand – the finger-marks are quite distinct.
WATSON:	Here, young man, drink this.
GILCHRIST:	Thank-you. (DRINKS)
HOLMES:	As to your medical credentials, I detected the odour of iodoform through the grime from several feet away. A close analysis of your hands – note the lack of dirt under the fingernails, Watson – reveals the stains and scarring common to anyone who performs chemicals experiments. My own hands bear the… (SUDDENLY DISTRACTED) same marks. What is your name, sir?
GILCHRIST:	Gilchrist, Mr Holmes. Crawford Gilchrist.
HOLMES:	(REGAINING COMPOSURE) I see. Well, if that drink has settled your nerves sufficiently, perhaps you would see fit to tell us your story.
WATSON:	And kindly omit nothing, Mr Gilchrist.
GILCHRIST:	Well, from the beginning, then… I've never been what you might call gregarious, gentlemen, always preferring my own company to being in a crowd. But since I began my medical studies at the University of London I found myself becoming increasingly envious of the popularity of Hindley Lewis.
HOLMES:	You mentioned his name earlier. A fellow student?
GILCHRIST:	That's right, Mr Holmes. He's the son of Sir George Lewis, the barrister.
WATSON:	A great man.
GILCHRIST:	I was once fortunate enough to see Sir George at work in the Central Criminal Court. His son Hindley is usually surrounded by a crowd of fawning admirers, and more than once I had been conscious of them staring at me and whispering, so I was astonished, then, when Lewis himself invited me to a "gathering"

	at an address on Knatchbull Road near Myatt's Fields.
WATSON:	Not a very salubrious area of London for the son of a barrister.
HOLMES:	But you kept the appointment?
GILCHRIST:	I did. It wasn't until I arrived and discovered that the address was a furniture warehouse that I began to think I'd been the victim of a childish prank. Just then, I heard my name and turned to see Hindley Lewis, beckoning to me from the side entrance of the building.
FX:	FADE IN LONDON BG
LEWIS:	Gilchrist, come and join us! We're waiting for you down here!
FX:	GILCHRIST TROTS OVER TO HIM
GILCHRIST:	Lewis! I- I'm surprised to see you here.
LEWIS:	Follow me down.
FX:	LONDON BG OUT AS THE WAREHOUSE DOOR SHUTS BEHIND THEM AND THEY DESCEND A SHORT FLIGHT OF STONE STEPS
LEWIS:	The others are waiting in the basement.
GILCHRIST:	The others?
LEWIS:	Yes, Craven and Hinton, you remember them? A client gave this place to my old man in lieu of payment. He didn't know what to do with it, so he was only too glad to pass it on to me. We've used it as a meeting-house ever since. Here we are. We have to keep it locked, you'll see why in a moment.
FX:	LEWIS UNLOCKS THE METAL DOOR AND PUSHES IT OPEN
GILCHRIST:	Good grief!

LEWIS:	Our little oasis of civilization. I dare swear you never expected to find anything like this.
GILCHRIST:	I've never seen anything so grand! It's like some sort of luxurious-
CRAVEN:	-Gentleman's club.
LEWIS:	Gilchrist, you've met Howard Craven, I think?
GILCHRIST:	Well, not really…
LEWIS:	And this is Edwin Hinton.
HINTON:	Mr Gilchrist.
GILCHRIST:	Crawford, please. You'll forgive me for asking, but why are the two of you… dressed as beggars?
LEWIS:	We are the Amateur Mendicant Society.
GILCHRIST:	The Amateur Mendicant Society? I've never heard of it.
LEWIS:	We shouldn't have been doing our job properly if you had, my boy. Its existence is a secret, known only to its twenty-or-so members.
CRAVEN:	Twenty-three, in fact.
LEWIS:	Just so, thank-you, Craven. You'll meet the others in time. Sir Edgar Glossop, the famous nerve specialist, founded the organization some nineteen years ago. Cigar?
GILCHRIST:	Er, no thank-you.
LEWIS:	Then I hope you'll permit me.
FX:	HE STRIKES A MATCH AND LIGHTS THE CIGAR
LEWIS:	Where was I?

GILCHRIST:	Sir Edgar Glossop.
LEWIS:	Oh yes. He and the nine other original members are no longer Amateur Mendicants; membership ceases with one's entry into public life. We are dedicated to the financial support of… promising young gentlemen.
GILCHRIST:	Financial support through begging?
LEWIS:	We prefer the term "Mendicancy".
GILCHRIST:	But I thought that all three of you belonged to wealthy families.
LEWIS:	Quite right, Gilchrist. There *is* plenty of money in my family. But it's my old man's money and the miser gives me as little as he can which, of course, I *could* live on, but not as a gentleman. Why should I have to wait until I'm in practice to enjoy the fruits of my present labours? Why should you or any of us?
GILCHRIST:	Well, I suppose if I had a little more money, I could help my father, move to better lodgings, afford new clothes.
LEWIS:	That's the spirit! We don't expect you to be earning too much in the early days. However, you'll receive a weekly share of the Society's takings, so you'll never make less than nine pounds a week.
GILCHRIST:	Nine pounds!
LEWIS:	All you have to do is select a site, set up shop as it were, then bring the money you make to the headquarters every Friday. You might see myself or one of the other members as you ply your trade. It's just a courtesy we extend to newcomers. You mustn't acknowledge us, or the game will be up. Should you choose not to join us -
HINTON:	-And the choice is entirely yours.
LEWIS:	(WITH COLD MENACE) Thank-you, Hinton. We would rely upon your discretion in this matter and insist that you speak of this to no-one.

GILCHRIST:	I… understand.
LEWIS:	But why, I ask you, would any sane man turn his back upon such a remarkable opportunity?
CRAVEN:	The Amateur Mendicant Society is made up of some of the most influential young men in London.
HINTON:	Your membership, Gilchrist, will virtually guarantee your success in whichever field of medicine you choose.
LEWIS:	Of course, I appreciate that your pride may be more important to you than the opportunity to make good all your debts and improve your lot…
GILCHRIST:	Er, well…
MUSIC:	UNDERCURRENT
WATSON:	This is Dr Watson. I'll tell you all about the strange fate that befell Crawford Gilchrist in just a moment.
MUSIC:	OUT

FIRST COMMERCIAL

GILCHRIST:	Need I say, Mr Holmes, that I agreed to become the twenty-fourth Amateur Mendicant? I swore an oath of allegiance, and if they had kept faith with me, I should always have done so with them.
HOLMES:	How long ago did you have your singular experience, Mr Gilchrist?
GILCHRIST:	Just two weeks.
HOLMES:	Please continue.
GILCHRIST:	I spent an uncomfortable fortnight – whenever my studies allowed - attempting to persuade members of the public to show me their undeserved pity. I was a terrible vagrant, and my takings

were so minuscule that I can't describe my surprise when, at the end of that first week, Hindley Lewis simply counted out some coins and dropped them into my palm.

HOLMES: One moment. Was Lewis the only member present?

GILCHRIST: Well, yes. But I may have seen others from time to time without realising it. One day, late on the first week, I observed Lewis in the company of an older gentleman I didn't recognise.

WATSON: His father, Sir George, perhaps?

HOLMES: Obviously not, Watson. Didn't you hear Mr Gilchrist say that he had seen the great man at work?

WATSON: All right, perhaps it was this nerve specialist - Sir Edgar Glossop, wasn't it?

GILCHRIST: Perhaps. Yet I don't believe I'd ever heard the name until Lewis mentioned it.

WATSON: No, now I come to think of it, neither have I, Holmes.

HOLMES: That is suggestive. It may even be highly significant. Can you describe this man in any detail?

GILCHRIST: He… was a large man, with an aristocratic bearing. Clean-shaven. He seemed very particular in his manner of dress. I recall his black frock-coat and top hat, but also…

HOLMES: Something else?

GILCHRIST: Yesss… he wore a pearl pin in his cravat.

HOLMES: (EXCITEDLY) A satin cravat?

GILCHRIST: Yes, Mr Holmes, I believe it was.

HOLMES: Did you observe his gloves?

GILCHRIST: I did. They were kid-skin, I think.

HOLMES:	Kid-skin? Think carefully, Mr Gilchrist, you are certain that they were kid-gloves?
GILCHRIST:	Yes. Yes, I am certain.
HOLMES:	Did he say anything to you, or did you hear anything he may have said to Lewis?
GILCHRIST:	No, but he started when he saw me, as though he recognised me. As a matter of fact, he gave me the largest coin in the whole of my brief career as a beggar.
HOLMES:	Describe to us, please, the manner in which that career came to an end.
GILCHRIST:	It was early yesterday evening, about six o'clock. I'd grown sick at heart about taking money away from those unfortunates with a genuine need to beg on the streets, and I returned to the lower basement on Knatchbull Road determined to tell Lewis I could no longer continue as a member of the Amateur Mendicant Society.
LEWIS:	(CHEERFULLY) My lad, this reaction is by no means an uncommon one. Indeed, I would have thought it exceedingly strange had you *not* voiced these concerns to me.
GILCHRIST:	(RELIEVED) I thought you might be angry, Lewis.
LEWIS:	'Course not. But you don't quite see the whole picture. Perhaps this will help you to understand.
GILCHRIST:	(A GASP FOLLOWED BY VIOLENT CHOKING AS HE IS THROTTLED) Help – Lewisss-
LEWIS:	That'll do, Craven. I think he'll behave now.
CRAVEN:	Yes, you'll be a good boy, won't you?
FX:	GILCHRIST IS HURLED TO THE FLOOR
LEWIS:	Welcome to your new home, Gilchrist. Come Craven, let's be off.

16

FX:	<u>THEY LEAVE, CLOSING & LOCKING THE DOOR. GILCHRIST GETS TO HIS FEET, SCRAMBLES AFTER THEM & HAMMERS ON IT</u>
GILCHRIST:	No, wait! Let me out of here! Let me out! For the love of God, pleeease!
MUSIC:	<u>STING</u>
HOLMES:	You were their prisoner?
GILCHRIST:	My cries for help went unheard – I might as well have been in a dungeon - but I made them in any case. All night I searched the room, in the foolish hope of finding some hidden doorway, or a tool with which I might take the door off its hinges, perhaps even a weapon. I was in a fearful state by the morning when Hinton appeared at the door, carrying a tray of food.
FX:	<u>DOOR IS UNLOCKED AND OPENED</u>
HINTON:	Crawford, Crawford, can you hear me? Crawford, I'm so sorry! I thought I had the nerve for this, but I can't go through with it, it's just… inhuman! The door is open, you must escape.
GILCHRIST:	(CONFUSED) What? What are you saying, Hinton?
HINTON:	Go, man! They'll be waiting for me! But, before you go… you must make it look like an escape. If they think I let you go, God knows what they'll do to me. (PAUSE) Well, come on, hit me, you fool!
FX:	<u>GILCHRIST THUMPS HIM, THE TRAY CLATTERS TO THE GROUND AND HINTON FALLS</u>
GILCHRIST:	(NARRATING) I didn't even see him fall, I simply ran. I reached Stockwell Park Road before I came to my senses. I knew I couldn't return to my lodgings. My journey here has been the most terrifying of my life. I had no notion there were so many unfortunates on the streets, and no way of knowing whether any of them might be impostors who wished me harm.

HOLMES:	(SIGHS) Well, it was a most intriguing case. A drink, Watson?
WATSON:	*Was*? Holmes, you don't mean to say you've solved it already?
HOLMES:	I have one or two calls to make before the day is out and I am in hopes that we will be able to bring this affair to a conclusion by tomorrow afternoon. Mr Gilchrist, you look quite done in after your adventures.
GILCHRIST:	I can't deny it.
HOLMES:	Watson, would you be so good as to allow this weary gentleman the use of your room for the night? I'm sure that one of these chairs will prove quite comfortable for you.
GILCHRIST:	Thank-you, Mr Holmes, that's very generous of you.
WATSON:	(UNDERTONE OF SARCASM) Yes, thank-you, Holmes – very generous of you.
MUSIC:	UNDERCURRENT
WATSON:	(NARRATING) So relieved was our client that he drifted off to sleep without the need for a sedative. I had just settled down in the sitting-room when Holmes returned from his errand.
MUSIC:	OUT
FX:	SITTING ROOM DOOR OPENS AND CLOSES
HOLMES:	How is our visitor, Watson?
WATSON:	Sleeping like a tot.
HOLMES:	Excellent. You know, it's quite serendipitous that I should happen to be reviewing some of my earlier cases this evening.
WATSON:	One of them has a bearing on this affair?
HOLMES:	The search for Lord Hammerford's wayward son, Lawrence, some six years ago.* He had become mesmerized by London's

baser pleasures and broke off contact with his family and friends. I was asked to locate Lawrence – no, that's not it - and restore him to father and home before- well…

FX: <u>* AT THIS POINT, HOLMES BEGINS ROOTING THROUGH THE PAPERS IN THE METAL BOX</u>

WATSON: Before what, Holmes?

HOLMES: Let us simply say that His Lordship was both a practical and a realistic man, Watson. Ah, here it is.

FX: <u>HE EXTRACTS A SINGLE PHOTOGRAPH</u>

WATSON: I understand. London's streets are rarely paved with gold, particularly if you're young and foolish. So, were you able to locate Lawrence?

HOLMES: I was not. I freely admit, Watson, I thought the task a simple one. But the pubs of Whitechapel and the opium dens by the docks refused to give up their prey as easily as I had anticipated. I was eventually forced to report to my client that his son could not, and most likely never would, be found. Lord Hammerford died nearly three years ago, a broken man. Really a most unsatisfactory business.

WATSON: I'm sure his Lordship agreed with you. But how does this tie in with our current investigation? Does it have something to do with that photograph?

HOLMES: His Lordship gave me this. It is a picture of his son. Look.

WATSON: Good God!

HOLMES: You recognise him, then, Watson?

WATSON: Of course! I mean, he's younger and noticeably cleaner, but there's no mistaking him. Holmes – this is Crawford Gilchrist!

HOLMES: I recognised the likeness at once, but thought it wisest to hear his story first.

WATSON:	But do you mean to say that all this time we've been listening to a pack of lies? But why? Is he in some way deranged?
HOLMES:	Well, that is certainly one possibility. His Lordship's affairs were put in the hands of Colonel James Damery. I have never met him, but I understand he has some reputation for handling delicate society matters.
WATSON:	Do you think that we should make him aware of young Lawrence's present situation?
HOLMES:	I hardly think it necessary, Watson. The description of the aristocratic gentleman who showed our client so much concern matches Colonel Damery precisely.
MUSIC:	STING AND UNDER
WATSON:	(NARRATING) The following morning saw all three of us waiting on the kerb at Baker Street. Crawford Gilchrist had washed, and was now wearing one of my old suits, which Holmes had "generously" donated.
FX:	SEGUE TO BUSY LONDON STREET
HOLMES:	Something the matter, Watson?
WATSON:	Just a bit stiff after spending all night on the couch.
HOLMES:	Be patient, Doctor.
WATSON:	Is that supposed to be a joke, Holmes?
HOLMES:	Our cab will be here shortly; no doubt the jolting motion of the vehicle will straighten you out again.
GILCHRIST:	But, Mr Holmes, you still haven't told us where we're going.
HOLMES:	*We* are not be going anywhere, Mr Gilchrist. *You* are going back to your lodgings.
GILCHRIST:	My lodgings! But the Society members might be waiting there

	for me!
HOLMES:	I am certain of it. Ah, here he is at last!
FX:	A CAB PULLS UP
HOLMES:	Good morning, Lestrade!
LESTRADE:	Morning, Mr Holmes, got your telegram.
HOLMES:	Well, gentlemen, shall we be off?
MUSIC:	SHORT BRIDGE
FX:	SEGUE TO TROTTING HORSE PULLING CAB UNDER
LESTRADE:	That's quite a story, Mr Gilchrist!
WATSON:	(SLYLY) Yes, *quite* a story.
GILCHRIST:	(DISTRACTED) What? I'm sorry, Doctor-
HOLMES:	We are just coming onto Courtfield Road. Driver, stop here!
FX:	CAB HALTS. LONDON BG
HOLMES:	Now comes the moment of crisis, Mr Gilchrist. I wish you to walk to your lodgings alone.
GILCHRIST:	Mr Holmes, I-
HOLMES:	It is more than likely that you will be waylaid as soon as you open the door to your room. Show no resistance whatsoever. Have courage and your ordeal will soon be over. Dr Watson, the inspector and I will never be far away.
GILCHRIST:	Very well, Mr Holmes. Wish me luck, gentlemen.
FX:	CAB DOOR OPENS & CLOSES. GILCHRIST'S FOOTSTEPS DIE AWAY

HOLMES:	We shall know soon enough whether events unfold as I have anticipated.
LESTRADE:	You expect this Hindley Lewis and his cronies to be lying in wait for him?
HOLMES:	You observe that cab, waiting by the kerb, Lestrade? They have obtained a Growler for the occasion.
WATSON:	How can you be sure it's them?
HOLMES:	It takes little in the way of deductive reasoning to identify the nervous cabman as Hinton, the gentleman who so obligingly set young Mr Gilchrist free. Even from this distance I can make out a bruise beginning to form around his left eye.
MUSIC:	OMINOUS UNDERSCORE
WATSON:	(NARRATING) It seemed less than a minute before two people hurried in a shambling fashion from the house. One was unknown to me, a tall young man with spiteful features. The second, apparently unconscious, was Crawford Gilchrist.
MUSIC:	OUT
FX:	ONE MAN RISES IN THE CAB OPENS THE DOOR
HOLMES:	Lestrade, stay where you are! You'll spoil everything!
LESTRADE:	This is clearly abduction, Mr Holmes. What's to prevent us from making an arrest right now?
HOLMES:	If you have a little patience, I expect to be able to hand you the entire gang. Wouldn't that be a more satisfying morning's work?
WATSON:	But Holmes, there are over twenty of them!
LESTRADE:	Twenty-three, your Mr Gilchrist said. Surely the three of us won't be sufficient to detain them all?
HOLMES:	(AIRILY) Oh, we three are very able fellows. I don't suppose the

entire Amateur Mendicant Society will pose much of a difficulty. And now I see that the gentleman I suppose to be Howard Craven has succeeded in bundling our unconscious client into the cab. They should be on their way any moment.

WATSON: Shall I instruct the driver to follow them?

HOLMES: No need, Watson, we already know their destination – Knatchbull Road.

MUSIC: SHORT ENDING BRIDGE

SECOND COMMERCIAL

MUSIC: UNDERCURRENT

WATSON: This is Dr Watson again. I'll return in one more minute with the conclusion of tonight's new Sherlock Holmes adventure.

MUSIC: OUT

THIRD COMMERCIAL

MUSIC: UNDERCURRENT

WATSON: Knatchbull Road was exactly as Gilchrist described it: the furniture warehouse, the metal door at the foot of the stairs… I no longer knew *what* to think.

MUSIC: OUT

FX: THREE PAIRS OF FEET ON THE STONE STEPS. THEY HALT AT THE END OF HOLMES' LINE.

HOLMES: (WHISPER) Be on your guard, gentlemen. Watson, perhaps you would be so good as to draw your revolver.

FX: HE RAPS ON THE METAL DOOR THREE TIMES, PAUSES, THEN KNOCKS TWICE AGAIN. THE DOOR UNLOCKS

HOLMES: Now!

FX:	<u>A BRIEF SCUFFLE ENSUES BETWEEN HOLMES, WATSON & LESTRADE ON ONE SIDE AND CRAVEN & HINTON ON THE OTHER. A COUPLE OF PUNCHES ARE THROWN.</u>
LESTRADE:	Right, you three, I am a police officer and I advise you to remain where you are!
FX:	<u>WATSON RACES TO A CORNER OF THE CHAMBER</u>
WATSON:	Holmes, it's Crawford Gilchrist! He's unconscious, but alive. I think he's been drugged.
LESTRADE:	You, young man, what have you to say for yourself?
LEWIS:	Nothing you would be capable of comprehending, officer.
HOLMES:	Mr Hindley Lewis, I presume? My name is Sherlock Holmes.
LEWIS:	Well, well, well. I've heard of you Mr Holmes. I only regret that we should be forced to meet under such disagreeable circumstances.
HOLMES:	Come, sir. You have been caught and your criminal enterprise exposed.
LEWIS:	Oh, caught, am I? All I see here is a student prank, quite a common occurrence in high-spirited youngsters.
WATSON:	You are a liar, sir. Crawford Gilchrist has twice been held against his will in these chambers.
LEWIS:	Hardly a prison cell, *sir*. And if Mr Gilchrist has misunderstood my playful intentions, then I know my friends will confirm my version of events.
CRAVEN:	Hear, hear. This, sir, is assault!
HOLMES:	Mr Hinton. I believe I can rely on you to speak the truth.

LEWIS:	(THREATENING) Edwin…
LESTRADE:	Quiet, you!
HOLMES:	Mr Hinton, I know of your doubts concerning the wisdom of this enterprise. I know also of the goodwill you have shown our client-
CRAVEN:	I knew you'd set him free, you cur!
LEWIS:	Shut up, Craven, you dolt!
HOLMES:	I am certain that Inspector Lestrade would take it into consideration if you were to make a full statement. (PAUSE) Very well. I shall tell you what I understand of the matter and you will tell me where I am in error. The story of the non-existent Amateur Mendicant Society began when Sir George Lewis, rather against the rules of his profession, unwisely related the details of the generous financial arrangement made for the late Lord Hammerford's errant son to his own son, Hindley. His Lordship was a realistic man who knew there was a strong possibility that, should Lawrence be found, he might not be as he once was. Under such circumstances, a sizeable monthly income would be paid to the person *or persons* taking on the duty of providing him with care and accommodation.
HINTON:	I… I don't know about Sir George's part in all this, Mr Holmes, but the rest is as you say.
HOLMES:	The remarkable resemblance between Crawford Gilchrist and the missing gentleman was a stroke of good fortune. Gilchrist could be passed off as Lawrence to Colonel Damery, the gentleman presently in charge of locating the lost inheritor.
HINTON:	We were expecting the Colonel today.
HOLMES:	In order that you might display to him the comfortable surroundings in which your dishevelled and insensible patient would spend the reminder of his days. I warned the colonel by telegram that the business was a clever fraud. He, in turn, obligingly provided me with the secret knock he had agreed

upon with Lewis.

LEWIS: (SMUG) I can never resist a touch of the melodramatic.

HOLMES: But would Gilchrist agree to such an obviously illegal scheme?
              And why should he profit by it when his features were all that
              you required? Lewis, not yet possessed of a medical degree but
              still influential in society, could claim the fee for taking care of a
              once promising young man, now reduced to a pitiful and
              mentally deficient wreck, forced out onto the streets.

WATSON: And that was why he devised the fiction of the Amateur
              Mendicants - so that Gilchrist, apparently living as a vagrant,
              might be seen by Colonel Damery and mistaken for Lord
              Hammerford's missing son.

HOLMES: Quite correct, Watson.

HINTON: (DISTRAUGHT) It's true, every word of it's true! May the Lord
              forgive us!

HOLMES: I was immediately suspicious of the fact that Gilchrist never saw
              more than three members of this alleged Society together at one
              time. That and your poor judgement, Mr Lewis, in identifying a
              non-existent nerve specialist as its founder member-

LEWIS: Ah, me!

HOLMES: -indicated that the entire enterprise was simply a ruse to ensure
              that my client would be seen apparently living on the streets.

GILCHRIST: (GROANS) What's happening?

WATSON: He's coming round, Holmes. Welcome back, Mr Gilchrist.
              You've missed a most remarkable story.

LESTRADE: And once you had convinced this Colonel Damery that Gilchrist
              was who you claimed he was, did you intend to keep him locked
              up here forever? Or did you...?

LEWIS: What you will never be able to understand, Inspector, is that it was nothing but a financial matter, purely financial. The joke of it is, I didn't lie when I said the old man gave me a pittance. It's cost us all we had to furnish this place and supply Gilchrist with coins at the end of each week. And for what? We couldn't even afford more than one cigar. (LAUGHS)

MUSIC: *DANSE MACABRE*

The Further Adventures of Sherlock Holmes –
The Ripper Inheritance
(Original Airdate November 28, 2004)

This became my first hour-long episode when I realised that the plot was too complex to be comprehensible in just 30 minutes. For all that, it's still told with a relatively small cast – economy should be every scriptwriter's watchword.

I can rarely resist the opportunity to include references not only to the Canon, but also to other noteworthy pastiches, in particular the Rathbone and Bruce movies. In *The Ripper Inheritance*, we have society beauty Anne Brandon, who shares her name with Ida Lupino's character from 1939's *The Adventures of Sherlock Holmes*. A later Rathbone/Bruce picture, *The Woman in Green*, revolves around a series of crimes known as "The Finger Murders", in which the killer removes one digit from each female victim to plant on various society figures for blackmail purposes. Here, Gudgeon, acting under Lord Ely's instructions, slices *all* the fingers from one hand of his victims, who are of both sexes. Nevertheless, how could I call his crimewave anything but "The Finger Murders"? Holmes' "German" informant Steiner, who drinks at the Angel and Crown in Whitechapel is obviously partially inspired by Max Steiner, landlord of the Angel in Crown in the 1965 film *A Study in Terror. This* Steiner is a neither German nor a landlord, however – he is revealed as a starving artist named Sidney Lanfield, who just happens to have the same name as the director of Basil Rathbone's first Holmes film, *The Hound of the Baskervilles*. For no very good reason, other than to create a grim atmosphere while writing it, Gudgeon's hiding place at 13 Miller's Court in Whitechapel is the address at which the body of Mary Jane Kelly, the final victim of Jack the Ripper, was discovered.

I was surprised to discover upon re-reading this script for this episode that Gudgeon – real name Archie Griffin, apparently – was responsible for the murder of a groom outside the Holborn Bar, presumably the crime Holmes was investigating at the start of *The Three Gables*. I wonder if this counts as the resolution of another unsolved case from the Canon?

This episode is the first in which I identified Watson's second wife as Kate Whitney, widow of the opium addict Isa Whitney from *The Man With the Twisted Lip*. She's mentioned again in my 2006 adaptation of *The Mazarin Stone* before finally appearing in the 2009 episode *The Adventure of the Invisible* Man, where she is played by the actress Cynthia Lauren Tewes, well-known to audiences as Julie the Cruise Director in the long-running TV comedy series *The Love Boat*. Anyone who possesses a CD of this episode will, I hope, have noticed that Watson does indeed take seventeen steps to reach his rooms.

The script was subject to a minor rewrite before it went on the air, as it was felt that Lord Ely simply gave up too easily once Holmes identified him as the murderer. It was my original intention that he wanted to marry Anne purely for financial reasons, but as I wrote the part, it seemed to me that he really loved the girl after all, which made his actions all the more terrible.

CAST:

ANNOUNCER (DENNIS BATEMAN)

HOLMES (JOHN PATRICK LOWRIE)

WATSON (LAWRENCE ALBERT)

MRS HUDSON (LEE PASCH)

INSPECTOR HOPKINS (JIM HAMER)

STEINER (DENNIS BATEMAN)

LORD ELY (JOHN ARMSTRONG)

ANNE BRANDON (BETH DEVRIES)

GUDGEON (DENNIS BATEMAN)

DIRECTED BY JIM FRENCH

FX:	OPENING SEQUENCE, BIG BEN
ANNOUNCER:	*The Further Adventures of Sherlock Holmes*, featuring John Patrick Lowrie as Holmes, and Lawrence Albert as Dr Watson.
MUSIC:	*DANSE MACABRE* UP AND UNDER
WATSON:	My name is Dr John H Watson, and the story I am about to tell you is one of the most remarkable adventures I shared with Sherlock Holmes. It began for us in the September of 1901. I had just returned to Baker Street after performing one of the saddest duties of my life – that of coffin-bearer at the funeral of an old friend, Isa Whitney.
MUSIC:	OUT
FX:	WATSON OPENS AND CLOSES THE FRONT DOOR
WATSON:	Mrs Hudson, I'm back.
MRS HUDSON:	(APPROACHING) Oh, Doctor, how are you?
WATSON:	(BLUFFING) Oh, I'm- fine. Really.
MRS HUDSON:	And how's *Mrs* Whitney coping?
WATSON:	Kate's bearing up remarkably well. She's had a lot to deal with over the years. When a loved one is sick for a long time, something like this… it's almost like a release.
MRS HUDSON:	(SOFTLY) I understand all too well, Doctor. And I know you do, too.
WATSON:	Thank-you, Mrs Hudson. Is Mr Holmes still here?
MRS HUDSON:	Still here? Why. He's only been up an hour!
WATSON:	Ever the man of action.
FX:	HE GOES UP THE STAIRS (THERE ARE 17, AS PER *SCANDAL IN BOHEMIA*)

MRS HUDSON:	The sooner the police come to him over these awful murders, the better for everyone. You know there's been another one?
WATSON:	(DISTANT) Yes, I saw it in the paper. Well, perhaps I can stir him into action.
FX:	<u>WATSON OPENS AND SHUTS THE DOOR TO THEIR ROOMS</u>
HOLMES:	Welcome back, Watson. I trust you had an enjoyable time.
WATSON:	As a matter of fact, Holmes, I very rarely enjoy myself at funerals.
HOLMES:	I take exception to that tone, Doctor. My life's work is founded upon the observation and retention of details. If you had told me you were going to a funeral, I would certainly have remembered it.
WATSON:	If you say so.
HOLMES:	Was I acquainted with the deceased?
WATSON:	No, though you saw him once, years ago. During the Neville St Claire case. His name was Isa Whitney.
HOLMES:	Of course, your friend the opium fiend!
WATSON:	Very sensitively put, Holmes. Yes, Isa was, in his lifetime, a slave to the drug. Put his poor wife through Hell.
HOLMES:	I must confess, I'm baffled as to why an intelligent man such as yourself, a doctor no less, should choose to form a friendship with someone addicted to artificial stimulants.
WATSON:	(DRY) I've wondered and wondered. (SIGHS, THEN SHRUGS OFF HIS DARK MOOD) You've seen the newspapers?
HOLMES:	On the contrary, I've seen nothing later than the Middle Ages this morning. I've been busy rewriting my monograph on the Polyphonic Motets of Lhassus.

WATSON:	Something the world's been crying out for, I'm sure.
FX:	<u>WATSON SINKS INTO A CHAIR AND UNFOLDS HIS NEWSPAPER</u>
WATSON:	This makes four.
HOLMES:	Four?
WATSON:	These crimes the press are referring to as the Finger Murders. There was another one last night, Aubrey Nelson, a bookseller from Camberwell. The others were, er…
HOLMES:	Eugene Lytton, Yvette Schumann and Percy Latimer. And each victim missing all the fingers on their right hand. Retention of details, Watson.
WATSON:	The police don't seem to know which way to turn.
HOLMES:	Well, at least that's consistent.
WATSON:	And the newspapers seem determined to have the public in a blind state of panic. They're saying this fellow has inherited the mantle of Jack the Ripper.
HOLMES:	In what sense?
WATSON:	His crimes are brutal, and like the Ripper's, there's no rhyme or reason to them.
HOLMES:	Ah, but the Ripper's crimes were not without reason.
WATSON:	I'm still waiting to hear all about that case, you know.
HOLMES:	Surely I told you, Watson.
WATSON:	Your remarkable memory is becoming more and more selective, my dear Holmes.
HOLMES:	Tell me, who is in charge of the investigation into these Finger Murders?

33

WATSON: Uh...* Inspector Forbes. Usually, when the police are baffled, they look to you for assistance. Why haven't they done so now?

FX: * HE EXAMINES THE PAPER

HOLMES: You don't remember Forbes, then?

WATSON: Should I? Oh, wait a minute, yes I do! The stolen Naval Treaty!

HOLMES: Precisely. (IMITATING COCKNEY ACCENT) "I've heard of your methods before now, Mr Holmes. You're ready enough to use all the information the police can lay at your disposal, and then you try to finish the case yourself and bring discredit on them."

WATSON: I don't imagine he was any too pleased when you let the thief get away, either.

HOLMES: Rest assured, Watson, so long as Forbes is in charge of the case, we won't be consulted.

FX: A KNOCK ON THE DOOR

HOLMES: Come!

FX: DOOR OPENS

MRS HUDSON: Excuse me, Mr Holmes, but there's a cab waiting for you.

HOLMES: I haven't ordered a cab. Watson, did you order a cab?

MRS HUDSON: The driver says he's here to take you to Scotland Yard. It's about the Finger Murders.

WATSON: Very good, Mr Hudson. Tell him we'll be down in a moment.

FX: DOOR SHUTS

WATSON: You're slipping, Holmes.

HOLMES: Let's hope it's not the beginning of a trend.

MUSIC:	BRIDGE
HOPKINS:	Good afternoon, gentlemen. I apologize for dragging you out, but you have my word this is an emergency.
WATSON:	Inspector Hopkins!
HOLMES:	(LOW) It seems you owe me an apology, Watson.
WATSON:	We were under the impression that Inspector Forbes was in charge of this investigation.
HOPKINS:	Inspector Forbes is, uh… Well, let me put it this way: The Police Commissioner demanded to know what progress he was making on these murders and Forbes told him to mind his own business.
WATSON:	*Can* an Inspector tell Sir Edward Bradford to mind his own business?
HOPKINS:	Oh, yes. (A BEAT) But only once. So now Forbes is being transferred to Liverpool, and I've inherited his workload. I've been instructed to use every resource at my disposal.
HOLMES:	And I am one of those resources?
HOPKINS:	If you'll forgive my presumption.
HOLMES:	My dear Inspector, I'm honoured. May I ask why we're having this discussion at Scotland Yard rather than in the comfortable surroundings of number 221b?
FX:	HOPKINS PLACES A PILE OF PAPERS ON HIS DESK
HOPKINS:	Because of these, Mr Holmes.
WATSON:	The official files.
HOPKINS:	They're not to leave the building under any circumstances. But I thought you'd like to take a look at them.
HOLMES:	Evidently, this fellow is causing you some difficulty.

FX:	HOLMES FLIPS THROUGH THE PAPERS AS THEY SPEAK, SOMETIMES RAPIDLY, SOMETIMES VERY SLOWLY

HOPKINS: Jack the Ripper had the whole of the autumn to bring London to its knees; this fellow has managed it in a few weeks.

WATSON: Fellow? I suppose we're certain the killer is a man?

HOPKINS: Do you know any women capable of hacking off all the fingers on a person's right hand?

HOLMES: I've known some women capable of a good deal worse, if provoked.

WATSON: Perhaps if we knew what he wanted the fingers for, we'd be a step closer to identifying him.

HOPKINS: They're probably no more than a grisly trophy to him, Doctor.

FX:	HOLMES CLOSES THE FILE

HOLMES: Well, what Inspector Forbes lacks in manners he more than makes up for in record-keeping. It appears that he was unable to find a connection between any of the victims.

HOPKINS: In all fairness to him, he wasn't able to find one because none exists. Three men, one woman… different classes, different nationalities, all murdered in different areas of London. The only thing they have in common is the way they were killed.

WATSON: Strangulation, after which the killer removes all the fingers from one hand. Is it always the right hand?

HOPKINS: In every case. Technically, it's the Fingers and *Thumb* Murders, but I suppose the journalists think that has less of a ring to it.

HOLMES: With your leave, Hopkins, I intend to mull the matter over at Baker Street – perhaps smoke a pipe or two.

WATSON: Heaven help us!

HOLMES: I find the thickness of the atmosphere helps my thought processes.

HOPKINS:	In that case, smoke away, Mr Holmes. And please let me know if you come up with anything.
HOLMES:	After the good doctor, you will be the first to know.
FX:	<u>INTERIOR OF A MOVING CAB</u>
HOLMES:	Did anything strike you about those photographs, Watson?
WATSON:	Yes, a ragged tear in the same position on the right hand of each victim.
HOLMES:	And your conclusion?
WATSON:	Well, clearly the weapon has some sort of flaw. I can't see how it helps us, though.
HOLMES:	At present, it doesn't, but we shall at least know it if we see it. And what about this weapon? A surgical instrument, would you say?
WATSON:	Not necessarily. Any butcher would have the right implements. I've seen Mrs Hudson wielding a few items that might do the job.
HOLMES:	Not a very comforting thought. Remind me to compliment her on her cooking this evening.
WATSON:	Just eat some of your vegetables, that's all she asks.
FX:	<u>CAB BG UP & OUT. BACK AT BAKER STREET, HOLMES SLAMS THE FRONT DOOR</u>
HOLMES:	This promises to be a four-pipe problem at least!
WATSON:	Four!
MRS HUDSON:	Mr Holmes, this letter dropped onto the mat just after you left.
HOLMES:	Indeed? Thank-you, Mrs Hudson.

FX:	HE TEARS OPEN THE ENVELOPE AND UNFOLDS THE LETTER
HOLMES:	Well, well. It never rains but it pours. Don't take your hat off, Watson, we're not stopping.
WATSON:	What does it say?
HOLMES:	The author of this letter invites us to meet him in the saloon bar of the Angel and Crown in Whitechapel. It seems he has some important information to impart about the Finger Murders.
MUSIC:	UNDERCURRENT
WATSON:	And I'll tell you all about our mysterious informant in just a moment.
MUSIC:	OUT

FIRST COMMERCIAL

FX:	TAVERN BG
WATSON:	Just look at this place, Holmes! I'd call it a low dive, but that'd be an insult to low dives.
HOLMES:	True, but we didn't come here to soak up the atmosphere, we came for the conversation.
WATSON:	How do you know this isn't some wild goose chase?
HOLMES:	I don't. Ah, look, Watson! The fair-haired gentleman with the moustache is attempting to attract our attention.
STEINER:	Over here, gentlemen, over here!
HOLMES:	Mr Steiner, I presume?
STEINER:	Mr Sherlock Holmes, I recognise you from your pictures! Und you, you are the other one, ja?
WATSON:	(COLDLY) Ja.

STEINER:	Sit down, please; I get you both drinks, ja?
FX:	HOLMES & WATSON PULL UP BARSTOOLS
HOLMES:	It is not our intention to socialise, Herr Steiner. You said in your letter that you had some important information for us.
STEINER:	Ja, but meeting the great detective – this is an honour! We should celebrate with a drink!
WATSON:	We are really very busy men.
STEINER:	Busy with the Finger Murders? (A BEAT, THEN HE LAUGHS) I've been waiting for the police to call you in. I was outside Baker Street this morning when the cab arrived from Scotland Yard; I heard the driver talking to Frau Hudson.
HOLMES:	How very enterprising of you. And why should this be of any interest to you, sir? If you have something to report, why not tell it to the police?
STEINER:	That is difficult. I am… known to the police. You see, I am not always such a good boy. But now I work on the docks, I stay out of trouble… But the police, if they ask me how I know who the Finger Murderer is-
WATSON:	You know who he is?
STEINER:	The third victim, Herr Latimer, he was murdered in Whitechapel, ja?
HOLMES:	So I believe.
STEINER:	So maybe that night I visit a lady friend who lives in Dorset Street. Maybe I see a man with blood on his hands und all down shirtfront. I was still in Friedrichshafen when the Ripper was in Whitechapel, but the story is in the German newspapers. A man walking the streets of Whitechapel, covered in blood… maybe the Ripper is back at work?
HOLMES:	Can you describe this man?

STEINER: I can describe him, ja. He was tall, taller even that you, Herr Holmes. Big Shoulders, und a big moustache.

WATSON: That description might apply to a few thousand Londoners.

STEINER: Then what about if I tell you his name und where he lives?

WATSON: What!

STEINER: I see he has been… "up to something", do you say? He stops at a horse trough und washes the blood from his hands. Then he draws his cape about him und walks off.

HOLMES: And no-one else witnessed this display?

STEINER: It was very late. I had to do a lot of explaining to Frau Steiner when I got home. You see, I followed him to an address in Belgrave Square.

HOLMES: The house number?

STEINER: 149. I go back there a day later; I ask questions of the groom. He tells me that living in the house is a Lord Ely.

WATSON: Lord Ely!

STEINER: If you want to know where to find him, he will be at Lady Conyngham's party tonight. You know Lady Conyngham, ja?

HOLMES: Herr Steiner, I take it you wouldn't mind if I asked you a few questions.

STEINER: But gentlemen, I tell you all I know! What is there to ask?

HOLMES: Only this: What is your real name, and why are you lying to us?

STEINER: What do you say?

HOLMES: You are most certainly not a dockworker, and your story beggars belief! In each murder, the fingers were removed after death, once the heart had stopped pumping. I doubt there would have been anything like the amount of blood you claim. So why are

40

	you lying?
STEINER:	I- I don't-
HOLMES:	You will either tell us the truth or sleep in the police station tonight; it's a matter of small consequence to me.
FX:	STEINER KNOCKS HIS CHAIR OVER AS HE ATTEMPTS TO ESCAPE
HOLMES:	Stop him, Watson!
FX:	THERE'S A STRUGGLE
STEINER:	(NOW WITH AN ENGLISH ACCENT) Let go of me, damn you!
FX:	STEINER LANDS A PUNCH ON WATSON AND RUNS OUT. SOME UNEASE AMONG THE PATRONS
HOLMES:	Watson, are you all right?
WATSON:	(SHAKEN) I'm fine, Holmes. Luckily, the fellow doesn't know how to throw a proper punch. Agh, he's vanished.
HOLMES:	Along with his German accent.
WATSON:	So I heard. Well, what do you propose we do now?
HOLMES:	We have been given a line of enquiry; we must see where it leads.
WATSON:	Lord Ely, you mean? Holmes, are you sure it's wise? Our informant isn't exactly reliable, you know.
HOLMES:	Very true, Watson. But if we find out more about the mysterious Mr Steiner along the way, so much the better.
FX:	TAVERN BG OUT. THROUGH TO A SOCIETY BALL. MUSIC, GENERAL CHATTER OF GUESTS
HOPKINS:	I can't say I feel very comfortable with this, Mr Holmes.

HOLMES:	I have my concerns also, Hopkins, but at present this is the only avenue open to us. We must follow it as far as it leads.
WATSON:	And if it leads nowhere?
HOLMES:	You really are quite the pessimist, today, Watson.
HOPKINS:	I suppose we know what this Lord Ely fellow looks like? I'd hate to cause more of a scene than necessary.
WATSON:	I've seen his picture in the society pages. He'll be wherever Miss Anne Brandon is.
HOLMES:	Oh?
WATSON:	Miss Brandon is the wealthiest, most beautiful woman in London today. She has a parade of suitors, but none so highly favoured as Lord Ely. If the bookmakers were taking odds on the match, I'd say it was a racing certainty.
HOLMES:	I had no idea you were so acutely alive to the goings-on in the higher echelons of society, Watson.
WATSON:	If you took your nose out of the crime news and the agony column once in a while, Holmes, you'd be surprised what you might discover. There she is! And there *he* is!
ELY:	(SLIGHTLY OFF MIC) Anne, my darling, why this torment? It can't be any more bearable for you than for me!
ANNE:	(SLIGHTLY OFF MIC) You presume a great deal, Gabriel.
HOPKINS:	(WHISPERS) The society pages have a point, don't they? She is a beauty.
ELY:	You can't possibly tell me there's someone else? I doubt if there's a better-suited suitor in the whole of London.
ANNE:	Again, you go too far, sir! I'm simply enjoying myself too much at present to consider *any* offers.
ELY:	It's not that oaf Lanfield? It *is*, isn't it?

42

ANNE:	Don't speak so harshly of him; Sidney isn't an oaf – he's a sensitive soul.
ELY:	I'd like to see just how sensitive he is when I get my hands on him.
HOPKINS:	Excuse me for interrupting. Lord Ely?
ELY:	Who the devil are you? And how were you allowed in dressed like that? You can't have been invited!
HOPKINS:	The police are welcome everywhere, my Lord.
ELY:	And is it the Yard's policy to spy on my wooing?
ANNE:	Gabriel, what's going on? What do these men want?
ELY:	That's what I'd like to know. Who exactly *are* you?
HOPKINS:	Inspector Stanley Hopkins, your Lordship.
ELY:	Hopkins, eh? I'll remember that name. And what about your friends? They look a little old to be your underlings.
HOLMES:	My name is Sherlock Holmes and this is Dr John Watson.
ELY:	(SUDDENLY ANXIOUS) Er, Anne, darling, why don't you go and keep your father company – he's looking quite lost on his own. I'll join you in a moment, once I've given these fellows a piece of my mind.
ANNE:	If you're sure, Gabriel. (DEPARTING) Good evening, gentlemen.
WATSON:	Miss Brandon.
ELY:	If this is about that Music Hall girl, yes, there was some talk of marriage, but there was never an *official* announcement.
HOPKINS:	I'm afraid we've come about something a little more serious than that, my Lord. You're aware of the recent series of killings in the metropolis?

ELY: The Finger Murders. Of course, who isn't?

HOPKINS: We've received information suggesting that you have some knowledge of these crimes.

ELY: (A FEEBLE LAUGH) This is a joke! Who are you really? (PAUSE) This… *isn't* a joke.

HOPKINS: Perhaps this isn't the best place to discuss the matter.

ELY: Someone's told you I have something to do with the Finger Murders, have they? Presumably, then, you'll want to search my home?

HOPKINS: At the moment, my Lord, I really just want to talk to you in private.

ELY: That's fine. I live just a short cab ride away, we can talk and you can search at the same time. The sooner this bloody stupid business is over and done with, the sooner I can get back here!

FX: SOCIETY BALL OUT. ELY CLOSES HIS FRONT DOOR

ELY: (ECHO) Gudgeon? Gudgeon? Where are you, Gudgeon? Damn the fellow.

HOLMES: (ECHO) Gudgeon is your manservant?

ELY: (ECHO) Not for much longer if he keeps disappearing like this. Well, gentlemen, my house is yours for the next- shall we say, an hour? Feel free to search anywhere. I'll be in the library.

FX: HE MARCHES OFF

HOPKINS: (ECHO) Well, Mr Holmes?

HOLMES: (ECHO) We've been afforded the opportunity, Inspector. And as I say - at present, this is our only avenue of enquiry.

WATSON: (ECHO) I think it'd be rude *not* to search now.

HOPKINS: (ECHO) All right. I'll start upstairs.

HOLMES:	(ECHO) While you're thus engaged, we'll question Lord Ely.
FX:	<u>ELY POURS HIMSELF A DRINK</u>
ELY:	I trust you'll understand if I don't offer either of you a drink.
WATSON:	Please understand, your Lordship, this is simply an opportunity to eliminate you-
ELY:	Oh, it's an opportunity to eliminate me, all right! I know full well who's behind this!
HOLMES:	Behind *what*, my Lord?
ELY:	Your Inspector Hopkins said you'd received information implicating me. Well, I know who gave you that information - Sidney Lanfield, am I correct?
WATSON:	I overheard you mention his name at Lady Conyngham's. He's a rival for Miss Brandon's affections?
ELY:	*He* thinks so. Anne is astonishingly tolerant of his attentions. So far as I'm concerned, he's just a damned nuisance.
HOLMES:	And is Mr Lanfield, by any chance, an artist?
ELY:	The worst sort of artist.
WATSON:	Untalented.
ELY:	On the contrary, very talented. But impoverished. Down through the generations, the Lanfields have always practised medicine, you see.
WATSON:	Of course! His father must be Sir Beresford Lanfield.
ELY:	The same. When his youngest son chose the paintbrush instead of the scalpel, Sir Beresford disinherited him. I understand his elder brother is the only relation who'll still speak to him.
HOLMES:	Any German blood in the family?

45

ELY:	His mother's German. Why?
HOLMES:	That explains his ability to imitate the accent, Watson.
WATSON:	And Lanfield wants to put you out of the way because he's in love with Miss Brandon too?
ELY:	He's more in love with her father's bank balance.
HOLMES:	You mean he wishes to marry her purely for the financial benefits?
ELY:	You put it a good deal more politely than I would, Doctor; I doubt there's anything pure about it. Miss Brandon is, you will have observed, a strikingly beautiful woman.
WATSON:	So this fellow wants Miss Brandon for her money, whereas you..?
ELY:	I am *Lord* Ely. If you still have any doubts as to my position in life, just look around you.
WATSON:	It's, er, a very impressive home.
ELY:	One of several. There is, of course, a family pile in the country. So you see, I'm interested in Anne because I feel a certain affection for her.
WATSON:	Affection? You wouldn't put it more strongly than that?
ELY:	You really are an astonishingly impertinent fellow, aren't you?
HOLMES:	Strangely enough, Dr Watson is usually regarded as the polite half of the partnership.
HOPKINS:	(APPROACHING) Excuse me, Lord Ely.
ELY:	Do I take it you've completed your search, Inspector Hopkins?
HOPKINS:	I have.
ELY:	Good. Now be off with you, and if I ever see the three of you

again, it'll be much too soon.

HOPKINS: I wonder, my Lord, if you'd care to explain this.

ELY: What?

HOPKINS: I discovered it in a cigar box filled with salt.

ELY: I don't understand…

HOPKINS: Tell me, what did you do with all the other fingers?

ELY: No! This is- this is a mistake!

HOPKINS: I'm afraid I'm going to have to ask you to accompany us back to the Yard.

ELY: This is impossible! It can't be happening!

MUSIC: UNDERCURRENT

WATSON: Lord Ely's expression, as we rode in a cab to Scotland Yard, was one of utter bemusement. He asked to be allowed to inspect the severed finger, but Stanley Hopkins refused to allow the cigar box to leave his possession even for a moment. It was not until Ely was locked and a cell, and we three were ensconced in the Inspector's office, that Holmes and I had the opportunity of examining the gruesome object.

MUSIC: OUT

HOLMES: Hm. Definitely a male finger.

HOPKINS: Why do you suppose we only found the one?

HOLMES: A very good question, Inspector. Why indeed? Watson, would you say this was done with the same implement used in the other killings?

WATSON: Let me take a closer look.* No, I would not. This was clearly done with something much smaller and sharper.

47

HOLMES: Just as I thought.

HOPKINS: You mean there's another murder we don't know anything about?

WATSON: I wouldn't say that, Inspector. You see, this finger smells faintly of rectified spirits - preserving fluid.

HOPKINS: But what does it mean?

HOLMES: It means that this didn't come from one of the victims; it was taken from a jar in a hospital laboratory.

WATSON: Lord Ely did say Lanfield's older brother was a doctor.

HOPKINS: Oh. Dear.

HOLMES: To put it mildly, Inspector. You know, you're really coming along, Watson. I must look to my laurels.

WATSON: Thank-you, Holmes.

HOPKINS: So this is some sort of practical joke?

HOLMES: Perpetrated by His Lordship's rival in love, Sidney Lanfield.

WATSON: Alias Steiner.

HOLMES: And we've done everything in our power to assist him with it. You have my most profound apologies, Hopkins.

HOPKINS: I wonder if it's too late to recall Forbes from Liverpool. Hang on a moment, Mr Holmes. This Lanfield chap's plan was to implicate Lord Ely in the Finger Murders.

HOLMES: Just so.

HOPKINS: But he must have known we couldn't make the charge stick. I mean, once another murder was committed, we'd know Lord Ely was innocent and release him.

HOLMES: I suspect Lanfield is interested solely in humiliating Ely by creating a public scandal. What better way than to have him arrested for the most notorious wave of killings since Jack the Ripper? Evidently, he thought I'd be easier to dupe than the official forces. And regrettably, he was correct.

WATSON: And, of course, the longer Ely remains behind bars, the more time Lanfield has to win the affections of the lovely Miss Brandon.

HOPKINS: Damn! A pretty bunch of fools we're going to look.

HOLMES: I failed to heed your warnings, Watson.

WATSON: And Lord Ely's. He was right when he told us who wanted to see him incriminated.

HOPKINS: I should have known from his expression of disbelief when I confronted him with the severed finger. He'd have to be a very good actor to be that convincing. You know, I really think I'd like to have a word with Mr Lanfield about this serious waste of police time.

HOLMES: We'll accompany you, if you don't mind, Inspector.

HOPKINS: There's still Lord Ely to deal with. I'm not looking forward to this. Oh, well, they say an apology costs nothing. I hope it's true.

WATSON: I'll take care of him for you, Inspector. Holmes, I trust you'll keep me informed of developments?

HOLMES: This isn't like you, Watson. You're quite sure?

WATSON: Quite. The temptation to repay him for that punch on jaw might be too great.

MUSIC: UNDERCURRENT

WATSON: I confess, I wasn't being completely truthful at that moment; I thought that after delivering Lord Ely to his home, I might pay a visit to the recently-widowed Kate Whitney… purely to offer my respects. It struck me that we had a good deal in common – both of the same age, both bereaved. A friendly chat would be most welcome.

MUSIC:	OUT
FX:	A BUSY LONDON STREET
ELY:	Watson! What the devil is the matter with you, man? I said, *we're here*.
WATSON:	(ROUSED FROM HIS REVERIE) Hm? Oh, splendid. Thank-you, cabbie.
FX:	THEY ALIGHT FROM THE CAB
ELY:	Here you are, driver. And don't expect a tip, either. I've never had such a bumpy journey.
FX:	THE DRIVER WHIPS THE HORSES AND THE CAB RACES OFF
ELY:	Arrogant dog. Whole world's going to rack and ruin. Nobody knows their place any more.
WATSON:	Don't ring just yet, your Lordship. I want to examine the lock with my magnifying glass.
ELY:	*You* have a magnifying glass?
WATSON:	(DEFENSIVELY) Yes, I do. You may not realise it, but you have *me* to thank for your liberty. No, no sign of any scratches, Lanfield must have got in by an unlocked window.
FX:	THE FRONT DOOR OPENS
GUDGEON:	I observed you on the step, sir.
ELY:	Oh, so you're home at last, are you, Gudgeon! Well, get out of the way, man, let me in!* It might interest you to know I've spent the last few hours in the company of the police!
FX:	*AS PER DIALOG, THEY ENTER. STREET BG DIMINISHES, BUT DOES NOT END – THE DOOR'S STILL OPEN.

GUDGEON:	(WARILY) Really, sir?
ELY:	Yes, the damned fools got it into their heads that I was responsible for this rash of murders! It was only thanks to Mr Sherlock Holmes-
WATSON:	(A DISCREET COUGH)
ELY:	Oh, yes, and this gentleman – that I was set free. And where were you all evening, Gudgeon?
GUDGEON:	Ah-
ELY:	Don't tell me, you were with that young lady of yours, weren't you? I can't pretend I approve. And the next time you're not at home when I require you, it'll be the last time!
GUDGEON:	Very good, sir.
ELY:	And you, what are you still doing here?
WATSON:	Well, I thought-
ELY:	Oh, you thought? You thought, did you? You thought that having got me out of jail, after putting me in there in the first place, that you'd be my new best friend for life, eh? Well, think again! I've no use for you or Holmes, damn the pair of you, now get out!
FX:	HE SLAMS THE DOOR SHUT. WATSON'S BACK OUT ON THE STREET.
WATSON:	Now I wish we hadn't paid off the cab.
HOLMES:	Not to worry, Watson, we can take mine.
WATSON:	Holmes, what are you doing here? I thought you'd gone to find Lanfield.
HOLMES:	Indeed I did. His residence on Brick Street isn't terribly far from Belgrave Square. I came on here at all speed.
WATSON:	Was he there?

HOLMES:	In a sense. But in another sense, he wasn't.
WATSON:	Holmes, you're talking in riddles. Things are complicated enough as it is.
HOLMES:	I'm afraid you won't have the chance to repay Mr Lanfield for his assault on you. Last night, he became the Finger Murderer's *fifth* victim.
MUSIC:	STING

SECOND COMMERCIAL

MUSIC:	UNDERCURRENT
WATSON:	We did not go back to Brick Lane - home to the recently deceased artist Sidney Lanfield - but to the mortuary, where the body of the man we had met the night before in the Angel and Crown was laid out upon a table.
MUSIC:	OUT
FX:	ECHO ON DIALOG THROUGHOUT
HOPKINS:	Mr Holmes has already confirmed this is the fellow you spoke to yesterday, Doctor.
WATSON:	Steiner, alias Sidney Lanfield. Yes, it's him all right, Inspector. Holmes, you knew he was an impostor from the first.
HOLMES:	I knew he was no dockworker, Watson. Observe the smoothness of the palms, and the traces of paint underneath the fingernails on the right hand.
WATSON:	That was why you asked Ely whether his rival was an artist.
HOLMES:	With a German background.
HOPKINS:	Dr Malachai's done a preliminary examination, and he's satisfied Lanfield was killed late last night.
WATSON:	Which eliminates Lord Ely as a suspect. The only time he was

out of our sight, he was locked up in a police cell.

HOPKINS: We found this chap dead on his doorstep; passers-by probably thought he was a drunkard and never looked twice at him.

WATSON: Hmm… Paint under the fingernails of the *right* hand. Inspector Hopkins, in all previous cases, the fingers were removed from which hand?

HOPKINS: The right, Mr Holmes.

HOLMES: And yet the fingers have been removed from Lanfield's *left* hand. Perplexing, isn't it?

WATSON: Is it possible that someone else committed this crime, someone trying to emulate the Finger Murders?

HOLMES: That was my first thought. But examine the cuts more closely.

WATSON: The same unique flaw in the knife. So what does it mean, then? Why this change?

HOLMES: The killer is sending us a message.

HOPKINS: And how do we decipher it?

HOLMES: Unfortunately, Hopkins, I haven't the faintest idea.

MUSIC: <u>FADE UP HOLMES PLAYING A SOLEMN PIECE ON HIS VIOLIN</u>

WATSON: Can't you play something more cheerful, Holmes?

HOLMES: This helps me to think.

WATSON: I can't say it has that effect on me.

MUSIC: <u>END</u>

FX: <u>HOLMES THROWS THE VIOLIN DOWN</u>

WATSON: Temper, Holmes.

HOLMES:	Never before have I had such a frustrating case, Watson! And never have I been so criminally slow!
WATSON:	Well, perhaps it would help to talk it through. What's troubling you?
HOLMES:	Where to begin? Lanfield comes to us in the guise of Steiner in order to falsely accuse Lord Ely of responsibility for the Finger Murders. Later that day, that selfsame murderer kills *him*.
WATSON:	I suppose it could be some incredible coincidence.
HOLMES:	I don't believe in coincidences.
WATSON:	Pardon me, but I beg to differ! I remember you saying… where is it?* Ah, yes! "If we could fly out of that window hand in hand, Watson, hover over this great city, gently remove the roofs and peep in at the queer things which are going on, the strange coincidences, the plannings, the cross-purposes, the wonderful chains of events-"
FX:	<u>WATSON FLIPS RAPIDLY THROUGH THE PAGES OF A BOOK</u>
HOLMES;	Yes, thank-you, Watson.
FX:	<u>WATSON SLAMS THE BOOK SHUT</u>
HOLMES:	I begin to see the disadvantages of using one's official biographer as a sounding-board.
WATSON:	I can't help it if I have a gift for retaining details.
HOLMES:	Nevertheless, I stand by my original assessment. The arm is coincidence is long, but not quite so long as that.
WATSON:	Then you're certain there's a link between Lanfield and the murderer.
HOLMES:	Precisely. No matter how tenuous, a link exists. Somehow, we must trace that link back to our quarry!

54

FX:	A KNOCK AT THE DOOR
HOLMES:	Go away, Mrs Hudson!
WATSON:	Come in, Mrs Hudson.
FX:	DOOR OPENS
MRS HUDSON:	A gentleman to see you, Mr Holmes.
HOLMES:	Send him away; I can't see anyone at the moment.
ELY:	Really, Mr Holmes, it's harder to get in to see you than it is to book a table at Marcini's.
WATSON:	Lord Ely! (COLDLY) Well, I must say, this is a surprise.
ELY:	This isn't a social call, I assure you, Doctor. Mr Holmes, I wish to avail myself of your services. (TO MRS HUDSON) Thank-you, my good woman, you may go.
MRS HUDSON:	Hmph!
FX:	DOOR SHUTS
HOLMES:	I'm afraid the hunt for the Finger Murderer demands my full attention, your Lordship. At present, I can't spare the time for any other matter.
ELY:	But my manservant has gone missing, Mr Holmes!
WATSON:	Gudgeon?
ELY:	I couldn't find the fellow this afternoon, and when I checked, I found he'd packed his things and vanished!
HOLMES:	Obtain another manservant. I'm certain there must be agencies for the acquisition of new staff.
ELY:	I'm… concerned for his safety.
WATSON:	His safety?

ELY:	Of course! There's a murderer on the loose!
HOLMES:	Yes, I could hardly fail to have noticed. Very well, Lord Ely, if I come across Gudgeon in the course of my investigations, I shall advise him of your concerns.
ELY:	Well, if that's all you can offer, I suppose it'll have to do. (DEPARTING) Send me a bill in due course, Holmes.
FX:	HE LEAVES
WATSON:	That was unexpected. From the dressing-down he gave his manservant this morning, he shows a surprising amount of concern for Gudgeon's well-being.
HOLMES:	Perhaps there's more to Lord Ely than meets the eye.
WATSON:	Sidney Lanfield certainly wanted us to think so.
HOLMES:	You're developing quite a mischievous sense of humour, Watson; I shall have to guard against it. Now, where was I?
MUSIC:	HOLMES BEGINS TO PLAY HIS MOURNFUL TUNE AGAIN
WATSON:	Oh, for heaven's sake!
MUSIC:	STOPS ABRUPTLY AS:
FX:	THE DOOR FLIES OPEN
HOPKINS:	Mr Holmes!
HOLMES:	Hopkins! I hope you didn't collide with Lord Ely over on your way up. I'd hate to think we'd done anything else to incur his wrath.
HOPKINS:	Lord Ely was here? What did he want?
HOLMES:	A trifling domestic complication, no more. You have something more interesting, I trust?

HOPKINS:	Perhaps, Mr Holmes, only perhaps. This telegram just arrived at the Yard.
FX:	THE TELEGRAM IS HANDED OVER
WATSON:	(READING) "Mr Hopkins, if you still want the F.M., you can find him at 13 Miller's Court, Whitechapel." F.M. – Finger Murderer.
HOPKINS:	I assume you'd both wish to accompany me.
HOLMES:	You assume correctly, Hopkins. But you're right to be on your guard. Our last sojourn to Whitechapel ended in disaster.
WATSON:	All the same, Holmes, if we're about to come face-to-face with our quarry, you won't object to my bringing my old service revolver along.
MUSIC:	STING

THIRD COMMERCIAL

FX:	HOPKINS RAPS ON THE DOOR. A DOG BARKS IN THE DISTANCE
HOPKINS:	No answer. A merry dance we're being led here.
WATSON:	The windows are so grimy it's difficult to make out details. I think there's somebody on the bed. They're either asleep or…
HOPKINS:	Right, we'll put our shoulders to the door.
HOLMES:	Don't you think the landlord might have something to say about that, Inspector?
HOPKINS:	If he rents out properties in Whitechapel, he shouldn't expect anything else. Alright. On the count of three. One – two – *three!*
FX:	THE DOOR IS SMASHED OPEN. HOPKINS TAKES A FEW STEPS OVER TO THE CORPSE.
HOPKINS:	He looks dead, all right. Still got all his fingers, though.

WATSON:	Holmes, I've seen this man before. It's Lord Ely's manservant, Gudgeon.
HOPKINS:	The manservant? You're quite sure, Doctor?
WATSON:	There's no doubt. I met him only this morning.
HOLMES:	And His Lordship wanted us to find Gudgeon after he went missing this afternoon. Most perplexing.
HOPKINS:	Wait a moment. *I* know this fellow, too! I didn't recognise him without the beard, but- yes, it's Archie Griffin! Used to be one of the Spencer John Gang. I wanted to talk to him about the killing of that groom outside the Holborn Bar. Fellow just vanished off the face of the Earth.
HOLMES:	You were looking for him among the dregs of society, Hopkins. Griffin chose a hiding place on a different level altogether. What brought him to Whitechapel, I wonder?
WATSON:	Is anybody who they claim to be in this case? Steiner is Lanfield, Gudgeon is Griffin…
HOLMES:	It seems he smoked a cigar and enjoyed a drink before he died. But I doubt he would have enjoyed this last drink. Sniff the bottle, Watson.
WATSON:	Prussic Acid. But did he take it willingly, or was it forced down his throat?
HOPKINS:	Gentlemen, look what I've found underneath the bed.
FX:	<u>HOPKINS PICKS UP A HEAVY KNIFE</u>
WATSON:	It's a cleaver. And the flaw in the blade would match the wounds on the victims' hands, I think. Now we know why Gudgeon wasn't in Belgrave Square last night – he was murdering Sidney Lanfield.
HOPKINS:	And then he kills himself in remorse for his crimes, or because he's afraid we're catching up on him. It's tidy.

HOLMES:	One loose end remains, however.
HOPKINS:	What's that?
WATSON:	Who sent the telegram?
HOLMES:	Hopkins, would you have any objections to my collecting up this cigar ash?
HOPKINS:	Be my guest, Mr Holmes.
HOLMES:	Thank-you. I'd also like to examine this bottle.
HOPKINS:	What do you have in mind?
HOLMES:	Too early to say. But I have a suspicion that all is not right here.
MUSIC:	SHORT BRIDGE
FX:	HOLMES IS SHUFFLING PAPERS ABOUT
WATSON:	Holmes, what will Mrs Hudson say about this mess?
HOLMES:	Whatever she likes, Watson. As long as she doesn't attempt to tidy anything away, I'm happy to let her voice her opinion.
WATSON:	What *is* all this?
HOLMES:	The official documents on the Finger Murders.
WATSON:	I thought these papers weren't allowed out of Scotland Yard!
HOLMES:	With Gudgeon's apparent suicide, they've become less possessive. It seems that Sir Edward is satisfied the case is at an end and has told Hopkins as much.
WATSON:	You're not so certain?
HOLMES:	I think it entirely likely that Gudgeon was murdered. In all likelihood, by the unknown person who notified us of his death.
WATSON:	I bumped into Dr Malachai at the club. He's completed his post-

mortem, and tells me that Gudgeon had consumed so much alcohol, he would have been completely insensible when he died.

HOLMES: So it would have been easy for someone to force him to drink prussic acid without much of a struggle.

WATSON: He might even have drunk it himself, not knowing what he was doing 'til it was too late.

HOLMES: I don't believe so. I found Gudgeon's fingerprints on the neck of the bottle.

WATSON: Well, doesn't that support my theory?

HOLMES: But there were no other fingerprints anywhere else, not even those of the man who sold it to him. Doesn't that seem peculiar to you?

WATSON: But if he was forced to drink poison, and then the killer wiped the bottle and placed Gudgeon's dead hand on it... Yes, I see what you mean.

HOLMES: So you see, this business is far from over. But without proof, my theories are just that – theories. That's why I'm going over the papers in the case. Hoping to find some connecting thread between the victims.

WATSON: And have you?

HOLMES: No. Eugene Lytton was a fishmonger, murdered in his shop three weeks ago. Yvette Schumann was a visitor to our shores, German by birth, found dead in her room at the Northumberland Hotel just three days later. A week and a half passed before the death of Percy Latimer, a journalist, killed in a Whitechapel alley, not far from the Angel and Crown. And lastly, Aubrey Nelson, just three days ago. And nothing whatsoever to connect them.

WATSON: I still think there's something to be said for my initial observation; once we find out what became of the fingers-

HOLMES: (ALERT) What was that you said, Watson?

WATSON: I said, I believe there's something to be said for my original

	observation.
HOLMES:	No, no you didn't. You said "my *initial* observation".
WATSON:	Well, does it matter?
HOLMES:	More than you realise. "The strange coincidences, the plannings, the cross-purposes, the wonderful chains of events…" Watson – you're invaluable!
WATSON:	Nice of you to say so, Holmes.
MUSIC:	SHORT BRIDGE
ELY:	I suppose you want to ask me about Gudgeon, gentlemen.
HOLMES:	Among other things, my Lord.
ELY:	Ask away, Holmes, I doubt there's anything I can tell you. The whole thing seems unbelievable to me. But they do say that life is stranger than fiction.
HOLMES:	Infinitely so. And I owe a Dr Watson a debt of thanks for reminding me about the intrusion of coincidence into our everyday lives. Your Lordship, I'm still unclear on the connection between Gudgeon and his victims. Perhaps you could enlighten me.
ELY:	Why does there have to be one? Clearly, the fellow was out of his senses.
HOLMES:	And yet, there was a connection between Gudgeon and Sidney Lanfield, was there not? Gudgeon was your servant, Lanfield your rival.
ELY:	I suppose that's a sort of a connection. Very likely he heard me complaining about Lanfield and fixed upon the fellow as his next victim.
HOLMES:	Why?
ELY:	Well, how the devil should I know? Obviously, Lanfield was just

	unlucky.
HOLMES:	I couldn't agree with you more. In fact, had I not witnessed the chain of events with my own eyes, I would not have believed just how unlucky he had been.
HOPKINS:	What do you mean, Mr Holmes?
HOLMES:	Lanfield broke into this house in order to plant evidence suggesting that Lord Ely was responsible for the Finger Murders. He could never have guessed in a million years that he was correct.
WATSON:	Holmes, are you certain?
ELY:	Is this some kind of sick joke?
HOLMES:	Come now, your Lordship. It's too late to play cat and mouse.
ELY:	I advise you to take great care, Holmes. Talk like that can get you sued.
HOLMES:	You were anxious to have your home searched, because you knew that with Gudgeon busy despatching your rival, you had nothing to hide. Your shock when Inspector Hopkins discovered the severed finger was quite genuine.
HOPKINS:	I did say he couldn't have been that good an actor. But the rest of it-
ELY:	Now, now, just wait a moment. You're saying Gudgeon murdered Lanfield and all the others?
HOLMES:	I believe that Gudgeon committed all five murders, yes.
ELY:	So if Gudgeon was the murderer, I can't be responsible! I'm beginning to wonder if you're quite "with it", Holmes. Sounds to me like you're losing your touch. First Lanfield dupes you, and now this insane outburst. Dr Watson, perhaps you'd better take Mr Holmes back to Baker Street. He seems in need of a rest.
HOLMES:	Dr Watson told me what occurred when Gudgeon met you on

	your return from Scotland Yard.
ELY:	Yes, he said he'd been walking out with his young lady.
WATSON:	As a matter of fact, my Lord, he didn't. That was what *you* said. Gudgeon merely agreed with you.
ELY:	Well, I suppose I just assumed it. There's no crime in that, is there?
HOLMES:	Not unless you knew what he was actually doing. Because you had masterminded those crimes.
ELY:	You really are insane. Gudgeon committed those murders and then killed himself.
HOLMES:	I'm afraid not. You see, I found the stub of an Indian Lunkah cigar in the room where he died. But the amount of ash I collected was equal to two cigars.
ELY:	So?
HOLMES:	Clearly, two cigars were smoked in that room. And since the stub of the second did not leave on its own, it follows that there must have been a second person present. And if you will allow me to take a look in your cigar box.
ELY:	(MOCKINGLY) You don't expect to find another finger, do you?

<u>FX:</u>   <u>HOLMES OPENS THE LID</u>

HOLMES:	No, simply this. Indian Lunkahs.
ELY:	So because a servant stole some of his master's cigars, and because whoever killed that servant smoked one of those cigars, I must therefore be Gudgeon's murderer? Rather specious logic, Mr Holmes.
HOLMES:	It is certainly circumstantial, I admit.
ELY:	Why would I want all those people dead, anyway? With the

exception of Lanfield, they were complete strangers to me. And how could I persuade Gudgeon to commit murder for me?

HOPKINS: Gudgeon was really Archie Griffin, a well-known criminal. He'd have killed his own grandmother for the right price.

ELY: So you say, but I didn't know that!

HOLMES: So *you* say. And as to your second question, Lord Ely, you answered it yourself. Why should you desire the deaths of total strangers? Because they *were* total strangers. All this time, we've been wondering why the killer removed the victims' fingers. Now we know: in order to convince Scotland Yard that several unrelated crimes were in fact a series of *related* crimes.

WATSON: And in order that the one crime that had been planned all along, the murder of Sidney Lanfield, might be hidden among that series.

HOLMES: Precisely, Watson. But events took an unexpected course when Lanfield, in the guise of Steiner, put us on his enemy's track. It became clear to Lord Ely that the best course of action would be to sacrifice his pawn, the man who committed these crimes on his orders.

HOPKINS: So he told Gudgeon to clear out and lay low in Whitechapel.

ELY: I did no such thing.

HOLMES: You subsequently poisoned Gudgeon and telegraphed Inspector Hopkins, telling him where the Finger Murderer could be found. You called upon us at Baker Street in order to make us believe that Gudgeon had vanished without your knowledge.

ELY: My patience is at an end, gentlemen, and so is this interview. You'll be hearing from my solicitors.

HOLMES: But Gudgeon was no mere dupe. He knew he could not entirely trust you, and so he laid a trail for us to follow.

ELY: Stuff and nonsense!

HOLMES:	I suspect that his selection of victims was of little interest to you; you imagined that the killings were as random as they were supposed to be.
WATSON:	But there *was* a connection?
HOLMES:	The victims prior to Sidney Lanfield, were Eugene Lytton, Yvette Schumann, Percy Latimer and Aubrey Nelson. Lord Ely, perhaps you would be good enough to tell me their initials.
ELY:	Why?
HOLMES:	Why not?
ELY:	Very well… E.L., Y.S., P.L…. My God.
HOLMES:	*And A.N.* E-L-Y-S-P-L-A-N - "Ely's plan". That was why the fingers of Lanfield's *left* hand were removed, to let us know that this killing did not conform to the usual pattern, and should therefore be examined more closely.
ELY:	Damn the fellow.
HOLMES:	I'm very much afraid it appears as though he's damned you first.
ELY:	I was right, you know. Whole world's going to rack and ruin. Nobody knows their place any more.
HOPKINS:	Then it's true.
ELY:	Oh, I could fight you, Inspector; perhaps I'd even win. But Anne would suffer terribly… and I couldn't bear that.
WATSON:	(FLAT) How noble of you.
ELY:	Inspector, when you see Anne, tell her… tell her that if she should ever happen to think of me… let it be as someone who loved her very much. That was why, you see. I couldn't risk losing her to Lanfield.
HOPKINS:	I'll tell her.

ELY:	(HIS FORMAL MANNER RESTORED) Thank-you, Inspector. I'm ready now.
MUSIC:	STING
FX:	HOLMES AND WATSON ARE WALKING DOWN A QUIET STREET. IT'S RAINING.
WATSON:	I think this must count as one of your greatest triumphs, Holmes.
HOLMES:	After one of my most dismal humiliations. I wonder if Lord Ely wasn't too far off the mark when he said I was in need of a rest.
WATSON:	Surely not!
HOLMES:	It's a time of change, Watson. Perhaps the twentieth century will have no need of me.
WATSON:	The world will always need Sherlock Holmes.
HOLMES:	And faithful old Dr Watson. The nights are drawing in. Perhaps now would be the perfect time to regale you with the true facts of the Jack the Ripper case.
WATSON:	Not just now, Holmes. There's, ah, somewhere else I have to be.
HOLMES:	I see. Well, give Mrs Whitney my regards.
WATSON:	Yes. Yes, I shall. Good-night, Holmes.
FX:	HE STROLLS OFF
HOLMES:	(TO SELF) Good-night, Watson. And good-bye.
MUSIC:	DANSE MACABRE

The Further Adventures of Sherlock Holmes –
The Moriarty Resurrection
(Original Airdate January 8, 2006)

The producers of *The Further Adventures of Sherlock Holmes* have one very strict rule regarding the use of Professor James Moriarty: Forget it. Earlier radio and film series were happy to have the Napoleon of Crime turn up as a recurring villain, but for this series, the Canon is King, and the Canon states that Professor Moriarty died at the Reichenbach Falls. The Canon also states that Holmes died, too, but *The Empty House* provides an explanation for that. Nor can the Professor torment our heroes in any case set prior to *The Final Problem*, since in that story, it's made plain that Watson has never heard of the man before. Of course, the Doctor seems quite familiar with him in *The Valley of Fear*, written years later but set some time before. The real reason for that discrepancy is, of course, artistic licence, but in the context of this fictional world, I had it that Watson had no idea of Moriarty's involvement in *Valley* until informed of it in this episode. So, no Moriarty outside those two Canonical tales. But Conan Doyle did mention that the Professor had two brothers...

I was never going to have Colonel James Moriarty taking over his elder brother's criminal empire, but I was happy to trick listeners into thinking so for as long as possible (the title doesn't refer to him, but to his wife, Cecile). I also wished to prolong the impression that the Professor might still be alive until part-way through of Act Two. For this reason, I suggested that the same actor, Nolan Palmer, should play both Moriartys, in order to muddy the waters even further. I had, however, originally included a line regarding the Moriarty's daughter, Bernice. It was my notion that Bernice was the result of an affair between Cecile and the Professor, and that she should have inherited her true father's criminal genius. But even back then, I suspected that this was a pretty cheesy idea, and I've never used it to this day. If you ever hear a show with this premise you'll know I've finally run out of steam and should probably call it a day. The point made by Holmes at the end of the episode, that the Professor's body was never recovered from the Falls, is a mere tease – don't expect him back any time soon, or, more likely, ever.

If, as I've already insisted, the word of the Canon is law, it was downright perverse of me to spend so much of the latter part of this play proving that the explanation of the final battle between Holmes and Moriarty presented in *The Empty House* is actually incorrect. As it's Watson who narrates the stories, it was important that he should have believed what his friend told him about it, and had no suspicions to the contrary until this case. That was my justification, in any case. Strange to think that we actually overturned the notion of what occurred at the Reichenbach Falls three years before depicting the Canonical version, which you'll find elsewhere in this book.

The seemingly obligatory Basil Rathbone movie reference is pretty obvious here: Moriarty's solicitor is Frederick Worlock, one of the stable of actors used in almost all of the Universal films. I also have a suspicion that he played Lestrade in the later episodes of *The New Adventures of Sherlock Holmes* radio series, but those shows never had cast lists, so I can't be certain. Watson's opening narration states that after his apparent death at the Reichenbach Falls, Holmes travelled the globe under the name Olaf Sigerson. In fact, *The Empty House* only gives his surname; the Olaf part comes from the Rathbone radio play *Murder Beyond the Mountains*, written by Anthony Boucher and Denis Green. Of course, it's one thing to cross-reference the works of others, but the series has a continuity of its own, which is why mention is made to an earlier episode, *The Diary of Anthony Moltaire*, scripted by producer Jim French.

I soon realised it was a mistake to insert the "I am a brain, first and foremost" speech from *The Mazarin Stone* into this script, when I came to adapt *The Mazarin Stone* for *The Classic Adventures of Sherlock Holmes* just a few months later. At that time, I simply had Watson moan, "Oh, not *this* again!"

Although Lestrade doesn't appear in this episode, I'm proud to say that I gave him a Christian name here. Both the BBC's celebrated Complete Canon series, masterminded by Bert Coules, and David Stuart Davies' stage play *The Death and Life of Sherlock Holmes* refer to the Inspector as Giles. But he always felt like more of a George to me, and I had Watson say so. Cecile Moriarty's real identity – Alicia Cutter – is a sly (if pointless) reference to the unsolved case of the vessel that sailed into a patch of mist and vanished. The name of the victim, Ormond Sacker, was, of course, used by Conan Doyle as the assistant of detective Sherringford Holmes in the first draft of *A Study in Scarlet*, entitled *A Tangled Skein* (a volume discussed in further detail in *The Adventure of the Two Watsons*). Looking back, the fact that I didn't save the name for a character of greater significance in some other episode is a source of even greater regret than my decision to use the *Mazarin Stone* quote. Oh, well.

CAST

ANNOUNCER (DENNIS BATEMAN)

HOLMES (JOHN PATRICK LOWRIE)

WATSON (LAWRENCE ALBERT)

MRS HUDSON (LEE PASCH)

INSPECTOR HOPKINS (WILLIAM HAMER)

PROFESSOR JAMES MORIARTY/COLONEL JAMES MORIARTY (NOLAN PALMER)

FREDERICK WORLOCK (DENNIS BATEMAN)

CECILE MORIARTY (KAREN NELSON)

DR MALACHAI (JIM FRENCH)

DIRECTED BY LAWRENCE ALBERT

FX:	OPENING SEQUENCE, BIG BEN
ANNOUNCER:	*The Further Adventures of Sherlock Holmes*, featuring John Patrick Lowrie as Holmes and Lawrence Albert as Dr Watson.
MUSIC:	A DEEPLY MOURNFUL PIECE ON THE VIOLIN UNDER
FX:	A RAGING TORRENT OF WATER CAN BE HEARD, FAINTLY
HOLMES:	(READING) "My dear Watson… I write these few lines through the courtesy of Professor Moriarty, who awaits my convenience for the final discussion of those questions which lie between us. I am pleased to think that I shall be able to free society from any further effects of his presence, though I fear that it is at a cost which will give pain to my friends, and especially, my dear Watson, to you. I have already explained to you, however, that my career had in any case reached its crisis, and that no possible conclusion to it could be more congenial to me than this. I made every disposition of my property before leaving England and handed it to my brother Mycroft. Pray give my regards to Mrs Hudson, and believe me to be, my dear fellow, very sincerely yours… Sherlock Holmes."
MUSIC:	OUT
FX:	A MIGHTY PUNCH CONNECTS WITH HOLMES' JAW
HOLMES:	Oof!
PROFESSOR:	Do you know, I thought you were never going to finish? I really have no idea why you feel the need to bid farewell to Watson anyway. He isn't worthy of your condescension.
FX:	HOLMES DELIVERS A BLOW OF HIS OWN. THE FIGHT CONTINUES DURING THEIR DISCUSSION, WITH FLYING FISTS AND THE INFREQUENT CONNECTIONS.
HOLMES:	I doubt you'd ever be capable of comprehending the reason, Moriarty.
PROFESSOR:	You and I, Holmes, we represent the next step in man's

70

evolutionary journey – homo superior.

HOLMES: Then how does it come about that we find ourselves battling like common thugs?

PROFESSOR: My dear fellow, you do the moment a great injustice! In such a contest of wills, cataclysm was inevitable. One must die, so that the other might live.

HOLMES: And since neither of us is willing to volunteer..?

PROFESSOR: Precisely. And I could hardly have chosen better than the Reichenbach Falls. (A YELL OF PAIN AS:)

FX: HOLMES' KNEE CONNECTS WITH HIS GUT

PROFESSOR: (WINDED) And what, may I ask, was that?

HOLMES: Perhaps you are unfamiliar with the Japanese art of Baritsu. I had occasion to study it when engaged upon an investigation for the-

PROFESSOR: No more talk, Holmes. It's time for you to die. (MORIARTY GROWLS, THE GROWL GROWING IN INTENSITY AS HE'S ABOUT TO POUNCE)

FX: THEY CLASH FOR A FINAL TIME. THE FALLS ROAR.

PROFESSOR &
HOLMES: (BOTH CRY OUT AS THEY FALL TO THEIR DEATHS)

FX: FALLS OUT

HOLMES: (CONTINUES TO CRY, THIS TIME ALONE)

FX: A RAP ON THE DOOR

WATSON: (OUTSIDE) Holmes! Holmes, what's wrong?

HOLMES: (BADLY SHAKEN) I'm quite all right, thank-you, Watson. It was just… the dream. Again.

MUSIC: *DANSE MACABRE* UP AND UNDER

71

WATSON:	My name is Dr John H Watson, friend and biographer of the great detective, Sherlock Holmes. In the April of 1891, the long battle between Holmes and the criminal mastermind Professor James Moriarty came to an end upon the slopes of the Reichenbach Falls in Switzerland. Holmes was, of course, triumphant, but in order to escape the wrath of Moriarty's right-hand man, Colonel Sebastian Moran, he was forced to fake his own death, and vanished from public life for three years, travelling the world under the name Olaf Sigerson. In 1894, he returned to London to see Moran arrested for the murder of the Honourable Ronald Adair. In the three months since the resumption of his duties as a consulting detective, he had not mentioned Professor Moriarty.
MUSIC:	<u>OUT</u>
FX:	<u>THE DOOR TO HOLMES' ROOM OPENS</u>
HOLMES:	(YAWNS)
MRS HUDSON:	Ah! So he gets up at last!
HOLMES:	Mrs Hudson, please guard against this disturbing tendency to sound like my mother. 'Morning, Watson.
MRS HUDSON:	*Good afternoon*, Mr Holmes.
HOLMES:	*Good afternoon*, Mrs Hudson. Have I had any visitors?
MRS HUDSON:	Only one, sir.
HOLMES:	And who was that?
MRS HUDSON:	Me. I tidied up while you were asleep.
HOLMES:	Watson, you didn't let her dust, did you?
WATSON:	Well, the place had become rather a state.
HOLMES:	Mrs Hudson, must I remind you that dust is an essential part of my filing system? From its thickness-

MRS HUDSON:	I've heard it all before, Mr Holmes. I didn't believe it then and I don't believe it now.
WATSON:	Take a seat, Holmes.* Feeling better, I trust?
FX:	HOLMES PULLS UP A CHAIR AND SITS DOWN
HOLMES:	Better? You talk in riddles, Watson, I'm not ill.
WATSON:	The nightmare. You were in quite a state.
HOLMES:	It sounds as though you may have been dreaming yourself, Doctor. I never have nightmares. Never.
WATSON:	Of course. My mistake.
FX:	A PLATE AND CUTLERY ARE PLACED ON THE TABLE
HOLMES:	And what is this, may I ask?
MRS HUDSON:	Breakfast, Mr Holmes.
HOLMES:	Breakfast. Not dinner?
MRS HUDSON:	Breakfast. Ham and eggs. And there are some kidneys in the dish if you'd care for them.
HOLMES:	Splendid! Well, it's taken you a good many years, but you've finally adjusted to my irregular timekeeping. My congratulations, Mrs Hudson.
MRS HUDSON:	Not really, sir. When I asked you on Monday what time you'd like breakfast, you said "one-thirty, the day after tomorrow". So here it is. (DEPARTING) I'll be up for the plates later.
FX:	SHE LEAVES
WATSON:	You might get the better of London's smartest criminals, Holmes, but you'll never be able to outwit your landlady.
HOLMES:	I'm seriously thinking of giving up trying.

FX:	THE DOOR OPENS AGAIN
HOLMES:	What is it now, Mrs Hudson? My supper from three nights ago?
MRS HUDSON:	A visitor, Mr Holmes. That nice Inspector Hopkins.
HOLMES:	Well, don't keep him waiting on the stairs. Show him in, by all means!
HOPKINS:	Thank-you, Mrs Hudson. Mr Holmes, Doctor.
HOLMES:	Hopkins, do take a seat.* Can I interest you in some ham and eggs?
FX:	HE ALSO PULLS UP A CHAIR
HOPKINS:	Er…
WATSON:	Holmes, that food is for you.
HOPKINS:	Well, I shouldn't like to deprive anyone of their dinner.
WATSON:	Breakfast.
HOLMES:	Nonsense, Hopkins. I am a brain, first and foremost. The rest of me is a mere appendix.
WATSON:	Rubbish!
HOLMES:	By no means, Doctor. Surely you admit that what your digestion gains in the way of blood supply is therefore lost to the brain.
WATSON:	The body is like a fire in the grate, Holmes; it'll go out unless it gets more coal.
HOLMES:	I hope you're not suggesting I should eat coal, Watson. I'm sure you wouldn't object to my at least sharing this sumptuous repast with our visitor?
MRS HUDSON:	I'll fetch you a plate, Stanley.
FX:	SHE LEAVES

WATSON:	"Stanley"! You're honoured, Hopkins. She never calls Inspector Lestrade by his Christian name.
HOLMES:	What *is* Lestrade's Christian name, incidentally?
HOPKINS:	Uh… Giles, I think.
WATSON:	Oh, I shouldn't have said so. No, he looks more like a George than a Giles. Next time he calls, you must ask him, Holmes.
HOLMES:	I'd really rather not. I should prefer our association to remain on a business footing. And speaking of business, do I take you have something of interest for us, Hopkins?
HOPKINS:	In a manner of speaking, Mr Holmes. I don't really know whether there's anything for you to investigate - I don't even know if you *could* investigate, but when I arrived at the scene and met *him*- well, I just knew I had to see you at once!
HOLMES:	Hopkins, it isn't like you to be so unintelligible. Whom, precisely, did you meet and why should I be so interested in that person?
HOPKINS:	I'm sure I don't need to ask if you're familiar with the name James Moriarty?
MUSIC:	UNDERCURRENT
WATSON:	And I'll continue my story in just a moment.
MUSIC:	OUT

FIRST COMMERCIAL

MUSIC:	UNDERCURRENT
WATSON:	And now to return to the story I call "The Moriarty Resurrection".
MUSIC:	OUT
FX:	TWO PAIRS OF FEET CRUNCH ALONG A GRAVEL PATH

COLONEL:	I want to see him crushed, Worlock. I want him begging for mercy at my feet.
WORLOCK:	James, I advise you to stop using such emotive language.
COLONEL:	I'll make him rue the day he ever heard the name Moriarty.
WORLOCK:	Given what you've already put him through, I'm quite sure he does that already. Can't you just leave the fellow alone now? You've had your sport with him.
COLONEL:	Never! I won't finish until I see him finished off!
WORLOCK:	James…
COLONEL:	He's my nemesis, Worlock. My arch-enemy. I want my hatred for everything he stands for to go down in history. In the future, whenever people talk of great feuds between two equally-matched opponents, they will talk of James Moriarty and Dr John H Watson!
WORLOCK:	(SIGHS) Dear, oh dear, oh dear. James, as your solicitor-
COLONEL:	As my solicitor, you're supposed to back my side of the argument.
WORLOCK:	And I do! Watson's behaviour has been disgraceful, no doubt about it. But what does Cecile think about all this?
FX:	THEY HALT. MORIARTY KNOCKS AT THE DOOR.
COLONEL:	Cecile agrees with my position entirely, as any good wife should.
FX:	THE DOOR OPENS AND THEY STEP INSIDE
CECILE:	Hello, dear. Hello, Frederick.
WORLOCK:	Cecile, my dear. (HE KISSES HER CHEEK) It's unusually brisk for Summer, don't you think?
CECILE:	There's a fire in the grate. Did I just hear my name mentioned?

WORLOCK:	Only in the most complimentary terms, I promise you. I'm surprised to see you answering your own door. Where's – um… what's the girl's name again?
CECILE:	Rosemary. She's not here today, her mother's sick.
COLONEL:	Supposedly.
CECILE:	James!
COLONEL:	Well, how many times has her mother been sick since we took her on? It seems to me that woman takes ill whenever her daughter doesn't feel like coming to work.
CECILE:	We can't very well call her a liar.
COLONEL:	Just watch me. A drink for Frederick if you wouldn't mind, dear.
WORLOCK:	Thank you, Cecile. A cup of tea would be lovely.
COLONEL:	Tea? Oh well, same for me, I suppose. Wait here a moment, old chap, there are some papers in my study I want you to see. (DEPARTING) They should help us with our case. Shan't be a moment.
FX:	THE STUDY DOOR IS SHUT AND LOCKED
CECILE:	Dr Watson again?
WORLOCK:	I'm afraid so, Cecile.
CECILE:	(SIGHS) It's all so tiresome.
COLONEL:	(BEHIND THE DOOR) Who the devil are you? How did you get in here?
WORLOCK:	What's going on in there?
COLONEL:	(BEHIND DOOR) What do you want here? Back! Get back!
CECILE:	James!

COLONEL:	(BEHIND DOOR) Put that down, damn you!
FX:	THERE'S THE SOUND OF A STRUGGLE BEHIND THE DOOR. WORLOCK TRIES THE KNOB AND HAMMERS ON THE DOOR.
WORLOCK:	James! Unlock the door! James!
FX:	A GUNSHOT FROM BEHIND THE DOOR
CECILE:	(SCREAMS)
(PAUSE)	
FX:	THE DOOR IS UNLOCKED AND OPENED
CECILE:	James!
COLONEL:	I'm… all right, my dear. Just a little winded. Don't come in here.
WORLOCK:	James, what happened?
COLONEL:	An intruder. A burglar, no doubt. Came in through the window, surprised me, we struggled over my service revolver.
WORLOCK:	Is he dead?
COLONEL:	He would have done the same to me.
WORLOCK:	James, we'd better have the police.
COLONEL:	Whatever you think best, Worlock. Just so long as we can get this fellow out of here with the minimum of fuss. I don't want Cecile being upset by the sight of him.
FX:	FADE OUT
HOPKINS:	That's how it happened, gentlemen. Or, at least, that's how the participants described it to me.
WATSON:	Colonel James Moriarty… the Professor's brother.

HOPKINS:	I understand you two are acquainted, Doctor.
WATSON:	Through our solicitors, mostly. Colonel Moriarty's done everything he could to dispel the rumours concerning his brother's position as king of the underworld. We've been at loggerheads ever since. And now he's killed a man, eh? I'd cancel my fishing holiday to see this case through to the end!
HOPKINS:	Apart from a brief stroll about ten-ish, the Colonel spent the morning at home, then went out to meet Mr Worlock at the station. The Colonel lives out in Chelmsford, you see. Worlock's gone back to his office in the city, and the body's been taken to the mortuary.
HOLMES:	Inspector, have you noticed that the servants always seem to be absent when something of this nature occurs? It's a most peculiar phenomenon.
FX:	DOOR OPENS
MRS HUDSON:	Here's your plate, Sta- Goodness, what happened to all the food?
HOLMES:	My apologies, Hopkins. It appears I was hungrier than I first thought.
HOPKINS:	Not to worry, Mr Holmes. Thank-you anyway, Mrs Hudson.
MRS HUDSON:	(DEPARTING) Up and down these stairs like I don't know what…
FX:	DOOR SLAMS
HOPKINS:	Do you think perhaps I should-
HOLMES:	Not at all - she enjoys the exercise. Why did the Colonel lock his study door, I wonder?
WATSON:	Have you asked him, Inspector?
HOPKINS:	More than once. And on each occasion, he damns my impudence.

WATSON:	That certainly sounds like the Colonel. I remember becoming engaged in a shouting match with him over supper at Kellner's. Why does the fellow have to be so deliberately abusive?
HOLMES:	At the moment, Watson, there is something of greater moment that concerns us – if you can restrain your indignation.
WATSON:	Shan't say another word.
HOPKINS:	It took all my skill to persuade the Colonel to part with his revolver. I have it here.
FX:	HOPKINS PLACES IT ON THE TABLE
HOLMES:	Military paraphernalia is the Doctor's department. If he's finished sulking.
WATSON:	I'm not sulking, Holmes, I'm examining. It's a Webley. I was just thinking how odd it is that a man as pompous as Colonel Moriarty should have allowed it to get in such a state. My own service revolver is in a far better condition.
HOLMES:	Most enlightening. If I may..? (A PAUSE WHILE HE EXAMINES IT) Ahh… Tell me Hopkins, is the Colonel left-handed or right handed?
HOPKINS:	Left or-? I'm sorry, Mr Holmes, I'm afraid I didn't notice. Do I take it you have your suspicions?
HOLMES:	I suspect only that I may be guilty of jumping to conclusions. It is possible that he is entirely innocent of any wrongdoing.
WATSON:	But in all probability, he isn't.
HOLMES:	(SIGHS) Watson, you must not allow this feud to cloud your judgement.
WATSON:	Need I remind you, Holmes, that the feud began when I stepped forward to protect your memory? When I thought you were dead, that is.
HOLMES:	And I assure you, my good fellow, that I am eternally grateful for

your loyalty.

HOPKINS: If you'll permit me, Mr Holmes, the Doctor does have a point. It might not be logical, but I can't help feeling that the Colonel isn't being completely truthful. *And* he's a Moriarty.

HOLMES: Among nice people, murder – like matrimony – generally has a motive. Find the motive and the thread of deceit will unravel before your eyes.

HOPKINS: So you *do* think he's trying to deceive us, then?

HOLMES: I cannot draw conclusions without data. However, it strikes me that investigating this case will prove exceptionally difficult. Moriarty has no love for Watson or myself.

HOPKINS: Now you understand my concern over consulting you.

WATSON: There's always the lawyer, Frederick Worlock. Although I don't know how much he'd be prepared to tell us.

HOLMES: But there is, at least one player in this drama who will tell us the absolute truth.

HOPKINS: *Mrs* Moriarty?

HOLMES: The murdered man, Hopkins.

MUSIC: BRIDGE

FX: ECHO THROUGHOUT SCENE. HOLMES, WATSON & HOPKINS ARRIVE

HOPKINS: Dr Malachai? Hello?

DR MALACHAI: Back so soon, Inspector? Why, Mr Holmes! And John! It's been a long time!

WATSON: Too long, Andrew.

DR MALACHAI: You're here about the Moriarty business, I take it? Well, the victim's clothes are there and the man himself is over here.

HOLMES:	I'll examine the clothes. Watson, would you be so good as to assist the doctor?
WATSON:	Of course.
DR MALACHAI:	I should put the time of death at between ten o'clock and noon. I'm afraid I can't be more precise than that.
FX:	<u>HOLMES GOES THROUGH THE VICTIM'S POCKETS</u>
HOPKINS:	The shooting occurred at noon, according to Worlock and the Moriartys. Found anything, Mr Holmes?
HOLMES:	Nothing in his pockets.
WATSON:	Perhaps the Colonel emptied them, so we wouldn't be able to identify his victim.
HOLMES:	Perhaps. But I prefer facts to theories, Watson. From the age and shabby condition of the clothing, I should say that in life, the victim was a vagrant.
DR MALACHAI:	That would certainly tally with his malnourished state.
WATSON:	And his hands. Observe the calluses and the dirt underneath the fingernails. What was his name, I wonder?
HOPKINS:	Sad to say, we'll probably never know, Dr Watson. All we can say for certain is that he surprised Colonel Moriarty in his study, and there was a struggle, during which the Colonel shot him.
HOLMES, WATSON & DR MALACHAI:	I shouldn't have said so.
HOPKINS:	Pardon me for jumping to conclusions! Mr Holmes?
HOLMES:	No powder burns around the bullet hole in the victim's clothing. He certainly wasn't shot at close quarters.
HOPKINS:	I see. Doctors?

DR MALACHAI:	John, would you care to..?
WATSON:	I wouldn't dream of it, Andrew; we're visitors in your domain.
DR MALACHAI:	No, no, I insist.
HOPKINS:	One of you, *please*!
WATSON:	Very well. The wound is far too large. I'd say the gun must have been fired from some feet away.
DR MALACHAI:	I concur.
WATSON:	Thank-you, George. Well, that settles it – Colonel Moriarty has a case to answer after all.
HOLMES:	Perhaps not a case, but certainly an important question. Hello, what's this?
HOPKINS:	What's what?
HOLMES:	A scrap of newspaper in the dead man's sock.
FX:	HOLMES UNFOLDS IT
WATSON:	Probably he had a hole in his sock and used the paper to keep out the cold.
HOLMES:	I would be in complete agreement with you, Watson, were it not for the fact that the hole is in the *other* sock. It's from the *Daily Gazette*, dated 12th August 1864.
WATSON:	1864!
HOLMES:	(READING) "The young woman who died of asphyxiation on the London Underground at Aldersgate has been identified as Miss Alicia Cutter of Norwood. Miss Cutter's aunt came forward to claim the body on Tuesday". Interesting.
DR MALACHAI:	The sulphurous atmosphere down there can be fatal to anyone with a breathing condition. The Underground is a death trap.

HOPKINS:	But what can it have to do with this matter?
HOLMES:	Quite possibly nothing at all, Hopkins, but this article clearly meant enough to the dead man that he kept it safe for thirty years. Where are his shoes, by the way?
DR MALACHAI:	In this bag, Mr Holmes.
FX:	HOLMES REMOVES THE SHOES FROM A PAPER BAG
HOLMES:	The laces have been untied, Malachai! How many times do I have to tell you people, never *ever* untie a knot! There is a world of information in a knot! How am I supposed to function as a detective when I am confounded at every turn!
FX:	HOLMES THROWS THE SHOES IN ANGER
WATSON:	Holmes!
DR MALACHAI:	Excuse me, Mr Holmes, but when I received the body, the shoelaces had already been untied.
HOPKINS:	And *not* by me.
HOLMES:	(CALMING DOWN) I see. Well, that changes matters. You have my profound apologies, Doctor.
DR MALACHAI:	Accepted, Mr Holmes.
HOLMES:	Well, I think we have discovered all that we can here. Good-day to you.
FX:	ECHO OUT. THEY DEPART, AND WALK DOWN A LONG CORRIDOR
WATSON:	(LOW) Holmes, are you sure you're quite all right?
HOLMES:	Of course I am, Watson. Why shouldn't I be?
WATSON:	The way you became so enraged with Dr Malachai, I just thought-

HOLMES:	Oh, that! The occasional scolding does these chaps the world of good. Keeps them keen.
WATSON:	I just thought I might not be the only one unnerved by the name Moriarty.
HOLMES:	My dear Watson, I trust you know me better than that. I never allow my emotions to cloud my judgement.
WATSON:	Of course. My mistake.
HOLMES:	Now, I suggest, we should beard the lion in his den. Brace yourself; this may prove to be our most problematic investigation to date.
FX:	OUT

SECOND COMMERCIAL

FX:	TRAIN BG
HOPKINS:	I wonder, Dr Watson, if you could explain something to me.
WATSON:	If I can.
HOPKINS:	How is it that Colonel Moriarty and the late Professor Moriarty were both called James?
WATSON:	Actually, there are *three* Moriarty brothers. The youngest is a stationmaster in the west of England.
HOPKINS:	You're not going to tell me-
WATSON:	Yes I am. James is a family name, you see.
HOPKINS:	All the same, though – to have three sons and christen them all James seems absurd.
HOLMES:	I believe their parents surmounted the difficulties by referring to the eldest son as James, the middle son as Jim and the youngest as Jimmy. Their solution shows more imagination than the naming of their offspring suggests.

HOPKINS:	So Colonel James Moriarty is really Colonel *Jim* Moriarty?
HOLMES:	It's my understanding that with the Professor's untimely death, he's moved up in the ranks and now occupies the esteemed position of James Moriarty.
WATSON:	But a blackguard by another other name would still smell as rank.
HOLMES:	(SIGHS) Watson, really…
FX:	TRAIN BG OUT
MUSIC:	UNDERCURRENT
WATSON:	Upon our arrival at Moriarty's home in Chelmsford, Stanley Hopkins went inside to break the news of our presence to the Colonel. Holmes and I, meanwhile, searched the garden for evidence of the intruder.
MUSIC:	OUT
HOLMES:	It seems he scaled the wall here, then lay in wait for some time.
WATSON:	To be certain the coast was clear, no doubt.
HOLMES:	But the coast was *not* clear, Watson. Mrs Moriarty was in residence, and the Colonel and his lawyer were just returning.
WATSON:	When you put it like that, it does seem curious.
HOLMES:	Then the fellow darts across to the house. Follow me.
WATSON:	Coming, Holmes!
FX:	THEY WALK RAPIDLY ACROSS THE GRASS
HOLMES:	Then he halts at this corner.
WATSON:	Perhaps he contemplated climbing this drainpipe and entering through an upstairs window.

HOLMES:	You're positively scintillating today, Watson. In any case, it seems he changes his mind. He walks toward the pond. Then he changes direction again, and returns to the house.
FX:	THEY WALK OVER GRASS AGAIN
WATSON:	To the open window of the study, where he discovers…
FX:	THE WINDOW IS OPENED
COLONEL:	(INSIDE THE HOUSE) What the bloody hell are *you* doing here!
HOLMES:	Good-day to you, Colonel Moriarty, I don't believe we've been introduced. My name is She-
COLONEL:	(INSIDE THE HOUSE) I know who you are! How dare you trespass on my property! The police are here, you know!
HOPKINS:	(INSIDE THE HOUSE) I'm afraid I didn't get 'round to telling him, gentlemen. As a matter of fact, Colonel, Mr Holmes and Dr Watson are here at my invitation.
HOLMES:	It would really be much easier to have this discussion indoors rather than through an open window. Would you mind?
FX:	HE CLAMBERS INTO THE ROOM
HOLMES:	Take my hand, Watson.
WATSON:	Thank-you, Holmes.
FX:	WATSON CLIMBS IN
COLONEL:	Damned impertinence! This is none of your concern!
WATSON:	Murder, sir, is the concern of every right-minded citizen.
COLONEL:	Murder? How dare you, sir! If there's a murderer in this room, he's standing at your side! Inspector, I demand that you arrest Sherlock Holmes for the killing of my brother!

CECILE:	(ARRIVING) James, what's the matter? Oh!
HOPKINS:	Mrs Moriarty? This is Mr Sherlock Holmes and Dr John Watson.
CECILE:	Dr Watson? You're *the* Dr Watson?
WATSON:	I am, madam.
HOLMES:	Now I know how it feels to be in your place, Watson.
HOPKINS:	I was in the process of asking the Colonel about the powder burn discrepancy, Mr Holmes.
CECILE:	Powder burns?
COLONEL:	It's nothing, Cecile, nothing at all. Please prepare a cup of tea for the Inspector.
CECILE:	Of course, James. Anything for the other gentlemen?
COLONEL:	The other gentlemen are leaving. Immediately. Please go, Cecile; this is man talk.
CECILE:	Very good, dear.
HOLMES:	I hope, Colonel, that you will at least allow us the opportunity to hear your explanation of how you managed to struggle with the intruder and yet shoot him from some distance away.
COLONEL:	It's perfectly simple. We grappled for a few moments, I got hold of the gun, I broke away, the fellow was about to pounce, so I shot him. Nothing suspicious in it – I was protecting my home *and my wife*.
HOPKINS:	May I ask why you didn't tell me this before?
COLONEL:	I didn't realise you wanted me to account for every blessed second! I assumed that my word would be enough! You're certainly eager enough to take everything these blackguards say as gospel.
WATSON:	Sherlock Holmes is no blackguard! As a detective, he worked

ceaselessly to bring down your brother's organization!

COLONEL: You know that for a fact, do you? Tell me, Doctor, how were you involved in your friend's tireless efforts?

WATSON: (LESS CERTAIN) Well… I was never actually involved.

COLONEL: How convenient.

WATSON: I was married at the time and Holmes didn't wish to place me in unnecessary danger. Isn't that right Holmes?

HOLMES: Hm? Oh, quite correct, Watson, yes.

WATSON: As a result, I was never present when a case concerning the Professor came to his attention.

HOLMES: Except for the murder at Birlstone Castle, of course. Moriarty planned the whole thing.

WATSON: Holmes, you never told me that!

HOLMES: I didn't want to place you in unnecessary danger, Watson.

WATSON: I had that story ready for publication! I'll have to rewrite the whole thing now.

COLONEL: You see how pathetic you sound, Watson? The truth of the matter is that Holmes planned to kill my brother and as his dull-witted assistant, you were there to furnish him with an alibi and promote his depiction of poor James as some sort of criminal mastermind instead of the harmless mathematics teacher that was!

WATSON: Harmless? I'll have you know, sir-

HOLMES: Watson, don't waste your breath.

WATSON: I'll have you know that Professor Moriarty pursued us from England to the Continent after Holmes destroyed his criminal empire!

COLONEL:	And you actually saw him pursuing you?
WATSON:	Yes! Well… I… I saw the train that he'd engaged pass us at Canterbury Station.
COLONEL:	(SARCASTIC) You saw a train.
WATSON:	Moriarty set fire to our Baker Street rooms!
COLONEL:	*Holmes* set fire to his own rooms! Don't be a jackass all your life, Watson!
CECILE:	(APPROACHING) Your tea, Inspector.
FX:	A RATTLE OF CUP AND SAUCER
HOPKINS:	Thank-you, Mrs Moriarty. I don't suppose you could organise some sandwiches by any chance? I'm afraid I missed lunch.
COLONEL:	Forgive me, Inspector, I thought you were conducting an investigation. I didn't realise you came here to dine. And now, if Dr Watson has quite finished making a fool of himself, perhaps he and murderous friend would get out of my house.
HOLMES:	I've no wish to cause further ructions, Colonel. Before we go, perhaps you might permit me to ask one question?
COLONEL:	What's that?
HOLMES:	Upon entering your study, why did you lock the door? You seem unwilling to provide the Inspector with an explanation.
CECILE:	I can answer that, Mr Holmes. James *always* locks the study door. It's his habit.
COLONEL:	Precisely. Guards against intruders.
HOLMES:	Do you often have intruders, Colonel?
COLONEL:	Well, I had one today, didn't I?!
HOLMES:	Indeed. And as ill luck would have it, in the very room you

always keep locked. It's a shame you don't take the same precautions with your window fastenings.

COLONEL: What are you implying, Holmes?

HOLMES: I imply nothing. I *infer*, however, that you are not being truthful. A locked door and an open window do not make for a secure household.

CECILE: I'm afraid it was I who unlocked the window, to let out the smell of James' Indian cigars. That's how that dreadful man got in; it's all my fault, you see. (SHE SOBS)

COLONEL: It's nothing of the sort, Cecile. Pull yourself together.

HOLMES: Forgive me, Mrs Moriarty, but I saw no signs of cigar ash in the study.

CECILE: Because I cleaned the study, Mr Holmes.

COLONEL: Satisfied?

HOLMES: Quite. Well, it seems I owe you an apology, Colonel. And you, most of all, dear lady. I observed the smoothness of your hands, you see, and it never occurred to me-

COLONEL: The maid's off sick, Holmes. That's why Cecile tidied my study. Now, if you're quite done fondling my wife's hands…

HOLMES: Once again, my apologies. As proof that I harbour no ill-will towards the Moriarty family, I will give you some free advice before we leave.

COLONEL: (SUSPICIOUS) What's that?

HOLMES: Change your newspaper vendor. You appear to be missing the first two pages of this morning's *Times*. Good-day to you.

MUSIC: UNDERCURRENT

WATSON: After that rather uncomfortable interview, I had imagined that we would return directly to Baker Street, but Holmes insisted that

we pay a call upon Moriarty's solicitor, Frederick Worlock, in his rooms on Crown Office Row.

MUSIC:	OUT

WORLOCK: I hope you don't take it amiss if I don't ask you to sit, gentlemen. Indeed, I don't know if I should even have opened my door to you.

HOLMES: We experienced similar hospitality at the home of your client, Mr Worlock.

WORLOCK: Oh, please don't mistake my reticence for animosity, Mr Holmes. I have the greatest respect for your accomplishments as a criminal investigator. I'm proud to say I saw you both give testimony during the Anthony Moltaire case. Quite a remarkable business – you saved that young man's life. That was over ten years ago, and I've followed your careers ever since.

WATSON: That's very gratifying.

WORLOCK: (STERN) However, I must act in the interests of my client; even if my client doesn't always know what's best for him. And I have nothing to add to the statement I gave to the Inspector.

HOLMES: We quite understand the difficulty of your position, Mr Worlock. In fact, I have only one question for you; in all your dealings with Colonel Moriarty, were you aware that he kept his service revolver in his study?

WORLOCK: The revolver? Well… no. I assume he must have kept it in a drawer and I simply didn't see it.

WATSON: Then how on Earth did the intruder see it? Moriarty claims they struggled over the weapon.

WORLOCK: There might be any number of reasons, Dr Watson. Perhaps the drawer happened to be open. Perhaps the Colonel had taken the revolver out of the drawer in order to clean it. Really, gentlemen, if that's the basis of your case against my client, then you don't appear to have a case. James Moriarty did not murder that man.

HOLMES:	You will be delighted to hear that I am in complete agreement with you, Mr Worlock.
MUSIC:	SHORT BRIDGE
MRS HUDSON:	Your tea, Doctor.
FX:	CUP AND SAUCER PLACED ON A TABLE. WATSON IS HANDLING A NEWSPAPER THROUGHOUT SCENE.
WATSON:	Thank-you, Mrs Hudson.
MRS HUDSON:	When would you care to dine, Mr Holmes?
HOLMES:	Well, how about tonight for a change?
MRS HUDSON:	I'll put the vegetables on, sir.
FX:	SHE LEAVES
WATSON:	Well, Worlock didn't say it in so many words, but I think he's in no doubt that the Professor was a villain of the highest order.
HOLMES:	I'll take some comfort in that if his brother ever succeeds in pressing his case for a libel action or a prosecution for wilful murder.
WATSON:	Holmes… What the Colonel said… it was all rubbish, wasn't it?
HOLMES:	My dear fellow, how could you doubt it?
WATSON:	I mean… you have told me everything that occurred between you and Professor Moriarty?
HOLMES:	At present, we have something of more recent vintage to occupy our attention.
WATSON:	Of course. I think it's painfully obvious that Cecile Moriarty is screening her husband. Tidying his study, leaving the window open… all very fishy.
HOLMES:	(THOUGHTFUL) Fishy…

WATSON:	Something, Holmes?
HOLMES:	I'm not sure. Perhaps not. Yes, I'm inclined to agree with you, Watson. Mrs Moriarty lacks our housekeeper's skill with a feather duster. I noticed a thin layer of dust on the mantelpiece. There was a space where some object had been removed recently... of course! Fool that I am!
WATSON:	Something the matter?
HOLMES:	Watson, did I understand you to say that you were planning a fishing holiday this weekend?
WATSON:	That's right, Holmes. Why do you ask?
HOLMES:	Might I have the loan of your net for a few hours?
WATSON:	What the devil for?
HOLMES:	The footprints we examined led to the pond for a reason, and not because someone wished to look at the fish.
WATSON:	Something was thrown in there, weighted down with the object from the mantelpiece!
HOLMES:	You're invaluable to me, Watson, with your instinctive grasp for the obvious. Well, do you wish to accompany me to Chelmsford or shall I go alone?
WATSON:	Just a minute, Holmes, just let me finish this page.
HOLMES:	Have my adventures become so dull to you that you'd prefer to stay home and read the *Times*?
WATSON:	Not at all, old fellow. But I remembered that the first two pages of Moriarty's *Times* were missing. I thought perhaps there might be something on them the Colonel didn't want us to see. Perhaps something connected with the death of that young girl, Alicia Cutter. I wouldn't be at all surprised to learn that he was responsible for it. The intruder, whoever he was, knew it, and that's why the Colonel killed him.

HOLMES:	And have you found anything?
WATSON:	Well- no.
HOLMES:	And nor shall you. Consider, Watson, the victim's shoelaces were untied. That, combined with the question of the missing news-sheets should tell you everything you need to know. Now let's be off, there isn't a moment to lose.
FX:	HOLMES OPENS THE DOOR
HOLMES:	(CALLS OUT) Mrs Hudson, cancel dinner!
MRS HUDSON:	(IN DISTANCE) Oh, Mr Holmes!
MUSIC:	SHORT BRIDGE
FX:	HOLMES DRAGS HIS NET ACROSS THE POND
WATSON:	Can't this wait 'til tomorrow morning? You still haven't told me what you expect to find. Not the missing pages from the *Times*?
HOLMES:	Hardly, Watson. I have no doubt they were destroyed. You'll recall that when Worlock arrive at the house, there was a fire in the grate? No – *this*.* It was weighted down with this Indian curio that was removed from the mantelpiece.
FX:	*HOLMES FISHES AN OBJECT FROM THE POND
WATSON:	The Colonel's Webley revolver! No, wait, it can't be! He gave it to Hopkins. We examined it at Baker Street!
HOLMES:	He gave *a* Webley revolver to Hopkins, but I fancy that *this* weapon belongs to the Colonel. Observe the grip: it's somewhat worn on the left side. Clearly, it was the property of a left-handed man.
WATSON:	And is Colonel Moriarty right-handed or left-handed?
HOLMES:	You saw his study. His pen tray was situated on the left side of his desk.

WATSON:	So he's left-handed.
HOLMES:	And the grip on the Webley he gave to Hopkins was worn on the right.
WATSON:	But the intruder dropped this revolver into the pond. How did he get hold of Moriarty's gun and the Indian curio *before* entering the house?
HOLMES:	It's all perfectly elementary, my dea-
FX:	A HAMMER IS PULLED BACK ON A RIFLE
COLONEL:	The revolver you're holding isn't loaded. But my hunting rifle is.
HOLMES:	Good evening, Colonel.
COLONEL:	Holmes. You killed my brother. Can you think of any reason why I shouldn't do the same to you?
MUSIC:	STING

THIRD COMMERCIAL

COLONEL:	I could shoot you as a common burglar and the law would be on my side. What's to stop me?
WATSON:	Possibly the fact that shooting three burglars in one day might look even more suspicious than it does already?
COLONEL:	Into the house, both of you!
FX:	THEY TRUDGE SLOWLY ACROSS THE GRASS
WATSON:	Holmes, what do we do?
HOLMES:	Remain calm, Watson, and use whatever intelligence the Lord has endowed us with.
COLONEL:	Quiet, both of you! Inside!

FX:	OUT
MUSIC:	SHORT BRIDGE
HOLMES:	If you have a telephone, Colonel, I'd be happy to place the call to Scotland Yard for you.
COLONEL:	No police, Holmes. Not tonight. Watson, you're armed, I take it?
WATSON:	What about it?
COLONEL:	Put the gun on the table.
FX:	HE DOES SO
WATSON:	Just what do you want, Moriarty?
COLONEL:	I want to hear your friend admit that the accusations he made about my brother were false; I want him to confess to murder.
HOLMES:	Very well. The accusations I made about your brother were false. I confess to murdering him.
WATSON:	Holmes, don't give him the satisfaction.
HOLMES:	If it makes our host feel better, Watson, we should oblige him, regardless of what the truth might be. He knows in his heart the kind of man Professor James Moriarty really was. He was possessed of hereditary tendencies of the most diabolical kind.
COLONEL:	I'm warning you, Holmes.
HOLMES:	A criminal strain ran in his blood, which was increased and rendered infinitely more dangerous by his extraordinary mental powers.
COLONEL:	Shut up!
HOLMES:	But it may go some way towards lessening your hostility to learn that I was not in fact responsible for your brother's demise.
WATSON:	What did you say?

97

FX:	<u>WE'RE BACK ON THE REICHENBACH FALLS</u>
PROFESSOR:	No more talk, Holmes. It's time for you to die. (MORIARTY GROWLS, THE GROWL GROWING IN INTENSITY AS HE'S ABOUT TO POUNCE. BUT SUDDENLY-)
FX:	<u>A RIFLE SHOT</u>
PROFESSOR:	(HE'S HIT. HIS CRY IS ALMOST ONE OF SURPRISE) Moran… you- fool! (HE GIVES ONE LAST, LONG CRY AS HE DESCENDS INTO THE CHASM)
FX:	<u>FALLS BG OUT</u>
HOLMES:	Moran fled as soon as he saw what he'd done.
COLONEL:	Sebastian Moran… killed my brother.
HOLMES:	Accidentally. He was aiming at me, of course. I believe that was the Professor's intention all along. He never meant for us to battle to the death. Such a conclusion would have been distinctly unscientific.
WATSON:	Holmes, why didn't you tell me any of this before?
HOLMES:	Forgive me, Watson, but I had my reasons.
COLONEL:	What were they? Why did you let the world- let *me* believe that you were responsible?
HOLMES:	Strange as it may seem, Colonel, it was for your brother's sake.
COLONEL:	For James' sake?
HOLMES:	He and I matched wits for many years. An accidental death caused by one of his own minions seemed so trivial, so undignified. I held Professor Moriarty in the highest esteem, you see – but only as a knave.
COLONEL:	To think: I introduced him to Moran; we were both members of the Bagatelle Club, you see.

HOLMES:	Don't berate yourself. You are no more responsible for your brother's death than you are for the death of the intruder this morning.
COLONEL:	What is this nonsense? Of course I was responsible for his death! He broke into my house and I shot the blighter!
HOLMES:	Your wife and Mr Worlock both heard you fire a revolver behind a locked door. But the shot was fired through the open window. I daresay I could find the bullet if I had sufficient time and more light.
WATSON:	Holmes, are you trying to say the man was already dead?
HOLMES:	Dr Malachai, the police surgeon, informed us that death occurred between ten o'clock and noon. Of course, your wife and Mr Worlock heard you fire a shot at noon, which enabled Hopkins to fix the time of death precisely. I'm curious, Colonel; what were you doing at around ten o'clock?
COLONEL:	What business is it of yours?
HOLMES:	Indulge me, please. *You* have the gun; the cards are in your favour.
COLONEL:	At ten o'clock, I was taking my morning stroll.
HOLMES:	Ah yes, the morning stroll. And as a man of precise habits, you do this every day at the same time.
COLONEL:	Certainly.
HOLMES:	So a patient man might, after several days' observation, know the best moment to enter your home? At a time when you were absent but the house was not completely empty?
COLONEL:	What are you driving at?
HOLMES:	Hopkins may be the smartest of his breed, but you know as well as I that you have nothing to fear from him. You share the blood of England's most notorious criminal, you see. How could he fail to be prejudiced? I doubt it ever occurred to him that a different

Moriarty might have been responsible for the shooting.

CECILE: You're every bit as clever as Dr Watson claims.

COLONEL: Cecile, go back to bed. I'm dealing with this.

HOLMES: You should never have allowed me to examine your hands, dear lady. When I did so, I saw the minute grains of gunpowder embedded in your pale skin. We all knew that Colonel Moriarty had fired a weapon but nothing was said about you having done so.

CECILE: I don't understand why you didn't just tell Inspector Hopkins there and then.

HOLMES: *Knowing* that you had fired a revolver is one thing. *Proving* that you had done so in order to kill- Really, it's quite irksome not knowing his name.

CECILE: Sacker. Sergeant Ormond Sacker of the Highland Brigade.

HOLMES: Thank-you. Once I realised the significance of the missing news-sheets, I knew where I could find my proof. It may please Dr Watson to know that Sacker did indeed climb up the drainpipe and enter the house through an open upstairs window as he suggested. Is that where you killed him, Mrs Moriarty?

CECILE: It was.

HOLMES: Had you simply concealed the body until after Worlock's visit, the crime might well have gone undetected. But the Colonel's sense of chivalry demanded that *he* take the blame. The more featureless a crime is, the more difficult it is to bring it home. But you laid so many false clues that the truth became easy to deduce.

CECILE: Go on.

HOLMES: Wearing your victim's shoes, you created a second set of footprints leading from the drainpipe to the window of your husband's study.

CECILE:	Bravo, Mr Holmes.
WATSON:	But the shoes were much too large for your feet, and so you had to stuff them with newspaper in order to make them fit! And that was why the laces were untied.
HOLMES:	Correct again, Watson. Even without the evidence of the newspaper, I would have realised the truth – the length of the stride in the two sets of footprints differed because of the difference in height. I'm only surprised it didn't occur to me sooner.
COLONEL:	It was an accident! The fellow surprised Cecile as she was reading. They struggled for his gun-
HOLMES:	I have no doubt that is what your wife told you at the time, but that is not how it happened. You know now that there was no close-quarters struggle.
CECILE:	I think James had begun to suspect; even so, I doubt he would ever have questioned me about it.
COLONEL:	Don't listen to him, Cecile.
CECILE:	It's done, James. And it's time you knew the truth. I owe you that much for everything you've done for me. And not just today.
HOLMES:	Might the truth have anything to do with this, Mrs Moriarty?* It is a story from the *Daily Gazette*, detailing the circumstances surrounding the death of one Miss Alicia Cutter some three decades ago.
FX:	*HOLMES UNFOLDS A PIECE OF PAPER
CECILE:	(A SMALL LAUGH) You should never believe everything you read in the newspapers, Mr Holmes.
HOLMES:	You are Alicia Cutter?
CECILE:	I am.
COLONEL:	Cecile, what are you talking about?

101

CECILE:	My first life, James. The life I had in India before we met. I was just a girl, but already my hand had been promised to Sergeant Sacker. He was of good family you see, and expected to progress in the service. My parents were… socially ambitious. But I was desperate and nearly out of my mind.
HOLMES:	But one member of your family was sympathetic to your plight. Your aunt.
CECILE:	Aunt Lucy. I was always her favourite. My worries had made me unwell you see, so I'd been sent to England to stay with her and recuperate in time for my wedding. I told Aunt Lucy everything. How I thought I might go mad, perhaps even kill myself. She was the one who came up with the plan.
COLONEL:	What plan?
CECILE:	A young girl had died on the Underground, but no-one had come forward to claim the body. She was about my age, so all Aunt Lucy had to do was identify the dead girl as me. Do you know, my parents never even came back to England for the funeral? And so, thanks to brave, wonderful Aunt Lucy, I was resurrected. First as Miss Cecile Braviner, and then as Mrs James Moriarty. I thought that you of all people, Mr Holmes, would understand. You died and came back to life, too.
HOLMES:	There is an important difference, Mrs Moriarty. I came back as myself. I have no secret past to conceal.
CECILE:	That was never an issue until today. Ormond Sacker. If my parents could have seen what he'd been reduced to, what would they have said?
WATSON:	How did he manage to track you down?
CECILE:	He didn't, Doctor – it was simply appallingly bad luck for both of us. It happened that one day I was travelling in a carriage that took a wrong turn through a rather disreputable area. Ormond saw me. After a few days, he managed to track me down to this house.
HOLMES:	He observed the comings and goings of the household, I

imagine, and fixed upon the best time to confront you.

CECILE: He said he saw me sat by an open upstairs window. He scaled the drainpipe. You can imagine my terror at seeing him again after thirty years. I did my best to disguise my panic. I put him at his ease. We talked. I managed to convince him that my feigned death had all been some gigantic misunderstanding and that I'd been unable to contact him afterwards. He swallowed every word of it. Why not? It was what he wanted to hear.

WATSON: But you still felt the need to kill him.

CECILE: He had this insane notion that we could still be together. That I would leave James and my new life for him – him! The last man in the world I'd want to be with, even if he were the King of England, and not some wretched beggar! I tried to dissuade him, but he was adamant. His gun was under his belt. I don't think it ever occurred to him that I might snatch it and use it on him. But I did. Then James returned from his morning constitutional. I told him I'd been surprised a burglar and used his own gun on him when we fought. I couldn't tell him the rest of it; it wouldn't have been fair.

COLONEL: Fair?

HOLMES: And so, rather hastily, you concocted a plan. You brought the body downstairs and placed it in the study, in order to perform that little charade for Mr Worlock's benefit. That was why you locked the door, Colonel; it wouldn't have done for him to walk in on you and spoil your little performance.

WATSON: And when you were collecting Worlock from the station, you, Mrs Moriarty, were laying a false trail with Sacker's shoes.

HOLMES: So you see, all is known.

COLONEL: By you two. But not by the police.

CECILE: James, no!

COLONEL: I'm sorry, Cecile. I have no choice.

103

WATSON:	Don't be a fool, man!
COLONEL:	Forgive me, gentlemen.
WATSON:	No!
FX:	THERE'S A SHOT
CECILE:	(A DEATH-CRY)
FX:	SHE FALLS TO THE FLOOR, DEAD
COLONEL:	She… should never have lied to me. I could have tolerated anything. But not that.
WATSON:	Colonel… *James* – give me the rifle.
COLONEL:	Take it, Watson – I'm finished now.
MUSIC:	BRIDGE
HOPKINS:	I really wish you'd called me in sooner, gentlemen. This could have been prevented.
HOLMES:	You have my most profound apologies, Hopkins. This was not the outcome I would have wished for.
HOPKINS:	I'm curious, Mr Holmes: why did she throw her husband's gun in the pond?
HOLMES:	Watson, would you enlighten the Inspector? I seem to have lost all enthusiasm for this case.
WATSON:	Certainly, Holmes. I suspect it was Cecile's idea, and her husband obliged out of blind devotion. She destroyed any evidence of Sacker's true identity, save for the newspaper article he kept hidden in his sock, but had we known that he carried a Webley, we might have deduced that he'd been a military man and there was just the faint chance that we could trace him. Fortunately for her, the Colonel's service weapon was also a Webley.

HOPKINS:	So he could claim Sacker's weapon as his own, and if we came to examine the grooves on the bullet, they'd match the gun he gave me.
WATSON:	But, of course, that meant they had to get rid of the Colonel's own gun.
HOPKINS:	Very cunning. But you were suspicious, Mr Holmes, when you saw that the Colonel was left-handed and the gun had belonged to a right-handed man. If only we'd known whether Sacker was left or right-handed, we could've sorted this out much sooner.
HOLMES:	An examination of his shoelaces would have told us that. When a right-handed person such as myself ties his shoes, the first loop is always on the left-hand side. With a left-handed person, it's the other way 'round.
WATSON:	The things you know, Holmes. And that was why you flew off the handle with Dr Malachai.
HOLMES:	I never fly off the handle, Watson.
WATSON:	Of course. My mistake.
HOPKINS:	Well, I'm grateful for your assistance, gentlemen. If you'll forgive me, I'd better be getting the Colonel into a cell.
HOLMES:	Good-day to you, Inspector.
FX:	HOPKINS WALKS AWAY
WATSON:	Well, not a very satisfactory conclusion, but a conclusion nonetheless.
HOLMES:	Do you really think so?
WATSON:	Is there any reason why I shouldn't?
HOLMES:	Watson, have you never thought it strange that after the battle at the Reichenbach Falls, Professor Moriarty's body was never recovered?

WATSON: I can't say I ever thought about it. I was more worried about you.

HOLMES: No doubt. But I have thought about it. Every night since then.

MD: OUT

MUSIC: *DANSE MACABRE*

The Further Adventures of Sherlock Holmes –
The Adventure of the Two Watsons
(Original Airdate October 19, 2008)

With *The Two Watsons*, my habit of naming characters after actors associated with previous Holmesian productions got completely out of hand. The play generated so much correspondence for this reason that the producers turned the spotting of these in-jokes into a competition, with a CD of previous episodes as a prize. As long as these indulgences don't distract from the plot, they're acceptable, but it was pretty plain that was no longer the case, and I needed to exercise some self-control in future.

For the record, the origins of the character names are as follows:

Hubert Willis – played Watson to Eille Norwood's Holmes in a series of silent pictures during the 1920s;
Basil St John – Christian and middle names of Basil Rathbone, perhaps the most famous cinematic Holmes of all time;
William Bruce – the real name of Nigel Bruce who, like his namesake, was indeed born in Mexico;
Edith Meiser – one cannot overestimate the importance of Ms Meiser as the dramatist who made Sherlock Holmes a permanent fixture on American radio;
Hillary Brooke – an actress who appeared in several of Rathbone and Bruce's films for Universal;
Samuel Hyams – the real name of actor Dennis Hoey, who portrayed Inspector Lestrade opposite Rathbone and Bruce;
Louis Hector – the first actor to play Holmes on television (*The Three Garridebs* in 1937), and Moriarty to Tom Conway's Holmes in the 1940s radio series;
Harry Cording – another member of the Universal stock company;
John Hawkesworth – the producer who brought the Jeremy Brett series to television;
Jerrold Hunter and Lloyd Brandon – characters from the 1939 film *The Adventures of Sherlock Holmes.*

Most of these characters are mentioned, but have no dialogue, aside from a little background murmuring. We hear do from several members of Sir Hubert's family, however, which presents a very common challenge for the radio dramatist – ensuring that the listener knows who's who. This requires the characters to address each other by name more frequently than anyone would in real life, but not so often that it becomes horribly artificial.

Given that Mary Watson passed away some time between *The Final Problem* and *The Empty House* (of causes unknown), it's become my habit to include some vague reference to her undiagnosed condition, in this instance concern over the proximity of a hospital were the couple to relocate to the Yorkshire Dales. Reading Watson's not-entirely flattering description of his wife-to-be in *The Sign of Four*, it was impossible not to imagine her being somewhat offended by it. Setting this episode shortly after the publication of *Sign* presented her with the opportunity to air her grievance.

As in *The Moriarty Resurrection*, I included a mention of an earlier show from the series; the search for Reverend Lantree to which Holmes refers relates to *The Man Who Believed in Nothing* by Jim French.

CAST:

ANNOUNCER (DENNIS BATEMAN)

HOLMES (JOHN PATRICK LOWRIE)

WATSON (LAWRENCE ALBERT)

MARY (MARY ANN DORWARD)

CONDUCTOR (DENNIS BATEMAN)

LLOYD BRANDON (DENNIS BATEMAN)

BASIL ST JOHN (RON HIPPE)

SIR HUBERT WILLIS (FRANK BUXTON)

WILLIAM BRUCE (TERRY ROSE)

EDITH MEISER (JAN DARCY)

DIRECTED BY JOHN PATRICK LOWRIE

| FX: | OPENING SEQUENCE, BIG BEN |

| ANNOUNCER: | *The Further Adventures of Sherlock Holmes*, featuring John Patrick Lowrie as Holmes, and Lawrence Albert as Dr Watson. |

| MUSIC: | *DANSE MACABRE* UP AND UNDER |

| WATSON: | My name is Dr Watson, and it was my privilege to share the adventures of Sherlock Holmes. But the story I am about to tell you began far from no. 221b Baker Street. In the Autumn of 1890, my wife Mary and I were enjoying an unseasonal but much-needed holiday in the Yorkshire town of Aysgarth, the scene of many of my happiest childhood experiences. |

| MUSIC: | OUT |

| MARY: | This is wonderful, dear! |

| WATSON: | Just what the Doctor ordered. *This* Doctor, to be precise. |

| MARY: | Wouldn't it be marvellous if we could retire here? |

| WATSON: | Retire? I think I should feel insulted. Surely I'm not so old as all that! |

| MARY: | You know that's not what I mean, John. |

| WATSON: | Of course I do. And yes, it would be wonderful. But… |

| MARY: | But what? |

| WATSON: | A holiday is one thing, Mary, but it *is* rather isolated here. What would we do if your health… took a turn for the worst? |

| MARY: | Then it's a good thing I know a doctor. |

| WATSON: | Well, it's something to think about for the years to come. |

| MARY: | Perhaps not so far off as all that. |

| WATSON: | I don't think you've looked at the practice accounts lately. |

MARY:	You're making money from your stories; you could give up medicine and write professionally.
WATSON:	It's a little early to be considering something so drastic, Mary. I've had two accounts of my adventures with Sherlock Holmes published, and neither to great acclaim.
MARY:	Yes, I've been meaning to talk to you about that. Now where is it?
FX:	SHE FLICKS THROUGH THE PAGES OF A BOOK
MARY:	Ah, yes! *The Sign of Four*: "Her face had neither regularity of feature nor beauty of complexion".
WATSON:	Who does that describe?
MARY:	Me.
WATSON:	You?
MARY:	Me.
WATSON:	Editorial interference, I'm sure I never said anything of the kind.
MARY:	I wonder.
FX:	SHE CLOSES THE BOOK
WATSON:	Mary, you are the most beautiful woman I have ever known, and if someone were to tell me that I would have to stay in this cottage with you for the rest of my days, I'd jump at the chance.
MARY:	And never go back to London?
WATSON:	Never.
MARY:	And never work with Mr Sherlock Holmes again?
WATSON:	(CHOKES)
MARY:	I thought as much.

WATSON:	It's not that I crave the excitement, or Lord knows, enjoy spending time away from you, but the more investigations I share with Holmes, the more material I have for my stories, and the sooner we can retire. I thought that's what you wanted.
MARY:	You should have been a lawyer, dear – you argue your case so well.
FX:	A KNOCK AT THE DOOR
WATSON:	Now who on earth can that be?
MARY:	It's probably the farmer, come to offer us more fresh eggs.
WATSON:	Wonderful! I'm famished.
MARY:	John, is food all you ever think about?
WATSON:	Not all, my dear; not all.
MARY:	(GIGGLES)
FX:	HE OPENS THE DOOR
HOLMES:	Good morning, Watson.
WATSON:	Holmes!
HOLMES:	May I come in? It's a trifle brisk outside.
FX:	HE ENTERS. THE DOOR CLOSES.
HOLMES:	My, but what a charming little cottage. Very rustic.
MARY:	(COLDLY) Mr Holmes, to what do we owe the pleasure of this visit?
HOLMES:	Mrs Watson, might I steal your husband away for a few days? I have a case in nearby Hambledown in which his assistance is required.
WATSON:	Well, I-

MARY:	No, Mr Holmes, you may not.
HOLMES:	I beg your pardon?
MARY:	You may not steal my husband away. Please understand, Mr Holmes, I'm terribly grateful for everything you've done for us.
WATSON:	Everything.
MARY:	But between John's practice and his adventures with you, we see little enough of each other!
WATSON:	It's true, Holmes.
MARY:	And now you expect him to just go gallivanting off with you in the middle of the first holiday we've had since our honeymoon? I'm sorry, Mr Holmes, but the answer is no.
HOLMES:	Yes, of course you're quite correct. Forgive me, Mrs Watson, it was selfish of me.
MARY:	I'm sorry for my bluntness, but I'm quite sure you're capable of dealing with any difficulties on your own.
HOLMES:	I hope you're right, Mrs Watson. Yes. Yes, I'm certain you're right. True, I can't be everywhere, and it would have been useful to have a second pair of eyes-
MARY:	Mr Holmes…
HOLMES:	Yes, of course. Well, if you'll forgive me, I must make haste. I only hope I'm not too late to prevent a tragedy.
WATSON:	Tragedy? What tragedy?
HOLMES:	(DEPARTING) Enjoy the rest of your holiday in peace.
MUSIC:	STING
FX:	A TRAIN BEGINNING ITS JOURNEY
CONDUCTOR:	May I see your ticket, sir?

HOLMES:	Here you are, conductor.
CONDUCTOR:	Hambledown? Very good, sir.
HOLMES:	Oh, by the way, if you see a gentleman with a moustache and the air of a medical man, kindly direct him to this compartment.
CONDUCTOR:	(NONPLUSSED) Certainly, sir.
FX:	WATSON OPENS THE SLIDING DOORS OF A CARRIAGE
WATSON:	Excuse me, conductor, but have you seen-
HOLMES:	Watson!
CONDUCTOR:	Hambledown, is it, sir?
WATSON:	(NONPLUSSED) Er, yes, that's right.
CONDUCTOR:	Have a pleasant journey.
HOLMES:	And to what do I owe this delightful surprise?
WATSON:	You said something about *preventing* a tragedy?
HOLMES:	There has already been one attempt upon the life of Sir Hubert Willis. Every minute's delay puts him in greater danger.
WATSON:	Very well – I'll be happy to assist in any way I can.
HOLMES:	Splendid! I knew you wouldn't let me down.
WATSON:	However, I must make one proviso.
HOLMES:	Name it, old fellow.
MARY:	Good afternoon, Mr Holmes.
HOLMES:	Ah.
FX:	OUT

MUSIC:	<u>BRIDGE</u>
FX:	<u>TRAIN BG AGAIN</u>
MARY:	Where, precisely, is our destination, Mr Holmes?
HOLMES:	Pendark Manor.
WATSON:	Pendark Manor?
HOLMES:	You're familiar with it, Doctor?
WATSON:	A little more than familiar with it, Holmes - I used to explore its ruins when I was a boy! Surely no-one lives there!
HOLMES:	It's been fully restored, Watson, and for the last six years has been home to our client.
MARY:	This Sir Hubert Willis.
HOLMES:	Indeed. He made his fortune as the owner of the Terai Tea Company in Ceylon, and retired to his home country to live out a life of elegant seclusion.
WATSON:	And what has happened to put him in danger?
FX:	<u>THE COMPARTMENT DOORS OPENS AGAIN</u>
BRANDON:	Excuse me, is anybody sitting there?
WATSON:	Please, help yourself.
BRANDON:	Thanks.
FX:	<u>DOOR SLIDES SHUT</u>
HOLMES:	I have no precise details other than that an attempt has already been made upon his life. No doubt when we speak to Sir Hubert-
BRANDON:	Sir Hubert? Not Sir Hubert Willis?
WATSON:	You know him?

BRANDON:	Yes, he's my great uncle. Well, *step*-great uncle, to be precise, but nobody ever says *step*-great uncle, do they? Lloyd Brandon's my name. But what's this about an attempt on Sir Hubert's life?
WATSON:	We are- investigators, travelling to Hambledown at his request.
BRANDON:	Investigators? All three of you?
MARY:	Quite so.
WATSON:	This gentleman is Sherlock Holmes; I am Doctor Watson, and the lady by my side-
BRANDON:	I say, you're not – Lady Molly of Scotland Yard?
MARY:	I am Mrs John H Watson.
BRANDON:	Oh. Oh well, never mind.
FX:	OUT
MUSIC:	UNDERCURRENT
WATSON:	This is Dr Watson. When we return, I'll tell you what surprises were in store for us when we arrived at Pendark Manor.
MUSIC:	OUT

FIRST COMMERCIAL

FX:	A HORSE-DRAWN CARRIAGE. THE PASSENGERS HAVE TO RAISE THEIR VOICES A LITTLE, AS THE WIND HOWLS.
WATSON:	Mr Brandon, are we nearly at Pendark Manor yet?
BRANDON:	We should be able to see it over the next rise, Doctor. Ah, there it is! Not far now.
MARY:	I shall be glad to be indoors! The weather is atrocious.
BRANDON:	Yes, I think snow might be on the way. I always smoke a cigar to

116

keep myself warm. Would you care for one, Dr Watson?

WATSON: No, thank-you.

BRANDON: Cigar, Mr Holmes? Mr Holmes?

HOLMES: Mm? My apologies, Mr Brandon. My mind was elsewhere.

MARY: You surprise me, Mr Holmes; John always told me that you were always very sensitive to your environment.

HOLMES: Indeed I am, dear lady. I was just musing over our destination: Houses, like people, have definite personalities – and this one is positively ghoulish.

MARY: Not a very scientific observation.

HOLMES: Not in the least. But true, nonetheless.

BRANDON: I'm sorry to hear you say so, Mr Holmes. You see, I was responsible for the renovation of Pendark Manor.

WATSON: Oh?

BRANDON: I'm an architect by trade, and this was my last really big commission – keep it in the family, you know.

WATSON: I didn't ask, Mr Brandon – Why exactly are you coming here today?

BRANDON: The same reason the rest of the family is here – to celebrate Uncle Hubert's 80th birthday.

MARY: And how many people do you expect will be at Pendark?

BRANDON: Oh, at least a dozen.

MARY: A dozen!

HOLMES: It seems we'll have our work cut out for us. How fortunate that I thought to ask you both to accompany me.

MARY:	*Most* fortunate.
FX:	<u>CARRIAGE OUT. THROUGH TO THE INTERIOR OF PENDARK MANOR - THE PARTY WALK UP A LONG CORRIDOR. THEY STOP AS ANOTHER SET OF FEET APROACH</u>
ST JOHN:	Lloyd? Lloyd, is that you?
BRANDON:	Basil! How are you, my old fellow?
ST JOHN:	Keeping well, keeping well.
BRANDON:	You're looking well. Managed to stay away from the… you know?
ST JOHN:	I wanted to talk to you about that. I wonder if you could spare me-
HOLMES:	We'll talk about it later, Basil. Mr Holmes, may I introduce Basil St John, another member of our far-flung clan.
HOLMES:	Mr St John.
BRANDON:	Basil, these are the detectives from London.
ST JOHN:	All of them?
BRANDON:	Uncle never does things by halves, old chap.
ST JOHN:	*Your* uncle – *my* grandfather.
BRANDON:	What a complicated assortment we are. His room's still down here?
ST JOHN:	Still. But for God's sake, don't just walk in on him – (DEPARTING) it's as much as your life is worth.
FX:	<u>THEY CONTINUE WALKING</u>
MARY:	Mr Brandon, I noticed that there was something you didn't want to discuss with Mr St John while we were listening.

BRANDON:	A personal matter, Mrs Watson. I promise you it can't have anything to do with the case my uncle wishes you to investigate.
MARY:	*We* shall be the judges of that.
HOLMES:	Really, I seem quite surplus to requirements. Perhaps I should have remained in London and sent a telegram asking the Watson Detective Agency to act on my behalf.
BRANDON:	The Watson Detective Agency?
WATSON:	It's Mr Holmes' idea of a joke, Mr Brandon.
BRANDON:	Ah. Well, let me just say that Basil has battled with certain weaknesses over the years, and leave it at that. Here we are.
FX:	FOOTSTEPS STOP. HOLMES KNOCKS ON THE DOOR
SIR HUBERT:	(BEHIND THE DOOR) Who's there?
HOLMES:	Mr Sherlock Holmes. Am I speaking to Sir Hubert Willis?
SIR HUBERT:	(BEHIND DOOR) You are. Who else is with you?
HOLMES:	My friend, Dr Watson, *his wife* and your great nephew, Mr Brandon.
SIR HUBERT:	(BEHIND DOOR) Very well. Wait a moment.
FX:	HE UNLOCKS & OPENS THE DOOR
SIR HUBERT:	Come in, come in.
HOLMES:	I can assure you that the firearm isn't necessary, Sir Hubert.
SIR HUBERT:	Oh, this.* Just a precautionary measure. Someone outside might have been forcing you to speak. I don't believe there's such a thing as being too careful, Mr Holmes.
FX:	*HE LAYS DOWN THE REVOLVER
BRANDON:	Mind still as sharp as ever, uncle.

SIR HUBERT:	Lloyd! How wonderful to see you again, my boy. How's business?
BRANDON:	Could always be better. Uncle, what's going on? Mr Holmes said there'd been an attempt on your life.
SIR HUBERT:	Yesterday, my boy. As I was taking a stroll with Basil.
WATSON:	Basil St John, your grandson?
SIR HUBERT:	*One* of my grandsons, Doctor. Met him, have you?
WATSON:	Just a moment ago.
SIR HUBERT:	He's a dear boy, but don't lend him any money. Now then, the attack... Lloyd, you know the gargoyle on the roof?
BRANDON:	Of course, I had it shipped all the way from Paris. I noticed it was missing. What became of it?
SIR HUBERT:	Smashed – and I was supposed to be underneath it. Basil pushed me out of the way just in time. He saw – a figure on the roof. By the time the family searched the roof, he... or she... was gone.
MARY:	Mr Brandon tells us that there are a dozen people here, Sir Hubert – is that your entire family?
SIR HUBERT:	Oh, by no means, my dear. I have seven children and numerous grandchildren, scattered all around the globe – Canada, Australia. Did you know that Willy was born in Mexico? Er, William Bruce, a cousin.
WATSON:	The publisher? I should be interested to meet him.
MARY:	Surely you can talk shop when matters are less pressing, dear.
WATSON:	You were the one who wanted me to retire on my writing income, remember? I thought perhaps a monthly magazine might be just the thing.
MARY:	Sir Hubert, who would stand to gain by your death?
SIR HUBERT:	You're a refreshingly blunt young lady, Mr Watson. Pretty, too, if

you don't mind me saying so. Who would profit by my death? Everybody. All my blood relatives, I mean. My fortune will be shared out equally, they all know that.

HOLMES: I believe I would like to examine the spot where that gargoyle originally stood.

WATSON: I'll join you, Holmes.

MARY: As shall I.

WATSON: Mary, I really don't think-

MARY: John, I insist. If I'm to accompany you on your little adventure, I want to play a useful part in it. Otherwise, I might just as well be at home, waiting for you to return.

BRANDON: I'd like to come along, too, Mr Holmes. If anyone's trying to kill my uncle, I want to be the first to lay my hands on them.

HOLMES: Really, this is too much! I'm used to having *one* companion on my investigations, and I seem to have inherited a whole chorus.

WATSON: Perhaps it would be best if Mr Brandon stayed behind to protect Sir Hubert.

SIR HUBERT: I have my protection, sir.

FX: HE PICKS UP THE GUN

SIR HUBERT: I am not a trusting man – I don't trust people, I don't trust the Church, and I don't trust banks. If anyone manages to break the door down, they'll find *this* waiting for them.

FX: HE COCKS THE HAMMER

SIR HUBERT: (LAUGHS)

MUSIC: BRIDGE

FX: THE WIND WHIPS AROUND THE ROOF OF PENDARK MANOR. HOLMES, WATSON, MARY AND BRANDON

121

TRUDGE ABOUT.

HOLMES: An unusual challenge, eh, Watson? It's usually our job to find the culprit after the murder has been committed.

WATSON: Now we have to prevent the murder from occurring.

HOLMES: I don't believe we've had such a promising commission since our search for the errant Reverend Lantree.

MARY: It's getting even colder. Look, it's starting to snow!

WATSON: Perhaps you should go back down, Mary – this cold air can't be good for you. Ask one of the servants to prepare you a lemon and hot water.

MARY: John, we've discussed this. Like it or not, I am staying.

HOLMES: Mr Brandon, where did the gargoyle stand?

BRANDON: Right here, Mr Holmes. Directly over the front door.

HOLMES: Quite a drop to the ground below. Acceleration of a falling body is 32 feet per second per second - anyone struck by a heavy stone object would be dead in an instant.

BRANDON: Have you a theory?

HOLMES: No, Mr Brandon, but I am forming one by degrees.

MARY: Do you really expect to find any clues up here, Mr Holmes?

HOLMES: Every contact leaves a trace, Watson. Forgive me – *Mrs* Watson.

BRANDON: Good luck finding a trace of *anything*. In a few minutes this entire roof will be covered in snow.

HOLMES: Very likely. But what's this? It's white, but it isn't snow. Ah, most interesting.

BRANDON: What have you found, Mr Holmes?

SIR HUBERT:	(FROM FAR OFF, HE SCREAMS)
BRANDON:	Uncle!
FX:	OUT
MUSIC:	STING
FX:	THEY DASH DOWN THE CORRIDOR
WATSON:	The door's unlocked!
HOLMES:	Watson, inside! Mr Brandon, take care of the lady!
MARY:	Mr Holmes, I demand-
FX:	THE DOOR SLAMS IN HER FACE
BRANDON:	It's for the best, I'm sure. I promise you, madam, I'm just as anxious to find out what's happened to Uncle Hubert.
MUSIC:	BRIDGE
HOLMES:	The dust on the windowsill is completely undisturbed. The murderer must have entered by the door.
WATSON:	And the door was locked from the inside. Why did he open it, for heaven's sake?
HOLMES:	A pertinent question, Doctor. What do you make of the body?
WATSON:	Oval bruises on the interior and lateral neck – strangulation, without a doubt. The killer used only one hand, the right hand. Muddy waters, Holmes.
HOLMES:	Too muddy, old fellow; as though someone were constantly stirring them up. Well, I think we've discovered all we can here.
FX:	HOLMES CLOSES THE DOOR OF SIR HUBERT'S ROOM
HOLMES:	The room must remain locked for the time being.

BRANDON:	Mr Holmes, what happened in there?
FX:	HE LOCKS IT
WATSON:	I'm sorry, Mr Brandon – your uncle has been murdered.
BRANDON:	(TEARFUL) Devil take it! Why didn't I listen to you, Mr Holmes? He might still be alive if I'd- damn!
BG:	VOICES CAN BE HEARD IN THE DISTANCE
MARY:	I'm so sorry, John; I should have stayed with him.
WATSON:	Your own life would have been in danger, Mary. I'd sooner you were by my side.
BRANDON:	It sounds as though the family are stirring. This isn't the sort of reunion I was hoping for.
HOLMES:	They will have to be informed.
WATSON:	And the police will have to be sent for.
MARY:	It's too late for that, dear – look at the snow.
WATSON:	You're right. We can't leave, but neither can the murderer. If we act quickly-
HOLMES:	I leave the enquiries to you, Watson. And to Mrs Watson, of course.
FX:	A GREAT MANY FOOTSTEPS ARE GETTING CLOSER
MARY:	Is anything the matter, Mr Holmes?
HOLMES:	One must not allow one's emotions to influence one's actions, Mrs Watson. But I must confess that I'm unused to losing a client. I am… troubled. Forgive me; I feel I need a rest. (DEPARTING) I wonder if I can find a servant to show me to my room.
BG:	THE FAMILY HAVE ARRIVED, AND ALL CHATTER AT

ONCE. WE CAN HEAR:

BRUCE:	What the devil is going on? I thought I heard a scream.
ST JOHN:	Lloyd, who are these people?
EDITH:	What is going on?
WATSON:	Ladies and gentlemen, *ladies and gentlemen*! I am a doctor from London, and I'm afraid I have some sad news to impart. If we could all convene in the library…
BG:	OUT

SECOND COMMERCIAL

MUSIC:	UNDERCURRENT
WATSON:	In Holmes' absence, it seemed it was up to me to inform an assortment of nieces, nephews, cousins, in-laws and grandchildren of the details of Sir Hubert's murder. I did not say that, because of the heavy snowfall, someone within Pendark Manor must be responsible for the crime, but that fact must surely have occurred to them…
MUSIC:	OUT
BG:	LOTS OF CHATTER
EDITH:	Dr Watson, Dr Watson, may I have a word?
WATSON:	Of course, Miss..?
EDITH:	Meiser. Edith Meiser. Mrs.
WATSON:	Mrs Meiser, what was it you wanted to ask me?
EDITH:	Not to *ask* you, Doctor, I want to *tell* you something – who murdered Uncle Hubert.
WATSON:	Go on.

EDITH:	It was Basil St John.
WATSON:	You seem very certain of that fact.
EDITH:	I *am* certain! Basil, you see, is an incurable gambler.
WATSON:	Yes, I imagined it must be something of the sort.
EDITH:	I don't know if you've ever gambled, Doctor…
WATSON:	Once or twice… when I was a younger man.
EDITH:	Well, it's a disease, a compulsion. And Basil needs more and more money to feed his compulsion.
WATSON:	And you think he murdered Sir Hubert for the inheritance?
EDITH:	He's a desperate man, Doctor. He has no steady income, and since he arrived here, he's approached practically everyone in this room for money – even me, and I spent my last penny on the trip to England, after I'd buried Mr Meiser.
WATSON:	I see. Would you mind telling me where you were when the first attempt was made on your uncle's life?
EDITH:	Where *I* was?
WATSON:	Yes, er, Mr Holmes would never forgive me if I weren't thorough.
EDITH:	Of course. Well, let me think. I suppose I was taking a stroll in the gardens. I haven't seen Pendark since I was a little girl.
WATSON:	Alone?
EDITH:	Yes.
WATSON:	I see. And when Sir Hubert was killed?
EDITH:	Enjoying a few hands of Bridge with Hillary – that's Hillary Brooke - and Samuel Hyams and Louis Hector. We didn't play for money, I hasten to add. Are you going to place Basil under

	arrest, Dr Watson?
WATSON:	I'm afraid I can't, Mrs Meiser. I'm not an officer of the law, and in any case, Basil St John didn't kill Sir Hubert.
EDITH:	But I'm certain-
WATSON:	You see, he was the one who pushed your uncle out of the way when the gargoyle fell.
EDITH:	Oh! Oh. I didn't know that.
WATSON:	So if he wasn't responsible for the first attempt, he certainly can't have committed the actual murder. You'll forgive me for saying so, Mrs Meiser, but perhaps it might be best if you left the detective work to the professional investigators.
BG:	CROSS- FADE TO FURTHER CHATTER
ST JOHN:	What's she been telling you?
WATSON:	I beg your pardon?
ST JOHN:	Edith. What's she been telling you?
WATSON:	I hardly think it would be appropriate for me to repeat a confidence, Mr St John.
ST JOHN:	There's no need, I already know – she told you that I murdered the old man for my share of the inheritance. Didn't she?
WATSON:	Well…
ST JOHN:	She told you that I was a gambler, and that I was hopelessly in debt. Well, that part's true at least. I do need money, more than I'd get from my inheritance. But despite all that, I loved the old man, and I didn't want to see him get hurt. I pushed him out of the way of that ruddy statue.
WATSON:	Gargoyle.
ST JOHN:	Whatever it was! That thing didn't fall by accident. Find the man,

or woman, who was on that roof, who dislodged that gargoyle, and you'll have your killer.

WATSON: We're in agreement on that point at least, Mr St John. As for your financial difficulties, might I suggest honest work?

BG: CROSS-FADE AGAIN

BRUCE: Where was I *when*, dear lady?

MARY: When the gargoyle nearly struck your cousin, and when he was murdered in his room.

BRUCE: And you need to know this why?

MARY: I am working for Mr Sherlock Holmes, the eminent detective.

BRUCE: Sherlock Holmes... name rings a bell. I seem to recall receiving a manuscript a couple of years ago, about a detective named Sherringford Holmes.

MARY: *A Tangled Skein*. Yes, that was written by my husband, John. He made a few changes to it later on.

BRUCE: Your husband's a writer? I thought he said he was a doctor.

MARY: He's a writer in his spare time – a very successful one. Perhaps you've read his first two novels, *A Study in Scarlet* and *The Sign of Four*?

BRUCE: I'm afraid not.

MARY: Oh. Mr Bruce, I'm afraid you didn't answer my question.

BRUCE: Did I? I'm so sorry, my dear. (A BEAT) What *was* the question?

MARY: Where were you at the time of the attacks upon Sir Hubert?

BRUCE: Where was I? Where was I? Taking a nap, perhaps? I get so little opportunity in London.

MARY: So you can't provide a satisfactory defence?

128

BRUCE:	I never imagined I'd need to.
BG:	OUT
FX:	A KNOCK AT THE DOOR
HOLMES:	Come!
FX:	WATSON OPENS THE DOOR
HOLMES:	(DISINTERESTED THROUGHOUT) Oh, it's you, Watson.
WATSON:	This must be the first time you've failed to identify my footsteps, old chap.
HOLMES:	I fear my failure to protect Sir Hubert must have dulled my senses.
WATSON:	Do I take it you won't be joining us for dinner, then?
HOLMES:	I should prefer not to.
WATSON:	Oh, Holmes! There's a murderer at large! Your talents are needed!
HOLMES:	They haven't been of much use so far. However, I have absolute faith in your ability to cope in my absence.
WATSON:	Very good of you to say so, Holmes. I've certainly managed quite well so far, I think.
HOLMES:	And what *have* you done?
WATSON:	Well, I gathered the entire family in the library - it's smaller than I remember it. But then, I was much younger, and the place was a wreck then. Anyway, I questioned them one by one and made detailed notes of everyone's statements. I thought you'd want to look through them.
FX:	HE WAVES THE PAPERS
HOLMES:	Yes, very good. Put them down somewhere, would you, old

	chap?
WATSON:	Very well.* One member of the family, a Mrs Meiser, was keen to accuse Basil St John of the crime – I thought her zealousness quite suspicious.
FX:	*HE LAYS THE PAPERS DOWN
HOLMES:	Did you?
WATSON:	Yes, but it turns out she can account for her whereabouts at the time of the murder.
HOLMES:	Pity. And it seemed such a promising line of inquiry. Did you speak to William Bruce?
WATSON:	Mary did. That's just reminded me of something – I seem to recall reading something in the *Times* about Bruce fighting a very costly libel action against Lord Underwood. Apparently, one of his publications accused Underwood of horse-faking.
HOLMES:	(TUTS) A dangerous thing, to make unsubstantiated accusations against someone as rich as Lord Underwood.
WATSON:	I quite agree. Funny it should have slipped my mind.
HOLMES:	So you were not able to plead your case to Mr Bruce, then?
WATSON:	Plead my case? Oh, the publishing thing. No, no, I didn't.
HOLMES:	You should. From my lack of success in this affair, I begin to think I should take down my brass plate and resign from the business of detection.
WATSON:	Oh, Holmes…
MUSIC:	BRIDGE
MARY:	Well, John, what did he say?
WATSON:	Nothing to indicate any enthusiasm for the case. To tell you the truth, Mary, I'm rather worried about him.

MARY:	Surely you must be used to his mood swings by now, dear; you've told me about them often enough.
WATSON:	Yes, but he's usually in a funk *between* cases, not *during* them. I'm afraid Sir Hubert's murder has hit him quite hard. He's lost all interest in detection – says he wants to chuck it all in and take up beekeeping, or some such nonsense.
MARY:	John, did you give him those notes?
WATSON:	Of course.
MARY:	But do you think you can remember what was in them?
WATSON:	Naturally. Why?
MARY:	What is it Mr Holmes says? "The truth can only be found by the painstaking elimination of the untrue."
WATSON:	That's certainly *one* of the things he says. What are you driving at, dear?
MARY:	Well, since we're stuck here for the time being, thanks to the foul weather, I suggest we make ourselves useful.
WATSON:	How?
MARY:	By solving this murder.
MUSIC:	UNDERCURRENT
MARY:	It's simply a question of applying logic. Now your Mr Holmes has a natural flair for that sort of thing, but with perseverance, we'll undoubtedly come to the same conclusions.
FX:	A FLURRY OF PAPERS
WATSON:	All right, then. Where to begin? Motive. Lloyd Brandon gave the impression that he needed money – he said that the renovation of Pendark Manor was his last big commission, and that was six years ago.

MARY:	But Lloyd Brandon isn't a blood relative, so he doesn't inherit. He wasn't here when the first attempt was made on Sir Hubert's life, *and* he was with us when the murder occurred.
WATSON:	I *know* that dear, I was just- Oh, look, let's start again, shall we?
FX:	WATSON CRUMPLES UP THE PAPER
MUSIC:	FADES OUT & IN
WATSON:	Now, this is a list of all the people under this roof, except Holmes and ourselves, of course.
MARY:	And Mr Brandon.
FX:	WATSON CROSSES OUT HIS NAME
WATSON:	And Mr Brandon. Now what?
MARY:	Oh – Sir Hubert was strangled with the right-hand, you said. Remove the names of all the guests who are left-handed.
WATSON:	Did you notice which ones are left-handed?
MARY:	Did you?
WATSON:	(SIGHS)
FX:	WATSON CRUMPLES UP THE PAPER
MUSIC:	FADES OUT & IN
WATSON:	Right, it's simply a question of accounting for everyone's whereabouts at the time of the first and second attempts upon Sir Hubert's wife.
MARY:	So, if anyone can provide an alibi for one crime or the other, we can cross them off the list.
WATSON:	Precisely. Now, let's see… Basil St John was with Sir Hubert when the gargoyle fell, so he's in the clear.

FX:	A PENCIL DRAWS A LINE ON PAPER
WATSON:	Miss Brooke, Mr Hyams, Mr Hector and Mrs Meiser were all playing Bridge with at the time of the murder – that lets them out.
FX:	FOUR NAMES ARE CROSSED OUT
MUSIC:	FADES OUT & IN
WATSON:	And lastly, Harry Cording and John Hawkesworth were playing billiards at the time of the first attack.
MARY:	With Jerrold Hunter watching!
FX:	WATSON CROSSES OUT THREE NAMES
WATSON:	And that just leaves…
MARY:	One name.
WATSON:	The name of the murderer.
MARY:	And it only took us- Good grief, is that the time?
MUSIC:	OUT
BG:	THE LOUD CHATTER OF THE ASSEMBLED CLAN
WATSON:	(LOUD) Ladies and gentlemen, ladies and gentlemen, may I have your attention, please.
BG:	CHATTER LESSENS
WATSON:	Thank-you. Ladies and gentlemen, it's less than twenty-four hours since we last assembled in the library. At that time, I had the unhappy duty of informing you that Sir Hubert Willis had been murdered. This morning, I am pleased to announce that I am able to name his murderer.
BG:	GASPS AND OTHER EXPRESSIONS OF DISBELIEF

MARY:	(LOW, CLOSE TO MIC) So glad you could join us, Mr Holmes.
HOLMES:	(LOW, CLOSE TO MIC) My dear lady, I wouldn't have missed this for worlds. He's really doing awfully well.
WATSON:	My method is based upon a logical process of elimination. In other words, anyone in Pendark Manor who cannot account for their movements at the moment Sir Hubert was nearly struck by the gargoyle *and* at the time of his murder must undoubtedly be a suspect.
BG:	MURMURS OF AGREEMENT
WATSON:	Now, I have taken statements from all of you, and I can now report that only one of you corresponds with that criteria, and must, therefore, be the murderer. And that someone is… Mr William Bruce.
BRUCE:	What the-? This is outrageous!
WATSON:	It is true, Mr Bruce, that you are desperately in need of money in order to fight the charge of libel levelled against you by Lord Underwood.
BRUCE:	What of it?
WATSON:	You murdered your cousin for that money.
BRUCE:	Are you quite mad?
WATSON:	First, you planned to crush him beneath the gargoyle you dislodged from the roof of Pendark Manor.
BRUCE:	Rubbish.
WATSON:	Then, after that attempt failed, you strangled him as Holmes and I were examining the scene of your first crime.
BRUCE:	You can prove all this, I assume?
WATSON:	Can anyone here provide you with an alibi?

BRUCE:	Well, no, but I'd hardly call that proof! Surely it's just as likely that someone from outside the house killed Hubert.
WATSON:	The sudden snowstorm means that no-one could have left after the murder. The killer is still under this roof. And logic states that you must be that killer, Mr Bruce.
FX:	<u>HOLMES CLAPS</u>
HOLMES:	Admirable, Watson, admirable! I'm pleased to see that the years you've spent observing my methods haven't been wasted.
MARY:	Have you anything to add, Mr Holmes?
HOLMES:	By no means. Your deductions seem entirely sound. I hardly think you need my advice, but I take it that you have made some arrangements regarding Mr Bruce's incarceration?
WATSON:	Incarceration? Well, I thought his room…
HOLMES:	The snow is melting, Watson. If he should get out via the window…
BRANDON:	There is the wine cellar, Mr Holmes.
HOLMES:	An excellent suggestion, Mr Brandon. Would you and Mr Hector see to it?
BRANDON:	Gladly. Come along, Willy.
BRUCE:	Get your hands off me! I won't stand for this! When the police get here, you'll see! I'm not a man to be handled in such a shoddy fashion! (HE IS LED AWAY, COMPLAINING LOUDLY)
MARY:	John? You look troubled. What's the matter?
WATSON:	We're wrong – William Bruce didn't do it.
MARY:	Why do you say that?
WATSON:	Because of the way Holmes capitulated. I know him too well.

MARY:	But we *must* be right! All the evidence points to Bruce.
WATSON:	Then we've overlooked something, dear. That's the difference between being a detective and being Sherlock Holmes.
MARY:	If he thought we were wrong, why didn't he say so?
WATSON:	Because he's planning something. (TO HOLMES) Aren't you, Holmes?
HOLMES:	Am I that predictable, Watson?
WATSON:	Perhaps I've finally learned to apply your methods – but only in regard to you, it seems. I take it I'm correct?
HOLMES:	It *is* true that I have formulated an opinion, and I expect that opinion to be substantiated by fact within the next few hours.
WATSON:	How long have you known?
HOLMES:	From the moment Sir Hubert was murdered.
WATSON:	(CHUCKLES) Of course. And you were never really planning to retire from detection to take up beekeeping?
HOLMES:	Certainly not. Beekeeping? What an absurd notion. Surely you know me better than that, Watson?
MARY:	John imagined that you were dispirited by Sir Hubert's murder.
HOLMES:	Well, it was undeniably a blow to my confidence, Mrs Watson. But this is not the time for remorse – it is the time for action.
WATSON:	Will you require my assistance?
HOLMES:	It may prove invaluable, old fellow. Men of my profession rely more on mind than limb, and there may be some danger. You have your old service revolver, I trust?
WATSON:	Of course.
MARY:	John, why on earth would you bring your revolver on holiday

with you?

WATSON: With a friend like Holmes, my dear, one learns to expect only the unexpected.

HOLMES: I accept the compliment, Watson, thank-you. Incidentally, Mrs Watson, I think it best if you do not accompany us on this little-

MARY: Not another word, Mr Holmes! I intend to see this thing through to the very end. And if there is any danger to be faced, John can protect me. Isn't that right, dear?

WATSON: Quite right.

HOLMES: Very well. I suggest you get all the rest you can, then. Our quarry will not make a move until tonight. The stage is set, and I think that we three may be able to contribute to a rather dramatic last act curtain.

WATSON: And where will this last act take place?

HOLMES: Surely you must know that, Watson? You told me yourself.

MUSIC: UNDERCURRENT

WATSON: And in just a moment, I'll be back with the solution to *The Adventure of the Two Watsons*.

MUSIC: OUT

THIRD COMMERCIAL

MUSIC: UNDERCURRENT

WATSON: It was past midnight when Holmes, Mary and I crept into the library of Pendark Manor. The entirety of Sir Hubert's family had retired to their rooms, but Holmes insisted upon absolute quiet as we settled down to wait behind a large writing desk.

MUSIC: OUT

WATSON: Ouch!

HOLMES:	(WHISPER) Hush, Watson.
MARY:	(WHISPER) John, what's the matter?
WATSON:	(WHISPER) Touch of cramp. Holmes, would you mind just moving a little to the left? I need to stretch my leg.
HOLMES:	(WHISPER) Stretch it later.
WATSON:	(WHISPER) How much later? How long are we expected to wait behind here?
FX:	THE DOOR CREAKS SLOWLY OPEN
HOLMES:	(WHISPER) No time at all, it seems. Have your revolver at the ready, Watson.
MARY:	(WHISPER) Someone's coming.
WATSON:	(WHISPER) I recognise her! It's Edith Meiser!
HOLMES:	(WHISPER) Remain where you are, Watson. Mrs Meiser is not our killer.
WATSON:	(WHISPER) Then what is she doing here at this time of night?
MARY:	(WHISPER) What does anybody do in a library, dear? She's looking for a book to read.
HOLMES:	(WHISPER) Bravo, Mrs Watson.
EDITH:	Mark Twain. This will do.
FX:	SHE LEAVES
MARY:	You see? She couldn't sleep, thought that reading something might help her to rest, and chose a book by an American author because it reminded her of home.
WATSON:	Yes, this is all very satisfying, I'm sure, but it doesn't assist us. Holmes, how much longer will we have to wait?

HOLMES:	I can't say for certain, old chap, but if it should be that Mrs Meiser's appearance has merely delayed-
FX:	THE DOOR OPENS
HOLMES:	Ah!
BRANDON:	(LOW) I think we can risk a light.
ST JOHN:	(LOW) Are you sure?
BRANDON:	(LOW) The whole house is asleep, and this'll take but a moment.
FX:	A MATCH IS STRUCK. THE DOOR CLOSES.
BRANDON:	(LOW) Splendid. Now then, where is it?
ST JOHN:	(LOW) Do you have to pull down one of the books to move it?
BRANDON:	(LOW) Rather obvious, don't you think? There's a secret lever… here.
FX:	THE LEVER IS PULLED, AND THE BOOKCASE SLIDES AWAY
WATSON:	(WHISPER) Great Scott.
MARY:	(WHISPER) A hidden safe!
ST JOHN:	(LOW) Do you know the combination?
BRANDON:	(LOW) Naturally.
HOLMES:	Since you installed the safe in the first place, Mr Brandon-
ST JOHN & BRANDON:	(EXCLAMATIONS OF SHOCK)
HOLMES:	Please don't move, or Dr Watson will shoot. As I was saying, since you installed the safe, it's only natural that you should have made a note of the combination.

ST JOHN: Lloyd, what do we do?

BRANDON: Say nothing, Basil.

HOLMES: Your confession will not be necessary. Dr and Mrs Watson, may
                I introduce you to the killers of Sir Hubert Willis, Mr Lloyd
                Brandon and Mr Basil St John.

MARY: But that's impossible.

BRANDON: Quite right. You should listen to the lady, Holmes; she talks a lot
                of sense. In any case, I thought Willy Bruce killed my uncle.

HOLMES: I'm afraid your theory, Mrs Watson, suffers from one fatal flaw –
                the belief that the person who attempted to kill Sir Hubert with
                the gargoyle is the same person who later murdered him. It's
                often a mistake to accept something as true, merely because it's
                obvious.

WATSON: You mean it was Lloyd Brandon who pushed the gargoyle off the
                roof?

HOLMES: Thus providing Mr St John here with a cast-iron alibi. How
                could he have killed his relative when he was present at the first
                attempt?

ST JOHN: Lloyd-

BRANDON: Shut up, Basil. But I wasn't even in Hambledown when the
                gargoyle fell, Mr Holmes. We met on the train, remember?

HOLMES: The simplest trick in the world, Mr Brandon, to sneak into the
                house and onto the roof unseen, leave Hambledown by the first
                available train, and then simply double back on yourself. And, of
                course, your innocence seemed even stronger when you were at
                my side at the time of the murder.

FX: WATSON PULLS BACK THE HAMMER ON HIS
                REVOLVER

WATSON: Ah-ah! Not one more step, Mr St John.

BRANDON:	Of course, I can't speak for Mr St John here, but surely you've already established the fact that I have no motive for murder. I'm not a blood relative, so I don't inherit anything.
HOLMES:	True, but you're not after the inheritance, are you? You're after the contents of this secret vault – a hidden fortune that only needs to be shared two ways. The moment Sir Hubert mentioned his mistrust of banks, I knew he must have a secret store, additional to his known wealth, and that it must be somewhere close to hand.
MARY:	And as the man behind the renovation of Pendark Manor, you, Mr Brandon, must have known about it.
BRANDON:	Well, all I can see that I'm guilty of so far is grave-robbing. How do you expect to prove a case for murder?
ST JOHN:	Yes, tell us that, Mr Detective.
HOLMES:	Very well. I am an expert in over 200 different varieties of tobacco, and the traces of ash I found on the roof match your own brand. You told us you like to smoke to keep out the chill. I imagine you did so as you hid behind the gargoyle, waiting for your uncle and Mr St John to appear.
ST JOHN:	And what about me, eh?
MARY:	I doubt very much that Brandon would stay quiet to save your hide, Mr St John.
HOLMES:	True, Mrs Watson, but Sir Hubert *did* trust his grandson, and that was his undoing.
ST JOHN:	What do you mean?
HOLMES:	He was very proud of his suspicious nature. Why, then, should he open his door to a potential murderer, and why lay down his weapon? Because he believed he was admitting the one man who couldn't possibly be guilty – the man who saved his life by pushing him out of the way of the falling gargoyle.
WATSON:	I think a jury would find that a very compelling argument.

HOLMES:	And if they require some more tangible evidence, you provided that yourself, Mr St John, when you strangled Sir Hubert.
ST JOHN:	When I- I never touched him.
HOLMES:	You shouldn't have used only one hand to perform the deed. I made a note of the measurements between the bruises, and I should be very much surprised if they do not match the span of your own right hand.
MARY:	Do you know, dear, I think I finally understand why you're in awe of Mr Holmes.
HOLMES:	Mrs Watson, would you do me a great favour, and free Mr Bruce from the wine cellar? I fancy that two new occupants will have need of it.
MUSIC:	STING
FX:	EXTERIOR SOUNDS. WATSON APPROACHES AND DUMPS HIS BAGGAGE IN THE WAITING CARRIAGE
WATSON:	That's the last of the bags, Holmes.
HOLMES:	Splendid, Watson – we can be getting on our way, then. Where's Mrs Watson?
WATSON:	Saying her goodbyes, promising to keep in touch – you know how women are.
HOLMES:	Actually, I don't, but I'm quite happy to take your word for it. Incidentally, my dear Doctor, I'm sorry that your theory came to nothing.
WATSON:	Ah, well. Better defeat in a good cause than victory in a bad one, as my old guv'nor used to say.
HOLMES:	If it's any consolation, the process was sound. You just-
WATSON:	I'm just not Sherlock Holmes.
HOLMES:	Would you want to be?

MARY:	(CALLING) I'll be there in a moment, dear.
WATSON:	(SOFTLY) No. No, I don't believe I would. (ALOUD) Well, Holmes, when are you going to tell me how you knew that Brandon and St John were in on it together? And how you knew where to find the hidden vault?
HOLMES:	It struck me from the first that for such a perilous enterprise as murder, the stakes did not seem high enough.
WATSON:	Sir Hubert's inheritance?
HOLMES:	A portion of it. Remember, the size of his family meant that the wealth would be spread quite thinly. It seemed to me that the risks outweighed the rewards – unless there were hidden rewards, about which we knew nothing.
WATSON:	But surely Brandon didn't need to kill his great-uncle - why didn't he just steal the money?
HOLMES:	Because the owner of Pendark would have called the police immediately, and Brandon would have been the only suspect. But with Sir Hubert dead, the vault might have gone undiscovered for years.
WATSON:	Logical, but horribly cold-blooded.
HOLMES:	The criminal mind travels in devious channels, Watson. One must admire its ingenuity, however much one may deplore its purpose.
WATSON:	But how did you know where to wait for them?
HOLMES:	Didn't you tell me that the library seemed smaller to you when you addressed the family there?
WATSON:	Yes, but-
HOLMES:	I have absolute faith in your senses, old chap.
WATSON:	Than-you, Holmes. I accept the compliment.

HOLMES:	They didn't make a move until you accused William Bruce of the murder. Once you'd done that, they believed they were safe.
WATSON:	At least we did *some* good. The only thing that troubles me now is having to face-
FX:	RUNNING FOOTSTEPS APPROACH
BRUCE:	(APPROACHING) Dr Watson! Dr Watson!
WATSON:	(TO SELF) Oh no. (ALOUD) Mr Bruce!
BRUCE:	Dr Watson, Mrs Watson explained the whole thing to me.
WATSON:	She did. She did?
BRUCE:	Yes, she told me how your accusation was all part of Mr Holmes' plan to draw out the real killers.
WATSON:	Yes! Yes, indeed!
BRUCE:	I must confess, I was more than a little annoyed at the time, not being let in on the scheme.
WATSON:	Mr Holmes likes to play things very close to the chest – it's his way.
BRUCE:	So your wife said, yes.
WATSON:	I see. Well, ah, I hope we didn't cause you too much distress, Mr Bruce.
BRUCE:	I don't think I'd care to repeat the experience, but it was worth a night's inconvenience to see those two blackguards go to the gallows.
HOLMES:	I think we can promise that. Once the snow cleared sufficiently, I sent one of the footmen to the nearest police station. St John and Brandon should be out of Pendark Manor and in a cell before the afternoon.
WATSON:	Incidentally, who inherits Pendark now that Sir Hubert is gone?

BRUCE:	You know, I've really no idea. I do hope Hubert left some sort of provision in his will, or we'll have the family tearing itself apart.
HOLMES:	I'm afraid such domestic complications are outside our province, Mr Bruce.
BRUCE:	I'd better go and check before all hell breaks out. Goodbye, Mr Holmes, Dr Watson.
WATSON:	Goodbye, Mr Bruce.
FX:	HE RUSHES OFF
WATSON:	Phew!
HOLMES:	It seems I'm not the only one with an ideal helpmate. I seem to recall, Watson, that when you informed me of your intention to marry, I said that I couldn't congratulate you. However, it seems that I was mistaken. I hope you will now accept my congratulations.
FX:	MARY APPROACHES
WATSON:	Thank-you, Holmes.
HOLMES:	I think there is someone else who deserves your thanks more, Doctor.
WATSON:	Of course. Thank-you, Mary.
MARY:	Don't mention it, John. And now I imagine you can't wait to get back home to start writing this case up for your collection.
WATSON:	Amazing deduction, my dear.
MARY:	Elementary, my dear Watson.
FX:	OUT
MUSIC:	*DANSE MACABRE*

The Further Adventures of Sherlock Holmes –
The Adventure of the Perfect Match
(Original Airdate June 29, 2009)

I felt as though this episode marked a turning point in my work on this series, although that certainly wasn't intentional. In fact, the only conscious decision was that, from now on, all my *Further Adventures* scripts would take their inspiration from the veiled references to unrecorded cases littered throughout the Canon, in this case "the atrocious conduct of Colonel Upwood in connection with the famous card scandal at the Nonpareil Club". But something just seemed to work particularly well here, resulting in a satisfyingly complex mystery which can be understood at the outset, but which includes small elements that can be picked up on later (Watson's minor battle over the use of the words "hanged" and "hung", for example). It's also probably the most economical script I'd written to date – save for the regulars and semi-regulars, there are only two additional characters in the story, a witness and the killer. The three victims all exist only in the listeners' imagination.

I wondered later on whether I shouldn't have had Julian Emery kill himself with the jack-knife Holmes used to affix his correspondence to the mantelpiece, but that might have been too much even for him to bear, and it would have robbed the mystery of an important clue. And, yes, Julian Emery *was* Watson's old school-friend in the final Rathbone/Bruce movie, *Dressed to Kill* (AKA *Sherlock Holmes and the Secret Code*, *AKA Prelude to Murder*).

Waxflatter the resting Shakespearean actor/cabbie was a deliberate move away from the typical chirpy cockney seen in too many scripts, mine included. It'd be nice to have him back some day, if I can come up with an appropriate situation. Waxflatter, as far as I can recall, takes his surname from the eccentric character played by ex-Watson Nigel Stock in the film *Young Sherlock Holmes*.

Holmes' "he's gone but he's still here" remark in the first scene is rather similar to a line in *The Ripper Inheritance*, something I'd forgotten in the intervening five years. Many times, I have difficulty remembering what I went into the kitchen for, so half a decade is pretty good going.

CAST:

ANNOUNCER (DENNIS BATEMAN)

HOLMES (JOHN PATRICK LOWRIE)

WATSON (LAWRENCE ALBERT)

MRS HUDSON (LEE PASCH)

LESTRADE (RICK MAY)

WAXFLATTER (DENNIS BATEMAN)

COLONEL UPWOOD (TERRY ROSE)

DIRECTED BY JOHN PATRICK LOWRIE

FX:	OPENING SEQUENCE, BIG BEN
ANNOUNCER:	*The Further Adventures of Sherlock Holmes*, featuring John Patrick Lowrie as Holmes and Lawrence Albert as Dr Watson.
FX:	OUT AS HOLMES AND WATSON CLOSE THE DOOR BEHIND THEM AND SET DOWN THEIR LUGGAGE
MRS HUDSON:	And how was Dartmoor, Doctor?
WATSON:	Eventful, Mrs Hudson – eventful.
MRS HUDSON:	Well, I hope you had a good rest while you were there.
HOLMES:	Hardly that, but certainly rewarding.
MRS HUDSON:	And that nice Sir Henry Baskerville? Oh, I hope he fares well.
WATSON:	He had a rather nasty turn before we left, but I trust his condition will only improve from now on.
HOLMES:	Any visitors while we were away?
MRS HUDSON:	Heavens, I almost forgot! A gentleman arrived for you this morning.
WATSON:	Will he call again?
MRS HUDSON:	He never left, Doctor – he was quite insistent on waiting for you.
HOLMES:	(SIGHS) Well, unless his problem is particularly compelling, he can come back later.
FX:	HOLMES MOUNTS THE STAIRS
WATSON:	Mr Holmes got drenched in the Grimpen Mire, Mrs Hudson – I think he may have caught a chill.
HOLMES:	(SLIGHTLY OFF-MIC) And for once, I am going to take my physician's advice and retreat to the warmth of my bed.
FX:	HE CONTINUES UP THE STAIRS. FAINTLY, WE CAN

WATSON: (CALLS OUT) I'll put our visitor off, Holmes. (TO MRS HUDSON) What's the gentleman's name, Mrs Hudson?

MRS HUDSON: He wouldn't give his name, Doctor. I don't think it'll be so very easy to persuade him to leave – he seemed very agitated.

FX: AT THE TOP OF THE STAIRS, HOLMES EXITS THE ROOM AND SHUTS THE DOOR

HOLMES: (OFF-MIC, AT THE TOP OF THE STAIRS) Watson? Would you join me, please?

WATSON: (CALLS) Something the matter, Holmes?

HOLMES: (OFF-MIC) Please, Watson.

WATSON: Very well.

FX: WATSON TAKES THE STAIRS AT A QUICKER PACE THAN HOLMES

HOLMES: (OFF-MIC, BUT BECOMING LOUDER AS WATSON APPROACHES) Mrs Hudson, would you prepare a strong cup of tea, please?

MRS HUDSON: (NOW SHE'S THE ONE OFF-MIC) Very good, Mr Holmes.

HOLMES: And take your time about it.

WATSON: Is our visitor in need of refreshment?

HOLMES: The tea is for Mrs Hudson. Our visitor has gone.

WATSON: Without anyone seeing him?

HOLMES: No-one saw him leave, Watson, because he's still here.

WATSON: Holmes, I think that chill has affected your reasoning, Holmes. How can he be gone if he's still here?

FX: HOLMES PUSHES THE DOOR OPEN

149

HOLMES:	See for yourself, old chap.
WATSON:	(GRAVELY) Good Lord.
MUSIC:	*DANSE MACABRE* UP AND UNDER
WATSON:	(NARRATING) Sherlock Holmes and I had returned from Dartmoor in triumph – we had brought to a conclusion the most perplexing case of our careers. Our reverie was not to last, however. Awaiting us in the consulting room of our Baker Street home was not yet another client with a fresh problem – but, seated in the basket chair, a young man of about five-and-twenty, his shirt-front stained claret red with the blood that had seeped from his throat... and lying at his feet, a murderously sharp shaving razor.
MUSIC:	OUT
LESTRADE:	(READS) "Mr Holmes... I came to see you today with the intention of informing you of today's terrible events – better you than the police."
HOLMES:	I'm sure our caller meant no offence, Lestrade.
LESTRADE:	(CONTINUES READING) "But now I realise that it is not for me to bring retribution upon another. Let their sins find them out in good time. They are surely as damned as I."
FX:	LESTRADE REPLACES THE LETTER
LESTRADE:	Not very informative for a suicide letter. Two in one day – must be the time of year for it.
HOLMES:	*Two* suicides, Lestrade?
LESTRADE:	Another case in Shepherd's Bush. Nasty business. I was thinking of asking your opinion on it, Mr Holmes, but you seem to have your hands full here.
WATSON:	Poor Mrs Hudson. This has been a terrible shock for her.
LESTRADE:	One of the police matrons is looking after her, Doctor. She says

	this poor fellow arrived here by cab.
WATSON:	That might be one way of tracing him – assuming he came directly from his home, of course.
LESTRADE:	Both your landlady and the page are adamant that no-one entered the house after him.
WATSON:	In other words, he did this to himself, whoever he is. Why would he call on a detective and then cut his own throat?
HOLMES:	Perhaps suicide was always his intention, Watson. The razor at his feet doesn't belong to either of us. Or perhaps he was disturbed in the act of shaving this morning - there are still traces of lather behind his ear.
LESTRADE:	What was it, I wonder, that made death preferable to life for him?
HOLMES:	That is what I intend to find out, Inspector.
WATSON:	Holmes, what about your cold?
HOLMES:	(SHARP) Watson, I can spare no time for such trifles!
LESTRADE:	Mr Holmes, you mustn't blame yourself for this, just because the man died in your home-
HOLMES:	I assure you, Inspector, I view this simply as a challenge to my deductive faculties.
LESTRADE:	Well, of course.
HOLMES:	The first challenge being to supply a name for this unfortunate gentleman.
WATSON:	Nothing on his person that might indicate his identity.
HOLMES:	Save that his hat bears the initials H.L., his boots are made by J J Godfrey of Pond Street, SW 1, he waxes his hair with Mr Brewster of Jermyn Street's Pomade, and smokes Egyptian Pasha cigarettes.

WATSON:	Apart from that, of course.
HOLMES:	Apart from that, we have traces of Dermatomycoses Seborrhoea on his shoulders.
LESTRADE:	Derma- (HE GIVES UP QUICKLY) What?
WATSON:	Topical eczema, Inspector – dandruff.
LESTRADE:	Well, why couldn't he just say dandruff?
HOLMES:	But none inside his hat – most interesting. And there's something else – there are bloodstains on his jacket. Here, on the lower part of the right arm.
LESTRADE:	What of it? He slit his own throat - wouldn't you expect him to have bloodstains?
HOLMES:	Damp bloodstains, Inspector – but these are quite dry.
WATSON:	Dry?
HOLMES:	And observe the shape.
LESTRADE:	Looks like... a thumb-mark.
WATSON:	So, some time earlier, before he came to Baker Street, someone grabbed him by the arm like so – someone with blood on their hand.
HOLMES:	"Let their sins find them out in good time". I think we may confidently say that sin was murderous in nature. We've never been launched so unexpectedly into a bleak and baffling mystery.
LESTRADE:	It seems that somewhere in London there's a murder that's yet to be discovered. But whose?
HOLMES:	I'll let you know that as soon as I've found out for myself, Lestrade.
LESTRADE:	I'd be very grateful if you could turn something up, Mr Holmes. Obviously, this is my responsibility, but-

WATSON:	But you have your other case in Shepherd's Bush. We quite understand, Inspector. Not to worry - we can be your very own Baker Street Irregulars.
MUSIC:	STING
FX:	INTERIOR OF A MOVING CAB
WAXFLATTER:	(SLIGHTLY OFF-MIC) Nearly there, gentlemen.
WATSON:	Thank-you, driver.
WAXFLATTER:	(SLIGHTLY OFF-MIC) Waxflatter, sir – Nigel Waxflatter.
WATSON:	Er, yes. (TO HOLMES) Hear that, Holmes? Nearly there.
HOLMES:	I can hear quite well, Doctor - my ears are nearly as well-trained as my eyes.
WATSON:	(TRYING HARD NOT TO GET ANNOYED) Hmm. You may not think I understand you, Holmes, but I do.
HOLMES:	Oh?
WATSON:	This isn't merely an exercise in deduction for you, is it?
HOLMES:	No, Watson, it is not.
WATSON:	You feel you have an obligation to that poor wretch.
HOLMES:	No, Watson, I do not.
WATSON:	Eh?
HOLMES:	I feel an obligation to Mrs Hudson. This man... (HE STARTS AGAIN) This *death* would not have come to her home were I not her lodger. I cannot adequately apologise, nor would I know how to... comfort her. The least I can do is to uncover the reason for this fellow's death. She deserves to know.
FX:	CAB BG OUT

FIRST COMMERCIAL

FX:	THE CAB PULLS UP
WAXFLATTER:	Bleek Street, good sirs.
FX:	HOLMES AND WATSON GET OUT OF THE CAB. QUIET STREET BG.
HOLMES:	And you're certain this is where he flagged you down, cabbie?
WAXFLATTER:	Please, I would prefer it if you did not address me by that term. This is merely a temporary position – I am an actor by vocation.
HOLMES:	Indeed.
WAXFLATTER:	He emerged from over there, number 47, at a quarter past the hour of nine in the morning. He was in quite a panic. I am always on the lookout for types, you see – my craft relies upon them.
WATSON:	And what did he say?
WAXFLATTER:	He said... (CLEARS THROAT, THEN, IN A BAD MELODRAMATIC DELIVERY) "Take me at once to Scotland Yard!" No, wait. I'd like to try that again.
WATSON:	(EAGER TO STOP HIM) And he subsequently asked you to take him to Baker Street instead?
WAXFLATTER:	He did. Regrettably, he would not be drawn upon the subject, but he provided me with sufficient inspiration, nonetheless. When I am next called upon to essay the role of an innocent man, trapped in a web of deceit not of his own making, I am quite confident-
HOLMES:	(CUTTING IN) Thank-you, driver. This is for your trouble.
WAXFLATTER:	(OFFENDED) I see. This is not the first time I have faced a hostile audience.
FX:	HE CRACKS HIS WHIP

WAXFLATTER:	On, Sophocles!
FX:	THE CAB MOVES OFF
WATSON:	Good grief! The sooner he gets an acting role, the better!
HOLMES:	I wonder whether it would be preferable to have a cab ride ruined, or an entire evening.
WATSON:	This is Shepherd's Bush, isn't it? Didn't Lestrade say he was investigating another suicide in this area?
HOLMES:	Curious. But come, let us see whether anybody is still home at number 47, and, if so, what they can tell us about our unfortunate caller.
FX:	STREET BG OUT
UPWOOD:	I've seen all the commotion, I know exactly why you're here.
WATSON:	You do?
UPWOOD:	I do, and I should tell you right now, I hardly knew the Lestersons – raised my hat to them in the street now and then, of course, but I never really cared for them. The "new" rich are so vulgar! And why he should want to do away with her, I've no idea. None of *my* wives ever gave me that much trouble.
HOLMES:	Colonel Upwood, if you imagine we are from Scotland Yard, you are mistaken.
UPWOOD:	You're not? Who did you say you were?
HOLMES:	My name is Sherlock Holmes. This is my colleague, Dr Watson.
UPWOOD:	Holmes? The detective? What- what is going on here? What do you want with me?
WATSON:	We'd like to talk to you about-
HOLMES:	(CUTTING IN) About the young man in this photograph. Your son, perhaps, Colonel?

UPWOOD:	My *step*son, Julian Emery – a good-for-nothing when his mother was alive, good for even less nowadays.
WATSON:	You two are far from close, then?
UPWOOD:	You're wise to leave the more testing deductions to your friend, Dr Watson. Julian is a weakling in every sense of the word, I despise the young wretch. Now you know what he is to me, perhaps you'll tell me what he means to the two of you.
HOLMES:	He came to our rooms in Baker Street earlier today.
UPWOOD:	Oh? And what did he say?
HOLMES:	What would you expect him to say?
UPWOOD:	(SUSPICIOUS OF THEM) Hmm... I don't think he said *anything* to you, Mr Holmes. In fact, I'm starting to wonder if he came to you at all. You have a lot of nerve.
WATSON:	Colonel, would you like me to examine that cut on your hand?
UPWOOD:	*No.*
WATSON:	May I ask how you sustained it?
UPWOOD:	*No.*
FX:	LESTRADE ENTERS THE ROOM
LESTRADE:	(APPROACHING) Good afternoon, gentlemen! It's a small world – I don't know when I've seen a smaller.
UPWOOD:	Lestrade!
WATSON:	You two are acquainted?
LESTRADE:	Acquainted, yes, but we don't travel in the same social circles. That's why I didn't recognise the dead man in your rooms.
HOLMES:	(ATTEMPTING TO SILENCE HIM) Lestrade!

LESTRADE:	But since you've got a picture of him there, Doctor, I suppose he must have been the Colonel's stepson.
UPWOOD:	Dead? Julian?
LESTRADE:	Surely Mr Holmes here already deduced that. (PAUSE) Didn't you?
UPWOOD:	I think I've said all I intend to say to any of you gentlemen.
FX:	LONDON STREET BG AGAIN
HOLMES:	For sheer addle-headedness, Lestrade, you've surpassed yourself!
LESTRADE:	Well, how was I to-
HOLMES:	*If* Colonel Upwood does know anything about his stepson's suicide, he certainly won't tell us now!
WATSON:	Inspector, why, exactly were you calling on the Colonel?
LESTRADE:	Talking to *everyone* on the street, Doctor – trying to find out more about the murder.
WATSON:	I thought you were investigating a suicide.
LESTRADE:	Murder *and* a suicide – didn't I say that?
HOLMES:	You heard the Colonel, Watson – a man named Lesterson murdered his wife.
LESTRADE:	Stabbed her in the back – then hung himself.
WATSON:	*Hanged*, Inspector. Pictures are hung, people are hanged.
LESTRADE:	As you like. But it doesn't make either of them any less dead.
HOLMES:	And where did these Lestersons live?
LESTRADE:	On the other side of the street – about 200 yards that way.
WATSON:	Unusually close – that's surely more than coincidence!

HOLMES:	It certainly becomes less likely.
WATSON:	Holmes, didn't you say the initials in our visitor's hat were "H.L."? But his name was Julian Emery?
HOLMES:	Lestrade, what was Lesterson's Christian name?
LESTRADE:	Hugh.
HOLMES:	"H.L."
FX:	STREET BG OUT. HOLMES AND THE OTHERS ENTER THE HOUSE. LESTRADE CLOSES THE DOOR.
LESTRADE:	Better not to use the front door, gentlemen – there are some nasty bloodstains in the hall I don't wish to disturb.
HOLMES:	Inspector, what is the nature of your history with Colonel Upwood?
WATSON:	I got the impression there was little love lost between the two of you.
FX:	HOLMES, WATSON & LESTRADE WALK ACROSS A WOODEN FLOOR
LESTRADE:	Oh, I've had my eye on the Colonel for some time – he's suspected of being the head of a gang of art thieves operating in this area. We placed an officer in the Colonel's card club, the Non... (HE CAN'T PRONOUNCE IT) Non...
WATSON:	Nonpareil?
LESTRADE:	You know it, Doctor?
WATSON:	Heard of it. But I can't believe it of Upwood – he was in the Scots Guards!
LESTRADE:	Perhaps you're right. Upwood never has any visitors, and he rarely goes out, except to the club, so we imagined he must make contact with the members of his gang there. But our man hasn't seen anything out of the ordinary – just fellows playing cards.

	Which, by the way, the Colonel is very bad at.
HOLMES:	Art thieves? I wonder...
LESTRADE:	(SLIGHTLY IMPATIENT) And just *what* do you wonder, Mr Holmes?
FX:	THEY HALT FOR A MOMENT
HOLMES:	These blank spaces on the wall – you see they're less faded by the sun?
LESTRADE:	You mean pictures were hanged there?
WATSON:	*Hung*, Lestrade.
HOLMES:	Missing pictures, a gang of art thieves?
LESTRADE:	A connection between Colonel Upwood and the Lestersons?
HOLMES:	But not necessarily between the Colonel and their deaths.
WATSON:	And Julian Emery's suicide?
HOLMES:	We're presented with an over-abundance of clues, Watson – too many to permit of any intelligent deduction.
MUSIC:	BRIDGE
LESTRADE:	(APPROACHING MIC) Through here, in the hallway – this is where it all happened. Nothing's been moved - except the bodies, of course. And the murder weapon – we found that lying next to Mrs Lesterson's body.
WATSON:	The pool of blood by the front door – does it belong to her?
LESTRADE:	It does. I imagine there was a violent row, she attempted to flee – he stabbed her before she could leave the house.
HOLMES:	(SLIGHTLY OFF-MIC) With the twin of this dagger mounted on the wall, perhaps. It's clearly one of a pair.

LESTRADE: That's right, Mr Holmes.

HOLMES: And then, no doubt filled with remorse, Lesterson hanged himself.

WATSON: How can you be so sure, Holmes?

HOLMES: The curtain sash has been sliced off with the knife used to kill Mrs Lesterson - there are traces of blood on the remaining portion of rope. I imagine he tied it to one of the stair-rods – even from here, you can see where the varnish has worn off.

WATSON: And with the other end wrapped around his neck, he jumped over the bannister.

LESTRADE: Precisely. The only thing missing is Lesterson's motive – why did he kill his wife? That's what I wanted to ask you about, Mr Holmes.

HOLMES: At what time did this occur, Lestrade?

LESTRADE: Some time before ten o'clock. The maid had been called away the night before to tend to a sick relative – she arrived back here at ten, saw her mistress dead, and raised the alarm.

WATSON: And three-quarters of an hour earlier, Julian Emery rushes from his own house a few doors away, takes a cab to Baker Street... And then slices his own throat.

HOLMES: This pool of blood – does nothing suggest itself?

LESTRADE: Should it, Mr Holmes?

HOLMES: Look here. Blood does not run around corners of its own accord, Inspector. Something was removed from this spot after the murder.

WATSON: A small book, perhaps, judging by the shape?

HOLMES: Doubtless you've searched the property for a volume of the appropriate size, Lestrade?

LESTRADE:	(WHO HASN'T) As a matter of fact, I was just about to instruct my officers to look for it.
HOLMES:	Splendid. Although I have little doubt that the killer took it with him – it may prove to be the key to unlocking this mystery.
LESTRADE:	The killer is Hugh Lesterson. Why else would he have hanged himself?
WATSON:	Then these bloody footprints are his.
LESTRADE:	Obviously!
HOLMES:	You've examined his shoes?
LESTRADE:	Well... no.
FX:	HOLMES WALKS UPSTAIRS
LESTRADE:	But his clothes are at the mortuary. It'll be an easy matter to verify that. Where are you off to?
HOLMES:	(SLIGHTLY OFF-MIC) More blood, Lestrade. Droplets on the stairs.
FX:	LESTRADE GOES UPSTAIRS TO JOIN HOLMES
LESTRADE:	(AS HE WALKS) Well, perhaps he stabbed her up there. She tumbled... probably... came to rest by the door.
HOLMES:	No. The drops are too small, and moving the wrong way.
LESTRADE:	How do blood-drops *move*?
HOLMES:	You see these tiny tails one each drop? They indicate direction. The drops came from the blade of the knife. It was taken upstairs *after* Mrs Lesterson was killed.
LESTRADE:	Makes sense – he used the knife to cut the sash after the murder – of course he had it in his hand.
WATSON:	(OFF-MIC) So how did it end up downstairs next to the body?
LESTRADE:	Ah.

FX:	<u>HOLMES AND LESTRADE WALK DOWNSTAIRS AGAIN</u>
WATSON:	(HIS VOICE GROWS LOUDER AS THEY APPROACH) Each new discovery presents us with more questions.
HOLMES:	We have an answer to one of our puzzles, Watson. This hat on the peg is a perfect match for the one worn by Julian Emery.
FX:	<u>HOLMES REMOVES THE HAT FROM THE PEG</u>
WATSON:	The one bearing Hugh Lesterson's initials on the lining.
HOLMES:	But if we check the lining of this hat, gentlemen, what do we find?
LESTRADE:	Dandruff!
WATSON:	And Emery had dandruff on his suit, but none in his hat.
HOLMES:	I have no hesitation in saying that *this* is the late Julian Emery's hat. He put it on the peg next to Lesterson's, and took the wrong one when he left. They were the same size, so it never occurred to him that he'd made a mistake.
WATSON:	So Emery was here – and recently!
LESTRADE:	But what was he doing here?
HOLMES:	The answer to that may be waiting for us at the mortuary, Lestrade – the dead, I find, are often more informative than the living.
MUSIC:	<u>STING</u>

SECOND COMMERCIAL

FX:	<u>ECHO ON DIALOG THROUGHOUT. WATSON IS PICKING UP SMALL IMPLEMENTS</u>
LESTRADE:	Well, Doctor?
WATSON:	(DEEP IN HIS WORK) Just a moment, Lestrade, just a moment.

162

Hugh Lesterson was a big fellow - build of a rugger player. Julian Emery was a positive weakling by comparison.

LESTRADE: What's Holmes doing over there with Lesterson's clothes?

WATSON: (DISTRACTED, TRYING TO CONCENTRATE) I haven't the faintest idea.

LESTRADE: Eh?

WATSON: (TRYING TO REASSERT HIMSELF) I mean, you'll find out in good time, Inspector.

HOLMES: (APPROACHING) I believe I've seen all I need to see here. Watson, have you concluded your examination?

FX: <u>WATSON REPLACES HIS INSTRUMENTS</u>

WATSON: I have, Holmes. And I'm quite certain Lesterson was strangled *before* he was hanged.

LESTRADE: Strangled?

WATSON: Oh, yes. See these horizontal marks on the neck? Observe the post-mortem bruising – there's no haemorrhaging in the ligature furrow.

LESTRADE: Gentlemen, how do I thank you? You've done it again! And the best of it is, I don't even have to worry about making an arrest – our man's taken care of his own execution!

HOLMES: Are you suggesting, Inspector, that Julian Emery murdered both Mrs and Mrs Lesterson?

LESTRADE: Why not? The hat shows he was in the house.

WATSON: But not necessarily at the time of the murder. I've only just discovered there *was* a third person there.

HOLMES: Actually, I'd discovered that fact a few moments earlier. The bloody shoeprints we examined are of a different size and shape than those worn by Mr Lesterson here. I did take the opportunity

163

to examine the late Julian Emery's boots...

LESTRADE: And?

HOLMES: The shoeprints seem to be a match. However-

LESTRADE: Well, that settles it, then! Emery did it.

WATSON: Why?

LESTRADE: Why? (HE'S NOT SURE) Well... it's obviously something to do with the art thefts... Yes! Emery was head of the gang, not his stepfather. We had the right address, but the wrong suspect! It was Emery who was responsible for taking the pictures from the Lesterson's home, they accused him, he murdered both of them, then he killed himself.

WATSON: Why?

LESTRADE: Remorse, something like that. Can you see a flaw in it?

HOLMES: Actually-

LESTRADE: Yes, sir, from now on, it's nothing but plain, ordinary policework – nothing you could use a magnifying glass on. And this explains why the blood drops on the stairs were going in the wrong direction.

HOLMES: Do go on, Inspector.

LESTRADE: After he stabbed Mrs Lesterson, he dragged her husband upstairs to stage the hanging. Then he realised how much neater it would be if the husband's fingerprints were on the knife. So he took it upstairs, placed it in the hand of his first victim, then brought it back downstairs again and put it next to the body.

HOLMES: I have no doubt it happened in just that fashion. Really, Lestrade, you're coming along.

LESTRADE: Thank-you, Mr Holmes.

FX: <u>LESTRADE LEAVES</u>

LESTRADE:	(DEPARTING) I'll be writing up my report, gentlemen – show yourselves out.
HOLMES:	(CHUCKLES) Apply my methods, Watson, and you'll probably find that they lead you in the opposite direction to that of our old friend, Inspector Lestrade.
WATSON:	It does seem strange that Emery, a man of slender build, should be able to overcome the substantially larger Hugh Lesterson.
HOLMES:	Substitute "impossible" for "strange" and your concerns mirror my own.
WATSON:	Then what are we overlooking?
HOLMES:	The perfect match, Watson. Let's see if we can catch up with Lestrade before he makes a fool of himself in front of the police commissioner.
FX:	ECHO OUT
MUSIC:	BRIDGE
FX:	STREET BG
LESTRADE:	Really, Mr Holmes, you can rely on me to take care of this.
HOLMES:	Yes, Lestrade, but I think you need a little unofficial help, just to supplement your usual happy mixture of cunning and audacity.
FX:	LESTRADE KNOCKS ON A DOOR
LESTRADE:	(SIGHS)
FX:	STREET BG OUT
UPWOOD:	A search warrant?
LESTRADE:	It's quite in order, I assure you, Colonel Upwood.
FX:	UPWOOD PUTS DOWN THE WARRANT

UPWOOD:	I see, And what exactly do you expect to find, Inspector?
LESTRADE:	A book. A book stained with blood.
WATSON:	A book given to the Lestersons by your stepson, Julian Emery.
LESTRADE:	Thank-you, Doctor, I was just about to say that.
WATSON:	Sorry, Lestrade.
LESTRADE:	The book was far too valuable for you to destroy, so it must still be here.
UPWOOD:	What the blazes are you talking about? *Julian* was in the Lesterson's house? Are you saying Hugh Lesterson didn't hang himself? You believe Julian was responsible? And for Rachel Lesterson's murder, too?
LESTRADE:	(AWKWARD) I... thought so at first, but...
UPWOOD:	But what?
LESTRADE:	Er... Mr Holmes?
HOLMES:	Colonel, you share your stepson's bootmaker?
UPWOOD:	No. *He* shared *mine* - J J Godfrey, Pond Street.
HOLMES:	And you wear the same size in boots.
UPWOOD:	Probably. I couldn't say.
LESTRADE:	Colonel, Mr Ho- *I* believe you made the bloodstained footprints at the Lesterson house!
UPWOOD:	I don't know anything about any footprints! If you discovered any, they obviously belonged to Julian!
WATSON:	You're remarkably quick to accuse your stepson, Colonel.
HOLMES:	I took the opportunity of examining your stepson's boots when I discovered his body in my rooms – there was not a trace of blood on the soles.

166

UPWOOD:	Doubtless he cleaned them before calling on you.
HOLMES:	It seems strange, does it not, that he should have removed the stains from the underside of his boots, but failed to clean the sleeves of his jacket?
WATSON:	Where he had bloodstains in the shape of fingers. But whose fingers?
UPWOOD:	How should I know? Lesterson's, presumably.
HOLMES:	Who simply stood by while your stepson murdered his wife? I think it far more likely that the husband was the first to die.
LESTRADE:	And the wife was killed as she fled, attempting to raise the alarm.
UPWOOD:	Lestrade, you have reached a new low. In your desperation to charge me with *something*, you've stooped to accusing me of a most heinous crime without a shred of evidence.
LESTRADE:	The book will be evidence enough.
UPWOOD:	*If* you find it, whatever it is.
HOLMES:	And if we do not, then we have only to examine the soles of your own boots, Colonel.
UPWOOD:	My-
HOLMES:	If the soles are bloody, and examination shows that they match the size and shape of the footprints left at the scene of the crime...
WATSON:	I imagine that will be enough to satisfy a jury.
LESTRADE:	Well, Colonel Upwood? What about it?
UPWOOD:	(SIGHS) Well?
HOLMES:	As your stepson predicted, your sins have found you out in the end.

MUSIC:	BRIDGE

MRS HUDSON: (STILL QUITE UPSET) And the book, Doctor?

WATSON: Oh, we found it – hidden inside a hollowed-out Bible. It was a notebook, used by the Colonel to list his gambling losses. But here's the interesting thing – they detailed money lost in games he had yet to play.

MRS HUDSON: I don't understand.

WATSON: Neither did I, Mrs Hudson. And neither did anyone at the Nonpareil Club – they all assumed Colonel Upwood was a poor card player. But he was losing intentionally – that was how he paid the members of his gang, right under everyone's noses.

MRS HUDSON: But surely, he- he must have been cheating. If he knew how much he was going to lose, I mean. Why didn't anybody at that club of his notice?

WATSON: Because people usually cheat in order to win. Colonel Upwood played to lose, so he didn't attract attention.

MRS HUDSON: You're very clever, Doctor.

WATSON: *Mr Holmes* is very clever.

MRS HUDSON: How is his cold, Doctor? Would he like a bowl of soup?

WATSON: I think he just needs rest, Mrs Hudson. He's been exerting himself quite a bit today, in spite of his condition. It was he who deduced the significance of the book, and also that Julian Emery must have given it to the Lestersons.

MRS HUDSON: So Mr Emery knew all about the art thefts?

WATSON: Well, the Colonel won't say, but he must have had some idea. Probably he turned a blind eye until his own neighbours were robbed. Before they had a chance to report it to the police, Julian called on them with the book.

MRS HUDSON: And when his stepfather found out, he... killed them both to get it back.

WATSON:	I'm afraid so, yes. He still had blood on his hands when he returned home – Julian Emery knew at once what must have happened. Colonel Upwood tried to stop him leaving the house – that's how the bloody marks got onto Julian's sleeve – but Julian used his razor to cut his stepfather's hand and get free.
MRS HUDSON:	He wanted to tell someone.
WATSON:	First the police, then Mr Holmes. But as he waited for us to return, it must have prayed on his mind that he was somehow responsible for what had happened. Eventually... well...
MRS HUDSON:	Oh, Dr Watson, if only I'd taken the time to talk to him! Perhaps I could have done something!
WATSON:	I don't believe so, Mrs Hudson. I think he'd quite made his mind up. He said in his note, he felt he was damned by what he'd done.
MRS HUDSON:	But you don't know that for certain.
WATSON:	Martha - none of this is your doing, none of it. And though it's no consolation, justice was done in the end and Julian Emery's death was not for nothing... Mr Holmes wanted you to know that.
MUSIC:	SAD UNDERCURRENT
FX:	WATSON ENTERS THE CONSULTING ROOM
HOLMES:	And how is our landlady, Watson?
WATSON:	She's a strong woman – she'll overcome this. But in the meantime, I've prescribed a few weeks in Lancashire with her sister.
HOLMES:	Perhaps it's for the best. You related the facts of the case to her?
WATSON:	I did. Bit I think she would have preferred to hear it from your own lips.
HOLMES:	*You* are the storyteller in this partnership, Watson, not I.

WATSON: Despite the impression you like to give, Holmes, you're not simply a calculating machine – and you're just as capable as anyone else of providing solace.

HOLMES: I... cannot, Watson. Not at this time.

WATSON: Why not?

HOLMES: The responsibility for this tragedy is mine entirely. Mrs Hudson did not advertise for a consulting detective as her lodger, but she took one all the same – and she has dealt with all the consequent disturbances when any landlady would have thrown me out onto the street. But this latest... disturbance... it goes beyond what any woman should have to bear. You were quite right, Doctor – she should go away, and soon. For my benefit as much as hers... for I think it will be quite some time before I am able to face her again.

MUSIC: SWITCHES TO *DANSE MACABRE*

The Further Adventures of Sherlock Holmes –
The Adventure of the French Compass
(Original Airdate December 26, 2010)

Beginning in 2007 with *The Adventure of the Improbable Snowman*, it's been one of my duties to provide Holmes and Watson with their annual Christmas mystery (including, naturally, a dramatisation of *The Blue Carbuncle*). *The Adventure of the French Compass* represents my effort for 2010.

Supposedly based on a reference in the Canon, this episode relates the detective's first encounter with Inspector Alec MacDonald. The date I selected for the episode, however, is later than the one W S Baring-Gould ascribed to *The Valley of Fear* (at which point Holmes and the policeman are well acquainted) in his famous chronology. Continuity is desirable, of course, until it becomes the enemy of creativity, which is why Conan Doyle didn't allow it to hold him prisoner or get in the way of telling a good story. There's mention of a couple of other "missing" tales here, one of which I'd forgotten entirely - the Manor House Case, which Mycroft Holmes questions his brother about during *The Greek Interpreter*, apparently involved coroner Dr Malachai in some capacity. I must remember to include him when/if I get around to writing it. The famous duellist François Le Villard (who was found stark staring mad with a matchbox in front of him containing a remarkable worm, said to be unknown to science) fought with the victim Antoine Burgoyne at some stage, and the outcome has a vital bearing on the solution of this case.

Imagine my surprise when, upon reviewing scripts for this collection, I realised that the body of Darius Crowthorne had been discovered on Bleek Street, scene of the murders of Mr and Mrs Lesterson in *The Perfect Match*. Anyone considering purchasing a house there should beware - it's one unlucky street.

Two individuals somehow work their way from real life into Sherlock Holmes' fictional world in this show. It turns out that Watson had the same tutor at medical school as Conan Doyle. Dr Joseph Bell was, of course, the inspiration for Holmes' deductive skills. And according to Solomon Crowthorne, his mistress was defended in her murder trial by real-life barrister Edward Marshall Hall. A colourful individual who was involved in many of Victorian England's most sensational crimes, it's easy to mistake Marshall Hall for a fictional character, and he fits very easily into the Sherlockian world. No doubt some day I'll arrange for them to meet, perhaps in The Manor House Case, where he turns out to be an old friend of Dr Malachai, thus killing two birds with one stone. Unless I forget, which seems quite likely.

CAST:

ANNOUNCER (DENNIS BATEMAN)

HOLMES (JOHN PATRICK LOWRIE)

WATSON (LAWRENCE ALBERT)

INSPECTOR MACDONALD (DENNIS BATEMAN)

DR MALACHAI (JEFFREY HITCHIN)

SOLOMON CROWTHORNE (STEVE MANNING)

GUS (JEFFREY HITCHIN)

JEAN LUMIC (DENNIS BATEMAN)

DIRECTED BY JOHN PATRICK LOWRIE

FX:	OPENING SEQUENCE, BIG BEN
MUSIC:	*DANSE MACABRE* UP AND UNDER
DENNIS:	*The Further Adventures of Sherlock Holmes*, featuring John Patrick Lowrie as Holmes and Lawrence Albert as Dr Watson. Tonight: *The Adventure of the French Compass*.
WATSON:	Sherlock Holmes did not, as a rule, enjoy Christmas. He resented such periods of enforced inaction. So I was more than a little surprised when, after spending most of the day at my club, I returned to Baker Street to find Holmes studying a parcel wrapped in plain brown paper...
MUSIC:	OUT
HOLMES:	It arrived by the last post. I think it extremely unlikely that this is an early Christmas present, Watson. Save yourself, I have no friends. And surely no-one else would buy me a gift.
WATSON:	Your brother Mycroft, perhaps? (PAUSE) Of course – a ridiculous suggestion. Well, don't keep me in suspense any longer, Holmes – open it, for heaven's sake!
HOLMES:	In good time. I have a healthy distrust of unexpected packages. Without opening it, I can't say for certain what it may contain, but I should prefer to deduce as much as I can before doing so. (PAUSE) Hmm... no ticking. Perhaps if I-
FX:	A SUDDEN, (VERY) LOUD KNOCKING AT THE DOOR
WATSON:	(A GASP, FOLLOWED BY A SIGH OF RELIEF) For a second, I thought-
HOLMES:	Yes, I know. (TO THE VISITOR) Come in!
FX:	THE DOOR OPENS AND MACDONALD ENTERS
MACDONALD:	I beg your pardon for disturbing you this evening. It's Mr Holmes, isn't it?
HOLMES:	That's correct. (TO WATSON) Watson, may I introduce

	Inspector Alec MacDonald.
MACDONALD:	Doctor.
WATSON:	Inspector.
MACDONALD:	You're Mr Holmes' physician?
WATSON:	Merely his biographer – Holmes is entirely uninterested in the state of his own health. But since you and he seem to know one another, I deduce you've worked together before.
HOLMES:	You deduce incorrectly, Watson. I made Mr Mac's acquaintance at the Yard's Christmas festivities a year ago. (TO MACDONALD) I hope you're not intending to drag us out to a similar celebration on such an inclement evening, Inspector?
WATSON:	Well, actually, that sounds rather-
MACDONALD:	Not to a celebration, gentlemen – to the mortuary.
HOLMES:	Excellent!
WATSON:	Inspector, can't it wait for a couple of days? Christmas is nearly upon us!
HOLMES:	I'm sure the good Inspector is aware of that, Watson.
MACDONALD:	When you see what I have to show you, Doctor, you'll understand the urgency.
MUSIC:	BRIDGE
FX:	ECHO ON DIALOG THROUGHOUT
DR MALACHAI:	Ah, John! The season's greetings to you. Forgive me if I don't shake hands – I'm just finishing up on our anonymous corpse.
WATSON:	Of course. (TO HOLMES) Holmes, you remember Dr Malachai?
HOLMES:	The Manor House Case, of course. This is the victim you were so anxious for us to see, Mr Mac?

MACDONALD:	That's right, sir.
HOLMES:	Hmm... how old would you say, Watson?
WATSON:	Thirty-five perhaps.
HOLMES:	Curious... he seems familiar.
MACDONALD:	You think you might know him, Mr Holmes?
HOLMES:	(HESITANT) I'm... not sure.
WATSON:	That's not like you, Holmes.
HOLMES:	No. No, it isn't...
DR MALACHAI:	His liver's in quite bad condition... But that's not what killed him. *This* did. I dug it out of his gut.
<u>FX:</u>	<u>MALACHAI DROPS A SMALL BULLET INTO A METAL BOWL</u>
DR MALACHAI:	The wound was a small one, but deep.
WATSON:	It's tiny.
HOLMES:	Fired from a derringer, perhaps?
MACDONALD:	Very likely.
WATSON:	And this was the only wound, Andrew?
DR MALACHAI:	It was. Fellow must've taken hours to die. I can only imagine the excruciating agony. Not the most joyous of thoughts at this time of year.
HOLMES:	A derringer is a small weapon, easily concealed... To shoot a man in the stomach, rather than the head of heart suggests- what?
WATSON:	That he wished his victim to suffer.
HOLMES:	Possibly, Watson. Or perhaps they were seated together...

MACDONALD:	...And the killer fired under the table!
WATSON:	A dispute at the card table, perhaps?
HOLMES:	Where was he found, MacDonald?
MACDONALD:	Bleek Street, sir. No gambling establishments that I'm aware of in that area. Very likely, he walked from the place where he was shot.
DR MALACHAI:	Walked until the last of his strength left him.
WATSON:	Were there any footprints, or a trail of blood to indicate the direction he came from?
MACDONALD:	Regrettably, there's been a fresh fall of snow since then, Doctor – any traces have been completely obliterated.
HOLMES:	Nor can we say how far he travelled - the weather has been so foul, no-one would have ventured out onto the street and seen this poor fellow's plight. (THOUGHTFUL) But whoever shot him couldn't have known that for certain... so why didn't he go after him, finish him off? You say you have no idea who he might be?
MACDONALD:	Nothing particularly noteworthy about his clothing or possessions, Mr Holmes – over here. Cigar...
HOLMES:	Burma cheroot.
MACDONALD:	Spectacles.
FX:	MACDONALD PICKS UP AND REPLACES THE GLASSES
HOLMES:	Steel-rimmed - American. As the rest of his wardrobe is distinctly English, I should say he has spent some time abroad.
MACDONALD:	Boots.
HOLMES:	Polished by a bootblack on the Belgrave Road – the russet-coloured cream is entirely distinctive. Right-handed, judging by the shoelaces. May I see the jacket? Ah, yes. The right pocket is

more worn than the left.

MACDONALD: (HARUMPHS) Trousers.

HOLMES: He's a bachelor – no woman would permit her husband to
                  venture out in unpressed trousers. Absence of a wedding ring
                  confirms this. In addition, I'd suggest from the mixture of old
                  and new clothing that the man was a gambler.

DR MALACHAI: Forgive me, Mr Holmes, but I'm afraid I don't see how you arrive
                  at your last deduction.

WATSON: Periods of good and bad luck, Andrew. The new clothes were
                  purchased when his luck was good-

DR MALACHAI: -and the old when his luck was bad. Yes, I see. That's really very
                  clever. And it seems to confirm your suggestion of a falling-out
                  between card-players, John.

WATSON: Yes, it does. No shirt among his clothing, I see. I must confess,
                  I've come close to losing mine on the horses once in a while, but
                  never literally.

FX: MACDONALD OPENS A DRAWER AND PRODUCES THE
                  SHIRT

MACDONALD: Ah, the shirt I put to one side for this particular moment,
                  gentlemen. You see, our victim was in the habit of making notes
                  on his shirt-cuff.

HOLMES: As I am myself – I suspect the laundry knows more about my
                  private affairs than Watson here.

MACDONALD: Take a look at what he wrote before he died.

WATSON: (READS) "Sherlock Holmes... 221B Baker Street" Holmes, we
                  was coming to see you!

HOLMES: Interesting. Now I understand why you were so anxious for us to
                  view the body, Mr Mac.

MACDONALD: And now that you've seen him, do you recall where you know

	him from?
HOLMES:	I'm afraid not. Strange, but... It's as though I knew him as a child. This is most annoying, I usually have an excellent memory for faces.
MACDONALD:	So, is there nothing you can do to assist me, Mr Holmes?
HOLMES:	I shall give it some thought. In the meantime, if you'll excuse us, there's a Christmas gift awaiting my inspection back at Baker Street.
FX:	ECHO OUT

FIRST COMMERCIAL

FX:	BACK AT BAKER STREET, HOLMES IS UNWRAPPING THE PACKAGE
WATSON:	I must say, Holmes, I'm a little surprised.
HOLMES:	Oh?
WATSON:	I really think you could have done more to assist MacDonald.
HOLMES:	I *am* assisting him, Watson. I simply prefer to work without the official forces of law and order breathing down my neck continually. That's the advantage of being unofficial – I tell as much or as little as I choose.
WATSON:	Are you quite certain you're assisting him? It looks to me as though you're just unwrapping that parcel.
HOLMES:	(SIGHS) Watson, have you been asleep throughout this entire case? Didn't you notice the victim's shirt-cuff?
WATSON:	With our address on it, yes.
HOLMES:	And did you also notice the similarity between that handwriting and the writing on this package?
WATSON:	(CATCHING ON) This was sent to you by the dead man!

HOLMES:	Whoever he may have been, he's given me the only Christmas gift I actually wanted.
WATSON:	A compass.
HOLMES:	A puzzle.
FX:	HOLMES SETS A HEAVY COMPASS DOWN
HOLMES:	*And*, yes, a compass.
WATSON:	Not even a note?
HOLMES:	Ah!
FX:	HE EXTRACTS A NOTE.
HOLMES:	(READS) "Mr Holmes... By the time you receive this, you will understand its importance. Keep it if you wish – I never had any use for it." Signed, D G Crowthorne.
WATSON:	Crowthorne – like the artist, Solomon Crowthorne.
HOLMES:	(HE'S GOT IT) Exactly like the artist, Watson! And now I know where I've seen him before!
WATSON:	You said you'd seen him as a child.
HOLMES:	Not him, Doctor, his portrait! Remember the exhibition last month at the Mountford Museum?
WATSON:	Crowthorne painted a portrait of his own son.
HOLMES:	*Darius* Crowthorne, as I recall. And that young man was, it seems, a potential client. For the first time in my career, I've been retained by a corpse.
WATSON:	I'm sure I don't need to ask whether you've noticed something unusual about the compass – there's a letter "O" instead of a letter "W".
HOLMES:	That's because it's a French compass. This case begins to assume

the colours of something truly recherché.

WATSON: Why would Crowthorne send us a French compass?

HOLMES: Undoubtedly, had he lived, he would have explained that to us by now.

WATSON: Perhaps the father might know.

HOLMES: An excellent suggestion, Watson – yes, perhaps he might.

MUSIC: BRIDGE

CROWTHORNE: (LAUGHS HEARTILY, ALMOST UNCONTROLLABLY)

HOLMES: Mr Crowthorne...

WATSON: It's shock, Holmes. He's just learned his son's dead.

CROWTHORNE: (CONTROLLING HIMSELF) No, no... it's not shock, Dr Watson. Merely amusement at the circumstances. You see, only yesterday, my son told me that as far as he was concerned, I might as well be dead. And now it's *he* who is dead. (SIGHS) The Lord is whimsical today. It must be something to do with the time of year.

WATSON: (NOW SLIGHTLY FROSTY) You didn't approve of your son, sir?

CROWTHORNE: He, Dr Watson, did not approve of *me*.

HOLMES: Specifically, your decision nine years ago to marry the woman accused of his mother's murder.

CROWTHORNE: A charge of which Cecile was proven entirely innocent.

HOLMES: You retained an excellent barrister – Mr Marshall Hall was able to convince a jury that what your late wife's doctor diagnosed as arsenic poisoning was actually gastritis.

CROWTHORNE: Yes. But Darius didn't see it that way, and we parted company.

180

WATSON:	But the murder- I mean, *the death* occurred nine years ago. And yet you saw your son yesterday.
CROWTHORNE:	No-one could have been more surprised than I, Doctor, I assure you. We exchanged few words, he simply said he wished to take something that had belonged to him during childhood. Something to do with something that had occurred or that he'd seen at the Turkish Baths – I don't recall. He found whatever it was, and left. I didn't wait to see him leave, I had guests - the festive season, you understand.
HOLMES:	We believe the item he removed was a compass.
CROWTHORNE:	I don't seem to recall Darius ever owning a compass – he always found his way about more than adequately. Went all the way to America once, Heaven knows why.
WATSON:	This compass may have been purchased in France.
CROWTHORNE:	Ah, now it comes to me! My memory, like my eyesight has become far from reliable over the years. Yes, it was during the time we lived in Marseilles – Claudia, Darius and I... It was a very happy time. Commissions were fruitful, my wife Claudia was-
HOLMES:	The compass, Mr Crowthorne.
CROWTHORNE:	Was a gift from Antoine Burgoyne, a neighbour. He took quite a shine to the boy. Why Burgoyne should have presented my son with a compass, I can't imagine – perhaps he expressed a desire to be an explorer for about five minutes, you know what boys are like.
HOLMES:	Why might your son have sent me the compass? What importance does it have?
CROWTHORNE:	None that I am aware of.
WATSON:	Perhaps he wished us to know something about Burgoyne?
HOLMES:	Well, Mr Crowthorne?

CROWTHORNE: All I remember is that he had a most faithful manservant – very quiet chap, I don't know that I ever heard his name.

HOLMES: Nothing more?

CROWTHORNE: Nothing. (A THOUGHT STRIKES) There was his tiresome boast of indestructibility, of course, but that's too absurd to even consider.

WATSON: Indestructibility?

CROWTHORNE: Oh, he used to say that he'd survived a duel with François Le Villard, some ridiculous affront to each other's honour. Claimed Le Villard shot him in the heart, and somehow he survived.

WATSON: Quite impossible.

CROWTHORNE: And more than slightly wearisome, Doctor. He'd display his old wound on every occasion. Quite inappropriate at the dinner table.

WATSON: And did it appear to be a bullet wound?

CROWTHORNE: How on Earth should I know?

HOLMES: Thank-you, Mr Crowthorne, we won't trouble you any further. One final question – your son's address?

CROWTHORNE: Somewhere on Raynor Road, I think.

HOLMES: Ah. Of course. Well, good day to you, sir. And our condolences.

CROWTHORNE: They're a little late in coming, Mr Holmes. So far as I'm concerned, the son I knew – the son I loved – died with my first wife.

FX: A QUIET LONDON STREET, VERY LITTLE TRAFFIC. HOLMES AND WATSON CRUNCH THEIR WAY THROUGH THE SNOW.

WATSON: At least we haven't had any more snow since this morning. Holmes, have you considered the possibility that there might be something hidden inside the compass?

182

HOLMES:	A treasure map, perhaps? A secret formula? The true identity of Father Christmas?
WATSON:	Surely it's at least worth considering.
HOLMES:	Indeed it is. But I should prefer to reach the limits of what reason and energy can supply before resorting to such destructive measures.
WATSON:	You weren't involved in the Crowthorne poisoning case, I take it?
HOLMES:	More's the pity, Watson. It seemed to offer some fascinating possibilities. Had the late Darius Crowthorne chosen to retain me then, we might be facing a very different set of circumstances today.
WATSON:	Could his murder be connected to his mother's death, do you think?
HOLMES:	Not if Solomon Crowthorne was correct about Darius noticing something at a Turkish Bath.
WATSON:	Unless he was lying. Do you suppose a man might murder his own son?
HOLMES:	I make it a habit never to suppose, Watson. I prefer to draw deductions from the facts. Perhaps we'll have amassed sufficient facts after we've paid a visit the Raynor Road Turkish Bath and Gymnasium.
WATSON:	And Darius Crowthorne lived on Raynor Road.
HOLMES:	You see how a thorough knowledge of the geography of London materially assists us in our investigation, Watson?
WATSON:	(CHUCKLES) Remarkable.
HOLMES:	Meretricious.
WATSON:	And a happy new year, I'm sure.

FX:	OUT
MUSIC:	SHORT BRIDGE
FX:	GUS IS WORKING HARD WASHING ITEMS IN A SINK

GUS: If you're hoping for a spell in the steam room, Mr Holmes, I'm afraid it's a little late in the day – I'm just washing the towels ready for tomorrow morning.

HOLMES: That's not what we're here for, Gus. We wanted to ask you about one of your customers – Darius Crowthorne.

GUS: Ah, Mr Crowthorne, Well, if you and Dr Watson are here, I suppose he must have done something, or else something must have been done to him.

WATSON: The latter, I'm afraid, Gus.

GUS: Aah, that's a shame. Such a polite young man. What's going on with the world, Doctor? The way we're going, we'll be lucky to see in the 20th century.

HOLMES: Gus, I believe something may have happened on Mr Crowthorne's last visit - something that troubled him?

GUS: I don't recall any incidents, sir. If anything, he seemed rather pleased when he signed the visitor's book and saw the name of an old friend.

WATSON: Oh?

GUS: A new member – Monsieur Burgoyne, French gentleman. Mr Crowthorne said he knew both Monsieur Burgoyne and his manservant during his childhood.

HOLMES: So we've been told. And how long has Burgoyne been a member of this establishment?

GUS: Only a few weeks, sir. I don't know for certain, you understand, but I believe he was attempting to escape a, er... romantic entanglement back home. You know what the French are like.

WATSON:	I don't, but Mr Holmes might – his grandmother was French.
GUS:	Right. Begging your pardon, sir.
HOLMES:	You may have it, Gus, if we're allowed to take a look at your visitor's book – I'd rather like to call upon Monsieur Burgoyne.
FX:	OUT

SECOND COMMERCIAL

FX:	A STRONG WINTER BREEZE. CRUNCHING THROUGH THE SNOW, MACDONALD APPROACHES.
MACDONALD:	No sign of anyone at home, gentlemen. It seems your Monsieur Burgoyne has fled.
WATSON:	It is Christmas, Inspector. It's entirely possible that he's attending a celebration somewhere.
HOLMES:	Well, with both Burgoyne and his manservant absent, I don't think there would be any harm in taking a look around.
MACDONALD:	Without a warrant, Mr Holmes?
HOLMES:	You're too scrupulous, Inspector. For my part, I confess my curiosity far outweighs finer considerations. Perhaps it would be best if you remained by the front door – to greet the householder, should he return.
FX:	HE SETS OFF THROUGH THE SNOW
HOLMES:	Come along, Watson.
MACDONALD:	(A RELUCTANT SIGH) No, I think I'd best accompany you gentlemen... You never know, we might find an open window.
FX:	WATSON AND MACDONALD JOIN HOLMES IN WALKING
HOLMES:	In which case, it would be your duty to enter and investigate – just to make sure no burglars have been at work.
FX:	HOLMES WANDERS OFF

MACDONALD:	Is it always like this, Doctor? Working with Mr Holmes, I mean?
WATSON:	It's never dull, Inspector. But modest though my talents are, they've not been without value to Holmes. For instance, I remember during the case of the seven swords of Osiris, we- (DISTRACTED) Holmes, where *are* you?
HOLMES:	(OFF-MIC) Do you notice that, Watson? Gleaming in the moonlight?
WATSON:	It's just the padlock on the coach house.
MACDONALD:	A brand-new padlock on a rather dilapidated old coach house, Doctor.
FX:	WATSON AND MACDONALD CATCH UP WITH HOLMES
HOLMES:	I wonder what would be worth protecting in here? Mr Mac, if you wouldn't mind facing in the other direction, I imagine this lock might listen to reason.
MACDONALD:	Eh?
WATSON:	If Holmes ever turned thief, Inspector, not even the Bank of England would be safe.
MACDONALD:	No, Mr Holmes. This is my investigation, and if there's a line to be crossed, I should be the one to cross it. Step aside, please. Now, let's take a look at this lo-
HOLMES:	MacDonald, no!
FX:	HOLMES PUSHES MACDONALD TO THE GROUND AS A SHOT GOES OFF
MACDONALD:	(SHAKEN) What... just happened?
WATSON:	A very good question. Holmes, where did that shot come from?
HOLMES:	Put your revolver away, Watson, the danger is passed. (TO MACDONALD) Let me help you up, Inspector. I apologise for pushing you to the ground in the first place.

FX:	<u>MACDONALD GETS UP</u>
MACDONALD:	(GROANS AS HE RISES) Think nothing of it, Mr Holmes. I have a feeling you might just have saved my life... but I confess, I'm not sure how.
HOLMES:	It suddenly occurred to me how else Darius Crowthorne might have sustained a bullet wound in the stomach. Look below the lock. It's quite safe now, I assure you.
FX:	<u>WATSON RAISES THE PADLOCK</u>
WATSON:	A wire... attached to- something, I can't make it out.
HOLMES:	It's a derringer, Watson – lodged in the door of the coach house. Any attempt to tamper with the lock causes it to fire. In the pursuit of criminals, one learns their devices. Now we know why Crowthorne's killer didn't pursue him through the streets – simply because he wasn't here at the time.
MACDONALD:	So this is definitely where he was shot.
WATSON:	Trying to see what was inside here – something Burgoyne was prepared to kill to keep secret.
MACDONALD:	I'd call that reasonable grounds for entering. (GRUNTS AS HE...)
FX:	<u>RAMS THE DOORS. NOTHING HAPPENS. HE RAMS IT A SECOND TIME. THE DOORS FLY OPEN (AND THE CHAIN SNAPS AND HITS THE GROUND). HAY UNDERFOOT AS THE THREE ENTER.</u>
MACDONALD:	Nothing.
HOLMES:	Nothing immediately apparent. What do you smell?
MACDONALD:	Horses.
WATSON:	Something else – decomposition. There's a body in here somewhere. Under the hay.

HOLMES:	Then I suggest we look for it.
FX:	THEY MOVE AROUND, SHIFTING THE HAY
MACDONALD:	I've found him!
FX:	MORE HAY IS BRUSHED ASIDE
MACDONALD:	Who is he?
WATSON:	Impossible to say – he's probably lain here for weeks, even with the cold, there's little left of his features. I imagine Burgoyne didn't bury him because the ground was too hard.
HOLMES:	I suggest a full examination be performed immediately.
MACDONALD:	Surely there's no need for that, Mr Holmes – you can see from the state of the back of his head what the cause of death was.
HOLMES:	Seeing is one thing – interpretation is an entirely different matter. I think it should be done without delay, Inspector. Will you contact Dr Malachai?
WATSON:	No need for that, Holmes – I'm quite capable of conducting the autopsy myself.
FX:	WINTER BREEZE OUT. THRU TO THE MORTUARY. ECHO ON DIALOG THROUGHOUT. WATSON PICKS UP AND REPLACES SMALL MEDICAL IMPLEMENTS.
MACDONALD:	Just what is it you expect the Doctor to find, Mr Holmes?
HOLMES:	Perhaps the key to this whole mystery.
WATSON:	Well, whatever it is, I haven't found it so far. There's a laceration of the saggital sinus – the wound track seems to stop at the falx cerebri... From its size and depth – and, of course, the location of the body, I'd suggest the murder weapon might have been a cabman's wheel-hammer.
HOLMES:	And the internal organs?

WATSON:	Looking now.
FX:	WATSON CUTS THROUGH THE VICTIM'S FLESH
WATSON:	Good Lord! Holmes, look!
HOLMES:	Remarkable.
WATSON:	You expected this?
HOLMES:	I considered it a possibility. There is no greater satisfaction for an investigator than to have a theory confirmed.
MACDONALD:	What is it, Dr Watson? What- where the blazes is his heart?
WATSON:	His heart...
FX:	WATSON LIFTS ANOTHER FLAP OF SKIN
WATSON:	...is on *this* side.
MACDONALD:	Impossible!
WATSON:	Not impossible, but incredibly rare – it's known as Dextrocardia situs inversus, the major organs are all on the opposite side.
HOLMES:	I believe Leonardo da Vinci was the first person to record a case in his anatomical sketches.
WATSON:	Yes, I remember my old tutor, Joe Bell, mentioning something of the sort. I bet Malachai would have given up his Christmas goose for an opportunity to see this.
MACDONALD:	Fascinating as this undoubtedly is, I don't see how it helps us.
HOLMES:	Forgive me, Mr Mac. You were absent during that part of the investigation. It explains how a man might be shot through the area where the heart is normally situated, and survive. Decomposition has obliterated any obvious trace of the duelling wound, but there can be no doubt that this is the body of Darius Crowthorne's old friend Monsieur Burgoyne. So, now we have the rope – we must draw the noose ever tighter.

FX:	ECHO OUT
LUMIC:	I appreciate the efforts you are making on my behalf, Mr Montague.
HOLMES:	(POSING AS AN ELDERLY MAN) Think nothing of it, Monsieur Burgoyne. Of course, the bank would ordinarily be closed over the Christmas period, but your telegram stressed the urgency of the matter.
LUMIC:	Just so, just so. I have been advised by my physician that the British climate is potentially ruinous to my health. I regret, therefore, that I must withdraw my money and leave the country immediately.
HOLMES:	You will be returning to France, no doubt?
LUMIC:	Ah... no. Somewhere else on the Continent. I have not yet decided.
HOLMES:	Well, Monsieur Burgoyne, if you will just sign here...
FX:	LUMIC SCRIBBLES ON A DOCUMENT
HOLMES:	And again here...
FX:	MORE SCRIBBLES
HOLMES:	Excellent!
FX:	LUMIC PASSES THE DOCUMENT TO HOLMES
LUMIC:	Here you are, Mr Montague.
HOLMES:	Thank-you, Monsieur. (AS HIMSELF) I must be careful not to smudge the fingerprints – they'll serve as proof that you are *not* the real Antoine Burgoyne.
LUMIC:	What? I beg your pardon?
HOLMES:	Your face reacts faster than your brain. I'm afraid we're neither of us who we pretend to be. My name is not Montague, and I am

not the manager of this bank. My name is Holmes.

FX:	THE DOOR FLIES OPEN AND MACDONALD AND WATSON ENTER

HOLMES: Ah, gentlemen, do come in! Dr Watson, Inspector MacDonald, may I introduce Monsieur Jean Lumic, manservant to the late Antoine Burgoyne.

MACDONALD: Monsieur Lumic. (TO HOLMES) Mr Holmes, you have my evidence?

HOLMES: The fingerprints are here, Mr Mac.

LUMIC: What is going on here? What sort of trick is this?

HOLMES: Forgive me, Monsieur Lumic, perhaps I should explain.

LUMIC: That is not my name!

HOLMES: If you insist. But you are certainly not Burgoyne. That individual's fingerprints were sent to me by a Mr Darius Crowthorne.

WATSON: They were on a compass which Burgoyne gave to Darius when he was a boy. He never had a use for it, and the fingerprints have remained intact.

HOLMES: Your plan should have been remarkably simple – your employer fled to England, a country he'd never visited before. If you were to kill your master, take his place *and* his fortune, who would know the difference?

WATSON: You and he were of similar appearance, and there were only two people in London who had ever known him - but Solomon Crowthorne's eyesight is failing, and his son hadn't seen Burgoyne since childhood.

HOLMES: But there was one aspect of Burgoyne's appearance you couldn't duplicate – his duelling scar, which he was in the habit of displaying on every possible occasion.

MACDONALD: And when Darius Crowthorne encountered you in the Raynor
                Road Turkish Bath, he noticed the absence of that scar.

HOLMES: He intended to consult me, but in the meantime, he foolishly
                decided to do a little investigating of his own, and fell victim to
                your ingenious little trap.

MACDONALD: And if it weren't for Mr Holmes here, I might have been your
                next victim. You should know, I take a very dim view of that.

LUMIC: I don't know anything about a trap.

HOLMES: Nonsense, sir! You are red up to your elbows in murder. And
                when you realised that your trap had been sprung, you decided to
                flee the country, though not before re-loading the derringer, of
                course. It was a simple matter to find out the name of your bank -
                or should I say, your *master's* bank.

WATSON: We explained the matter to Mr Montague, the manager. And
                when you contacted him, he contacted *us*.

HOLMES: And very graciously offered the use of his office for this little
                subterfuge. If any lingering doubt as to your true identity
                remains, I imagine these forged signatures should settle the
                matter.

MACDONALD: Well, Monsieur Lumic? Do you have anything to say?

LUMIC: Only that... It was not greed. It was not envy. It was duty. I did
                my duty by that man for more than thirty years, with nothing
                more than a curt nod as acknowledgement of my devotion. Who
                would do right by me? No-one. So I did it for myself. I simply
                wanted what I deserved.

MACDONALD: And I'll see that you get it. Stand up, please.

MUSIC: BRIDGE

FX: LONDON STREET BG. A CAB PULLS AWAY

HOLMES: I should say we are extremely fortunate, Watson.

WATSON: At this moment, I don't feel particularly fortunate. In fact, it's so

192

cold, I can hardly feel anything at all.

HOLMES: Most of the inhabitants of this great city use this time to indulge themselves and their families, convincing themselves that this is a time of "goodwill to all men" - utterly blind to the crimes that go on all around them.

WATSON: I, for one, envy them.

HOLMES: How can you be so naïve, Doctor? I should think you of all people should know better than that.

WATSON: Holmes, Lumic had a choice. We all have a choice. And if we choose to make all men our friends, even if only for a few days... well, better a few days than none at all. I don't call that naïve, Holmes, I call it optimistic.

HOLMES: A fair point. Perhaps... perhaps Lumic isn't the only one guilty of a crime. Wouldn't you say it was a crime to take a good friend for granted?

WATSON: (CHUCKLES) You know, MacDonald purposely refrained from inviting us to the Yard's celebrations...

HOLMES: He's a very perceptive fellow – he'll go far.

WATSON: But I shouldn't think he'd mind if we were to pay a brief visit on our way back to Baker Street. Do you?

HOLMES: No, Doctor. No, I shouldn't think he'd mind at all.

BG: OUT

MUSIC: *DANSE MACABRE*

The Further Adventures of Sherlock Holmes –
The Adventure of the Parisian Assassin
(Original Airdate April 24, 2011)

Should this story, loosely based on Conan Doyle's story *The Lost Special*, have been part of *The Further Adventures* or *The Classic Adventures*? Tough call. In some countries, both *The Lost Special* and *The Man With the Watches* are published in collections of the complete Canon. Holmes plays no active part in either tale, but his presence is felt; he is undoubtedly the "amateur reasoner of some celebrity" who presents his solutions to both cases via the newspapers. It was pretty clear upon first reading this story that, in having the detective and his faithful friend play a more active role in the proceedings, I should have to supply a great deal of original material.

The inclusion of Mycroft Holmes in this episode seemed essential, since his brother's solution to the mystery is just plain wrong, and surely his only intellectual superior could point him in the right direction. But I hit a snag when it occurred to me that, as a representative of the British Government (if not its embodiment), the elder Holmes would have good reason to see that the mystery went unsolved. Eventually, I came up with the simple explanation that Mycroft takes pity on Sherlock, and assists him so long as he is content that there is no danger of the *status quo* being upset.

Those familiar with the original story will notice that I changed the name of the culprit from Herbert de Lernac to Huret, as part of my mission to chronicle all Holmes' unrecorded cases. In this way, while the Master is responsible for the capture of the notorious "Boulevard Assassin", it is for a completely different, though no loss heinous, crime. Watson mentions the award presented to Holmes, but, as is typical of the great detective, he has no real interest in such honours.

I would love to think that Conan Doyle intended Huret's British advisor to be Moriarty's younger brother, but the gap of a decade and-a-half between the publication of *The Lost Special* and *The Valley of Fear* (when we learn of the existence of this West Country station master) makes it unlikely.

CAST:

ANNOUNCER (DENNIS BATEMAN)

HOLMES (JOHN PATRICK LOWRIE)

WATSON (LAWRENCE ALBERT)

MRS HUDSON (LEE PASCH)

MYCROFT (TERRY EDWARD MOORE)

JAMES BLAND (DENNIS BATEMAN)

LOUIS CARATAL (TERRY EDWARD MOORE)

HURET (DAVID NATALE)

POTTER HOOD (DAVID NATALE)

DIRECTED BY JOHN PATRICK LOWRIE

FX:	OPENING SEQUENCE, BIG BEN

MUSIC:	*DANSE MACABRE* UP AND UNDER

ANNOUNCER: *The Further Adventures of Sherlock Holmes*, featuring John Patrick Lowrie as Holmes and Lawrence Albert as Dr Watson.

WATSON: (NARRATING) In broad daylight, upon a June afternoon in the most thickly inhabited portion of England, a train and its occupants disappeared as completely as if some master of chemistry had volatilized it into gas. An engine, a tender, two carriages, a van, and five human beings - all lost on a straight line of railway. Thus it was that Sherlock Holmes and I found ourselves in the Liverpool office of the West Coast Railway Company at the request of a Mr James Bland...

MUSIC:	OUT

HOLMES: And these five missing people are?

BLAND: The driver, John Slater, the guard, James McPherson, the stoker, William Smith - a new hand, incidentally – and two passengers.

HOLMES: Monsieur Louis Caratal and his strange companion.

WATSON: It seems odd to me that no-one has come forward to report them missing.

HOLMES: Describe them to us, Mr Bland.

BLAND: Caratal was a small man, middle-aged and dark, with a marked stoop. He carried a small black dispatch box in his left hand, fastened to his wrist by a strap. I didn't attach any importance to it at the time.

HOLMES: But subsequent events have endowed it with some significance. And the companion?

BLAND: A man of imposing physique. His name did not transpire, but he was certainly a foreigner - either a Spaniard or a South American, I should say. His position was certainly one of dependence.

WATSON:	How can you be so certain of that?
BLAND:	His deferential manner, Dr Watson, his constant attention. Monsieur Caratal came to my office on the 3rd of June, while his companion remained outside...
FX:	<u>A STRONG WIND BLOWS OUTSIDE</u>
CARATAL:	I have arrived this afternoon from Central America, Mr Bland, but I regret to say that affairs of the utmost importance demand I should be in Paris without the loss of an unnecessary hour.
BLAND:	Paris? Well, I'm afraid you've missed the London express, Monsieur. Perhaps a special could be provided, but- well, how do I put this?
CARATAL:	Money is of no importance, and time is everything. If your company can speed us on our way, you may make your own terms.
BLAND:	I... I see. Well, I'll have a word with the traffic manager, Mr Potter Hood – no doubt a train will be ready to start in three-quarters of an hour. It'll take that time to insure that the line is clear.
FX:	<u>WIND OUT</u>
WATSON:	Then an agreement was reached?
BLAND:	Fifty pounds five shillings, Doctor.
HOLMES:	A rate of five shillings a mile.
BLAND:	The engine, No. 247 on our register, was attached to two carriages, with a guard's van behind.
HOLMES:	But you had only two passengers, Mr Bland. What purpose could the other carriage serve?
BLAND:	Solely to decrease the inconvenience arising from the oscillation. The second was divided into four compartments - a first-class, a first-class smoking, a second-class, and a second-class smoking.

HOLMES:	And which compartment was allotted to the travellers?
BLAND:	The first, Mr Holmes, the one nearest to the engine.
WATSON:	And the other three were empty.
BLAND:	That's right. Monsieur Caratal and his companion demanded to be shown the carriage, even though I assured them that the better part of an hour must elapse before the line could be cleared.
HOLMES:	And there were no other incidents before the special pulled out?
BLAND:	Well, actually... A request for a special isn't a very uncommon circumstance in a rich commercial centre, you understand... but that *two* should be required upon the same day...
WATSON:	Who requested the second?
BLAND:	A Mr Horace Moore, a gentleman of military appearance. In fact, I'd hardly dismissed Monsieur Caratal before he arrived...
FX:	THE STRONG WIND AGAIN
"MOORE":	It's absolutely imperative that I don't lose an instant in starting for London! It's an emergency! My wife-
BLAND:	I quite understand, Mr Moore. This must be quite distressing for you. I promise, I'll do everything possible.
"MOORE":	Thank-you, thank-you!
BLAND:	I'm afraid, however, that a second special is out of the question - the ordinary local service has already been deranged by the first.
"MOORE":	But my wife-
BLAND:	There *is* an alternative. If you were willing to share the expense of Monsieur Caratal's train, perhaps you could travel in the other empty first-class compartment.
"MOORE":	Why, yes, that would be perfect!

FX:	WIND OUT
BLAND:	It was difficult to see any objection to such an arrangement, yet when the suggestion was made to him, Monsieur Caratal absolutely refused to consider it for an instant. The train was his, he said, and he would insist upon the exclusive use of it.
WATSON:	Rather ungentlemanly behaviour.
BLAND:	Mr Moore left the station in great distress. I imagine he must have taken the ordinary slow train which leaves Liverpool at six o'clock.
HOLMES:	And when did the special train containing Monsieur Caratal and his gigantic companion steam out of the station?
BLAND:	Four thirty-one exactly. The line was at that time clear, and the special should have reached Manchester before six o'clock. At a quarter after six, I received a telegram stating it hadn't yet arrived.
WATSON:	The special may have run off the metals.
HOLMES:	Let's leave jumping to conclusions to the official forces, Doctor. It seems hardly possible that the local train could have passed down the same line without observing such an accident.
BLAND:	And yet, where can the train be, Mr Holmes? This is unique in my thirty years of experience! Absolutely unprecedented and inexplicable!
WATSON:	It seems obvious to me that there's been a wreck.
HOLMES:	And how did the special run off the metals without disturbing the line, Watson?
WATSON:	When one has eliminated the impossible, Holmes, whatever remains must be the truth.
HOLMES:	I doubt I could have phrased it better myself.
WATSON:	No doubt we'll have a wire to say that they've found the train at

the bottom of an embankment.

FX:	<u>THE DOOR FLIES OPEN. HOOD RUSHES IN.</u>

HOOD: Mr Bland!

BLAND: Ah, Hood, splendid! Mr Holmes, Dr Watson, this is our traffic manager, Mr Potter Hood.

HOLMES: You have something to report, Mr Hood?

HOOD: 'Deed I do, Mr Holmes! They've just found the body of John Slater, driver of the special train!

MUSIC: <u>STING</u>

FIRST COMMERCIAL

FX: <u>OUTDOOR BG – IT'S A WINDY DAY. HOLMES, WATSON, BLAND AND HOOD MILL AROUND, DISTURBING THE BUSHES.</u>

WATSON: The injuries to Slater's head appear to be cause of death. I'll have to make a full examination, of course.

BLAND: Perhaps the driver fell from his engine, pitched down the embankment, and rolled among these gorse bushes.

HOLMES: Or perhaps he was *pushed* from his engine, Mr Bland.

BLAND: And still no trace of that missing train, gentlemen.

HOLMES: There is more evil here than I have ever encountered before. Mr Bland, I imagine you have at your disposal a map of the area, showing this stretch of railway?

BLAND: Certainly, Mr Holmes, certainly. In my office.

FX: <u>OUTDOOR BG OUT. BACK IN BLAND'S OFFICE, HOLMES UNROLLS A MAP.</u>

HOLMES: Now... the country seems to have been dotted with ironworks and

	collieries.
HOOD:	Some are being worked and some have been abandoned.
HOLMES:	Thank-you, Mr Hood. And no fewer than twelve have small-gauge lines which run trolley-cars down to the main line. These can, of course, be disregarded. But there are seven which have, or *had*, proper lines running down and connecting with points to the main line...
HOOD:	So as to convey their produce from the mouth of the mine to the great centres of distribution.
HOLMES:	In every case these lines are only a few miles in length. Out of the seven, four belong to collieries which are worked out, or at least to shafts which are no longer used. These are the Redgauntlet, Hero, Slough of Despond, and Heartsease mines.
BLAND:	Ten years ago, the Heartsease was one of the principal mines in Lancashire, Mr Holmes. But the rails nearest to the main line have been taken up to prevent accidents - there's no longer any connection.
HOLMES:	Then these four side lines may be also be eliminated from our inquiry.
WATSON:	So there remain three other side lines leading to... er... (READS) "the Carnstock Iron Works", "the Big Ben Colliery" and "the Perseverance Colliery".
HOLMES:	Of those, the Big Ben line isn't more than a quarter of a mile long.
HOOD:	And it ends at a dead wall of coal waiting removal from the mouth of the mine.
HOLMES:	And the Carnstock Iron Works, Mr Hood? Might you know anything about that?
HOOD:	As a matter of fact, I do, Mr Holmes - the line was blocked all day by sixteen truckloads of haematite.
WATSON:	Nothing could have passed?

HOOD:	It's a single line, Doctor.
WATSON:	Which leaves the Perseverance line.
BLAND:	No, no, not the Perseverance. It's a large double line, which does a considerable traffic - the output of the mine is very large.
HOLMES:	And on the day the special was lost - this traffic proceeded as usual?
BLAND:	Oh, yes. Hundreds of men including a gang of railway plate-layers were working along the line.
HOLMES:	A line of two and a quarter miles in length.
HOOD:	It's inconceivable that a train could have gone down there without attracting attention.
WATSON:	It's rank lunacy, Holmes. How does a train vanish into thin air in broad daylight? The thing's preposterous.
BLAND:	Mr Holmes, can you give us any hope at all?
HOLMES:	As the good doctor has already noted, it is one of the elementary principles of practical reasoning that when the impossible has been eliminated the residuum, however improbable, must contain the truth.
BLAND:	(AFTER AN AWKWARD PAUSE) And?
HOLMES:	It is certain that the train left Kenyon Junction.
BLAND:	Of course!
HOLMES:	And it's certain it did *not* reach Barton Moss. It's in the highest degree unlikely, but still possible, that it may have taken one of the seven available side lines. It's obviously impossible for a train to run where there are no rails, so we may reduce our improbables to the three open lines, despite the objections we've considered.
HOOD:	Just what are you suggesting, Mr Holmes?

HOLMES: A secret society of colliers, which is capable of destroying both train and passengers.

WATSON: Secret society? Sounds somewhat improbable.

HOLMES: But not impossible, Watson- remember the affair of the Valley of Fear. I confess, I'm unable to suggest any other solution. (TO BLAND) I should certainly advise the company, Mr Bland, to direct all their energies towards the observation of those three lines - Carnstock, the Big Ben, the Perseverance - *and* the workmen at the end of them.

BLAND: (CLEARLY A LITTLE DISAPPOINTED) But... is that all?

HOLMES: Careful supervision of the pawnbrokers' shops in the district might bring some suggestive facts to light. Please keep me advised as to fresh developments. In the meantime, business demands our presence in London.

MUSIC: BRIDGE

FX: WATSON OPENS A NEWSPAPER

WATSON: The newspapers are offering a variety of suggestions to the mystery. One or two of them are feasible enough.

HOLMES: Oh?

WATSON: Some chap suggests the train might have run off the metals and be lying submerged in the Lancashire and Staffordshire Canal.

HOLMES: I understand why this theory appeals to you, Doctor, being so close to your own.
WATSON: Well, it's certainly worthy of consideration, isn't it?

HOLMES: Not to anyone who took the trouble to learn the depth of the canal before ever leaving London. Is this the best that the readers of the *Times* can offer?

WATSON: Well, an "amateur reasoner" calls attention to the bag the travellers brought with them. He believes some novel explosive of immense and pulverizing power might have been concealed in

203

	it.
HOLMES:	And the obvious absurdity of supposing that the whole train might be blown to dust while the rails remained uninjured reduces any such explanation to a farce.
FX:	A KNOCK AT THE DOOR
HOLMES:	Come!
FX:	MRS HUDSON ENTERS
MRS HUDSON:	Telegram for you, Mr Holmes.
HOLMES:	Ah, thank-you, Mrs Hudson.
FX:	HOLMES OPENS THE TELEGRAM
WATSON:	Well, has Mr Bland located the train?
HOLMES:	(INTRIGUED) No... no, this is something else, Watson. It's from Mycroft.
WATSON:	Mycroft? What does *he* want?
HOLMES:	He wishes to talk to me about Monsieur Louis Caratal, passenger on the lost special. I wonder why...
MRS HUDSON:	Perhaps the gentleman is a friend of Mr Mycroft's, sir.
HOLMES:	Get your hat and coat, old fellow, we're going out. (TO MRS HUDSON) Mrs Hudson, we shall have to turn dinner into supper, I'm afraid.
MRS HUDSON:	(CRESTFALLEN) Oh, Mr Holmes – and I'd got you a nice piece of mackerel!
MUSIC:	BRIDGE
MYCROFT:	(DISPARAGINGLY) "A secret society of colliers?" Really, Sherlock!

HOLMES:	My brother and I have never been close, Watson, yet he seems to know my thoughts and words, no matter where I might be.
MYCROFT:	Don't think your fame with the masses alters anything! I'm profoundly disappointed in you – your so-called solution has as much sense as the various conjectures put forward in the public press. There are larger issues at stake here than your realise, Sherlock.
HOLMES:	Then kindly enlighten me. I'm used to the chilly atmosphere of high places.
MYCROFT:	It is impossible for me to give you the full particulars, sufficed to say that the country is in the throes of a political crisis. That crisis has its origins in France.
WATSON:	In France?
MYCROFT:	Surely you must be aware of the famous trial in Paris, connected with a monstrous scandal in politics and finance. The honour and careers of many of the chief men in France are at stake.
WATSON:	And how does this affect England?
MYCROFT:	They are our allies, Dr Watson. The impact of any blow that befalls them will eventually be felt here.
HOLMES:	This is all very fascinating, but apart from his nationality, what is the connection to Monsieur Caratal?
MYCROFT:	You've seen a group of ninepins standing, all so rigid, and prim, and unbending. Then there comes the ball from far away and... (MAKES THE SOUND OF THE PINS FALLING) there are your ninepins on the floor. Imagine some of the greatest men in France as these ninepins.
HOLMES:	And Caratal was, no doubt, the ball, coming from far away, bearing evidence kept in a locked dispatch box.
MYCROFT:	You have it, Sherlock.
WATSON:	Mr Holmes, just who is Caratal?

MYCROFT:	He is well-known as a financier and political agent in Central America. His companion is Eduardo Gomez, a man of violent record.
WATSON:	Then this Gomez may be behind it all!
MYCROFT:	There is evidence to show that Monsieur Caratal employed Gomez as a guard and protector. Little good it did him. Powerful forces determined that he should *not* arrive in Paris. Those forces have the command of an unlimited amount of money. Do you understand, Sherlock?
HOLMES:	I believe I do.
MYCROFT:	Now, I could settle the whole matter without leaving the Diogenes Club, of course, but I feel I owe you the opportunity to redeem yourself.
HOLMES:	If you wish to avoid any political upheaval, Mycroft, why are you assisting me? What if I should recover the evidence Caratal was conveying to France?
MYCROFT:	Oh, I'm quite satisfied that the evidence has been destroyed by now and the crisis will pass; I'm simply indulging your curiosity. Think over what I've said, Sherlock.
FX:	HOLMES AND WATSON ARE IN A MOVING CAB
WATSON:	I must say, Holmes, I thought your brother was being rather high-handed.
HOLMES:	To you, Watson, Mycroft is a sterling character. To me, he's like a caged tiger – with very sharp claws. And he can afford to be high-handed because he happens to be correct. He sees the fatal flaw in my method.
WATSON:	Impossible!
HOLMES:	Ah, the key word - "impossible". As in "when you have eliminated the impossible, whatever remains, however improbable-"

WATSON:	"-Must be the truth."
HOLMES:	But I failed to consider that my adversary might be possessed of limitless resources.
WATSON:	And that which might seem impossible under ordinary circumstances now becomes possible.
HOLMES:	Everyone's entitled to make a mistake – Scotland Yard does sometimes. I'm entitled to at least one.
WATSON:	So what now, Holmes?
HOLMES:	I'm on my way to the beginning of a working hypothesis. We return to Liverpool, Watson – and we begin again.
FX:	<u>CAB OUT. THRU TO EXTERIOR BG. HOLMES, WATSON AND BLAND ARE WALKING THE TRAIN LINE.</u>
BLAND:	Mr Holmes, I thought we'd eliminated this line as a possibility!
HOLMES:	So we had, Mr Bland, so we had. But in the absence of data, it's permissible to theorize in directions which don not conflict with such data as does exist.
BLAND:	Eh?
HOLMES:	Consider... an organization with an unlimited sum of money and but a single aim – to stop Caratal reaching Paris at all costs. They knew he must commission a special train.
WATSON:	They bought off several officials, amongst whom the most important was James McPherson, the guard most likely to be employed upon a special.
HOLMES:	Smith, the stoker, was also in their employ.
BLAND:	And Slater, the engine-driver?
HOLMES:	No doubt been he'd approached, but found to be either obstinate or dangerous.

WATSON:	Or both.
HOLMES:	Everything had been prepared days before - only the finishing touches were needed. The disconnected side line had been repaired. They'd only have had to replace a few rails to connect it to the main line - that could be done without danger of attracting attention. When the special arrived, it ran off upon this side line so easily, the jolting of the points would have been entirely unnoticed by the two travellers.
BLAND:	But the line only leads to...
WATSON:	To the abandoned Heartsease mine.
HOLMES:	As you told us, Mr Bland, once one of the largest coal mines in England. This unused line runs through a deep cutting – no-one could have seen the train unless they'd been standing on that edge. They removed the boards which covered the old mine, and cleared the entrance. The rails run very close to the shaft for the convenience of loading the coal - they had only to add two or three lengths of rail in order to lead to the very brink of the shaft.
BLAND:	(HORRIFIED) The very brink... Then the train is-
WATSON:	Down there, Mr Bland – along with its unfortunate passengers.
FX:	BG OUT

SECOND COMMERCIAL

FX:	ECHO ON DIALOG THROUGHOUT
HURET:	Mr Holmes, come in, come in! How very good of you to call upon me.
HOLMES:	I felt certain of finding you at home, Monsieur Huret.
HURET:	Have you been to Marseilles before?
HOLMES:	Not since the Boulevard Assassinations of 1887. And certainly not to the police cells.

HURET:	(TUTS) All my accomplishments in the field of crime over the years, and I find myself arrested for the murder of some merchant whose name I don't even recall. I have you to thank for that, I believe. Tell me, Mr Holmes, to what do I owe the honour of this visit?
HOLMES:	The Lost Special – of all the criminals in Europe, you are the only one capable of carrying out such a daring operation.
HURET:	I would say I am flattered, if your statement were not entirely accurate.
HOLMES:	A few questions remain unanswered.
HURET:	You wish to make a record of my statement?
HOLMES:	Naturally.
HURET:	Splendid! Take out your notebook, please.
FX:	<u>HOLMES FLICKS THROUGH THE PAGES OF A NOTEBOOK</u>
HURET:	There were great financial as well as political interests at stake, and so a syndicate was formed to manage the business.
HOLMES:	They had ample warning that Caratal was coming long before he left South America, and knew the evidence he held would certainly mean ruin to all of them.
HURET:	So they looked round for an agent who was capable of wielding this gigantic power - a man in a million. They chose Huret, and I admit that they were right. A man I could trust was dispatched instantly to South America to travel home with Caratal. Had he arrived in time the ship would never have reached Liverpool...
HOLMES:	But it had already started before your agent could reach it. Nevertheless, you were quite prepared for Caratal's reception in Liverpool.
HURET:	You must not underrate the difficulties of my undertaking, Mr Holmes, or imagine that a mere commonplace assassination

would meet the case. I was to destroy not only Monsieur Caratal, but Caratal's documents, and his companions also. Do what he would, I would be ready for him. If he took an ordinary train, an express, or a special, I would be ready.

HOLMES: Surely you couldn't do all this yourself, Monsieur Huret. What do you know of the English railway lines?

HURET: Money can procure willing agents all the world over. My English ally knew the London and West Coast line thoroughly, and he had the command of a band of workers who were trustworthy and intelligent.

HOLMES: He it was who bought the services of McPherson and Smith?

HURET: At a price which would make them independent for a lifetime. I have found that the English are more expensive to buy.

HOLMES: But you couldn't buy John Slater, the engine-driver.

HURET: No, not he.

HOLMES: And once that special was ordered, your plan went into effect. Beginning with the appearance of "Mr Moore", the gentleman who desired to travel to London on the same train, in order to be at his wife's sickbed.

HURET: I've always had a flair for accents. It was my intention to board the train, shoot Caratal and his bodyguard, and then destroy the papers in the dispatch box. Caratal was on his guard, alas. But like all great organizers I had an alternative course of action prepared.

HOLMES: Your assistant controlled the points, in order that he might superintend the switching off of the train?

HURET: Having once seen it safely onto the side line, he handed over responsibility to me. I and two armed companions were waiting at a point which overlooks the mouth of the mine. The train was running with frantic speed, rolling and rocking over the rotten line, while the wheels made a frightful screaming sound. I was close to them, I could see their faces. Caratal was praying, I think. And Gomez roared like a bull who smells the blood of the slaughter-house. He saw us standing on the bank, tore at Caratal's wrist and threw the dispatch-box out of the window in our direction.

HOLMES: He was offering the evidence in return for their lives. You did not oblige.

HURET: The train was now as much beyond our controls as theirs. Gomez ceased howling when he saw the black mouth of the mine yawning before them. I wondered how a train running at a great speed would take the pit into which I'd guided it, and I was much interested in watching. One of my colleagues thought it would actually jump it. Fortunately, it fell short, and the buffers of the engine struck the other lip of the shaft with a tremendous crash. The funnel flew off into the air.

HOLMES: I found it.

HURET: Did you? The remains of the engine choked the mouth of the pit for a minute or so. Then something gave way in the middle, and the whole mass of iron, smoking coals, brass fittings, wheels, and wood-work all crumbled together and crashed down into the mine. We heard the rattle as the debris struck against the walls, there came a deep roar as the remains of the train struck the bottom. Then and all was quiet.

HOLMES: And having carried out your plan so successfully, it only remained to leave no trace behind you.

HURET: Except for the funnel, unfortunately. I can't imagine how we came to overlook it. My little band of workers ripped up the rails and disconnected the side line, replacing everything as it had been before. They were equally busy at the mine. The shaft was planked over as it used to be, and the lines which led to it were torn up and taken away. Then, without flurry, but without delay, we all made our way out of the country.

HOLMES: I couldn't help but notice a criminal mastery in the stroke of your brush, Monsieur Huret.

HURET: I accept your praise.

HOLMES:	But there was one flaw in all your admirable combinations - John Slater, the driver.
HURET:	It was the plan that McPherson should chloroform Slater, but he did his business so clumsily that the fellow fell off the engine, and broke his neck in the fall. A man who has had as many triumphs as I can afford to be frank, and I must agree with you. John Slater is the single flaw in one of those complete masterpieces which are only to be contemplated in silent admiration.
HOLMES:	Was McPherson punished for his actions?
HURET:	I understand it was his intention to emigrate to America, and then – after a suitable period – to send for his wife. Perhaps it would be a kindness, Mr Holmes, if you were to visit her and assure her that there is no impediment to her marrying again.
HOLMES:	I understand. You secured the bag of papers Gomez threw out of the window, and took them to your employers.
HURET:	Not all. I kept one or two as a souvenir of the occasion. Be sure you write that down, Mr Holmes. I have no wish to see them published; but, still, it's every man for himself in this world, and what else can I do if my friends won't come to my aid when I need them?
HOLMES:	Then the purpose of your statement is blackmail?
HURET:	It is not out of mere pride or boasting that I give this information - if that were my object, I could tell a dozen actions of mine which are quite as splendid... I do it in order that certain gentlemen in Paris may understand that I, who am able to tell about the fate of Monsieur Caratal, can also tell in whose interest and at whose request the deed was done.
HOLMES:	Unless the reprieve you're awaiting comes very quickly.
HURET:	These men in Paris, they know Huret the Boulevard Assassin, and they are aware that his deeds are as ready as his words. I have been true to my employers, and I have no doubt they will be true to me now.

HOLMES:	And they will know when this statement is published.
HURET:	Of course.
FX:	HOLMES TEARS UP HIS NOTES
HOLMES:	But you have given me no statement, Monsieur.
HURET:	I see. So that is how it is to be. You play the game well, Holmes. I would shake your hand, but I fear I might miss and accidentally throttle you to death.
FX:	ECHO OUT. THRU TO BUSY STREET BG
WATSON:	Well, did he say anything?
HOLMES:	Nothing unexpected, Watson. Monsieur Huret seems quite resigned to his fate – now. A brilliant antagonist – it's a pity his talents were so misdirected.
WATSON:	The arrest of Huret is the talk of Paris. There's talk that you might receive the Order of the Legion of Honour.
HOLMES:	(NON-COMMITTAL) How gratifying.
WATSON:	Don't really care, do you?
HOLMES:	Not particularly.
WATSON:	If I had to deduce the reason, I'd say you were preoccupied with the question of Huret's accomplice. I imagine he refused to give you his name?
HOLMES:	He did.
WATSON:	It would have to be someone with a considerable knowledge of the workings of the English railways. It's occurred to you, of course, that the late Professor Moriarty's youngest brother is a station master?
HOLMES:	It has, Watson – and I find the implications of that notion all too chilling.

FX: STREET BG OUT

MUSIC: *DANSE MACABRE*

I had every intention that *The Mystery of Edelweiss Lodge* should be a standard half-hour episode, but I'd incorporated so many elements that telling the story in under an hour would render it incomprehensible – as it is, I wasn't able to dedicate enough time to the break-in during the final act as I'd have liked. I had the notion, however, of spreading the adventure over two weeks for a change. It wasn't entirely unprecedented – several episodes of Imagination Theater's private eye series *Harry Nile* had been presented that way, and my massive dramatisation of *The Hound of the Baskervilles* (one of my proudest achievements on this series) was serialised in three hour-long weekly instalments. In the end, though, it was decided that the story should run for a single hour, but I've included the original two-part script in this volume.

My habit of using names from other Holmesian productions was now well under control, and all of the characters have their origins in my Ideas Book. The scene of the crime, however, is a different matter – Edelweiss Lodge was the base of operations for the kidnappers in William Gillette's classic stage play. At the time I was working on this episode, I was also playing the role of Dr Watson's manservant Parsons in an audio adaptation of that play recorded for the Sherlock Holmes Society of London, and available for download from their website. Doubtless, it was bouncing around in my mind when I finally settled on a title. The episode had previously been called *The Adventure of the Missing Manuscript*, with which I was never really very happy; for one thing, the alliteration made it sound more like a job for Perry Mason (whose cases I've also been fortunate enough to adapt for the radio), but it also gave the game away in referring too soon to the key piece of evidence that damns Jack Bruno.

Having failed to make an appearance in *The Amateur Mendicant Society* way back in 2003, Inspector Peter Jones finally gets his moment in the sun here. I was very impressed with Steve Manning's performance in the role, and I may well use the character again. Holmes mentions a previous encounter with Peter's brother, Athelney, prior to *The Sign of Four*. My 2004 episode, *The Adventure of the Serpent's Tooth* did indeed concern a firm of assayers named for the actors who played the detective and the doctor for BBC radio during the 1950s and '60s. As I say, it's all under control now.

I haven't the faintest idea what the double murder case Holmes and Watson were investigating in Lanarkshire might have been – I seem to recall it was my original intention that they should have just returned to London following the conclusion of *The Boscombe Valley Mystery* (*not* a double murder, of course), but I couldn't make the dates work out. It was undoubtedly because Watson handed over his practice to Dr Anstruther in that particular story that I originally decided to give his obliging neighbour more than just a name-check in this episode. I christened him Rupert, but not for any more logical reason than my decision to give Lestrade the forename George.

Sir Ronald Ramsgate, author of *Recollections of an Eventful Life*, is named for the guardian of the Crown Jewels in the 1939 film, *The Adventures of Sherlock Holmes* (funny how we keep coming back to that one in particular – it's not even my favourite Rathbone movie). Ernestine Proctor's jealous lover, Harold Saintsbury, takes his name from stage actor H A Saintsbury, who portrayed Holmes on stage many times in the early part of the 20th Century, and in a silent film version of *The Valley of Fear* (now lost to the world, alas). Real-life creeps in once again with Watson's mention of Robert James Lees, a psychic involved in the Jack the Ripper investigation. Donald Sutherland portrayed him in my favourite Holmes movie of all time (probably my favourite movie *period*), *Murder by Decree*. Speaking of movies, this script was written after the release of the Guy Richie film (which I regard as a terrific romp, by the way), which is probably why Holmes states that Watson's desire to punch him on the nose – as Jude Law does to Robert Downey Jr in the movie – would be uncharacteristic.

Holmes claims to have been in San Francisco before his association with Watson. This was intended as a nod to W S Baring Gould's assertion in his famous 1962 "biography", *Sherlock Holmes of Baker Street*, that the detective had toured America with the Sassanoff Shakespearean Company. As a rule, I try not to rely on this book as much as some other pastiche authors – there are certain speculations I just don't agree with – but I'm nothing if not changeable, which is why I included in my adaptation of *The Three Gables* Baring-Gould's assertion that gossip-monger Langdale Pike was one of Holmes' pals from University. I've also never felt completely comfortable with pastiches either including Sir Arthur Conan Doyle as a character or endlessly referring to him as the "literary agent", but when the plot required that Ernestine consult an oculist, it was impossible to pass up the opportunity. I thought I'd been subtle enough to avoid using his name, but apparently not – my memory constantly overestimates my abilities.

I wonder whether the fire at Arnsworth Castle is in any way related to the "Arnsworth Castle business" Holmes refers to in *A Scandal in Bohemia*. Did he learn a lesson about the advisability of engineering a fake alarm of fire rather than a real one, or did he play on the fears of the Castle's residents, having already faced a conflagration in their residence? I don't suppose I'll know until I get around to writing about it. Stay tuned.

PART ONE CAST:

ANNOUNCER (DENIS BATEMAN)

HOLMES (JOHN PATRICK LOWRIE)

WATSON (LAWRENCE ALBERT)

INSPECTOR PETER JONES (STEVE MANNING)

DR RUPERT ANSTRUTHER (DAVID NATALE)

ERNESTINE PROCTOR (ANNA LISA CARLSON)

JACK BRUNO (JEFF STEITZER)

DIRECTED BY JOHN PATRICK LOWRIE

MUSIC:	*DANSE MACABRE* UP & UNDER
ANNOUNCER:	*The Further Adventures of Sherlock Holmes*! Featuring John Patrick Lowrie as Holmes, and Lawrence Albert as Dr Watson. Tonight: *The Mystery of Edelweiss Lodge, Part One*.
WATSON:	I consider myself extremely fortunate that, during the early years of my practice, I was able to assist my friend Sherlock Holmes in his investigations thanks to the generosity of my neighbour, Dr Rupert Anstruther. But our friendship would prove to have unexpected repercussions...
MUSIC:	OUT
ANSTRUTHER:	Good to see you back, old fellow. Good hunting, I take it?
WATSON:	Good hunting, and very good game indeed – a double murderer.
ANSTRUTHER:	Double? I look forward to reading about it.
WATSON:	It'll probably be a while before it sees print – certain confidences have to be kept. Rather a delicate matter.
ANSTRUTHER:	(CHUCKLES) When isn't it?
WATSON:	I'll tell you as much as I can over a glass of whisky at the club. Thank-you for looking after my patients while I was away, Anstruther.
ANSTRUTHER:	Don't mention it, old man.
WATSON:	I'll do the same for you some day.
ANSTRUTHER:	Oh, I never go anywhere. Not all of us are meant for a life of adventure. Mrs Gorton's shingles are playing her up again, by the way.
WATSON:	All right, I'll pay her a visit tomorrow. There must be some way I can repay the favour, though.
ANSTRUTHER:	You could introduce me to Mr Sherlock Holmes.

WATSON:	Ah. I think you should know, Holmes isn't the most sociable of men.
ANSTRUTHER:	I don't want to share a drink with him, Watson, I want to consult him.
WATSON:	Consult him?
ANSTRUTHER:	Yes. I'd like him to find out who murdered one of my patients last night.
MUSIC:	STING
HOLMES:	I'm afraid my knowledge of the case if a trifle vague, Dr Anstruther. Watson and I were engaged in a case in Lanarkshire, and the London papers are not easy to come by.
ANSTRUTHER:	I'm happy to provide you with any details, Mr Holmes. I just want to know why anybody should want to murder Willoughby Proctor.
HOLMES:	Your patient, I understand.
WATSON:	You're quite certain it *was* murder, I suppose?
ANSTRUTHER:	I may not have your experience in such matters, Watson, but it took hardly any time at all to confirm that he'd met his end as the result of cyanide poisoning.
HOLMES:	Cyanide – not an easy thing to come by. Proctor was a butterfly collector, perhaps?
ANSTRUTHER:	His daughter, Ernestine. Before she lost her sight. It seems that Willoughby was done away with in the night. At a guess, someone doused a handkerchief in cyanide, and placed it over the old man's mouth and nose as he slept.
WATSON:	Ghastly!
HOLMES:	But intriguing. And from your befuddlement, Dr Anstruther, I take it that there was no-one who might have wished your Mr Proctor any ill will?

ANSTRUTHER: That I couldn't say for certain, Mr Holmes. He made his fortune from a metalworks in Kent, I believe.

WATSON: And a businessman is likely to have enemies.

ANSTRUTHER: No, what puzzles me, is why anybody should bother to kill a dying man.

HOLMES: Dying. Willoughby Proctor was dying?

ANSTRUTHER: Pancreatic cancer, beyond any treatment. I called upon him at his home, just two weeks ago. More as a friend than a physician, since there was nothing further I could do for him.

HOLMES: And that home is where?

ANSTRUTHER: Edelweiss Lodge, in Hampstead.

WATSON: Anstruther, was his condition known?

ANSTRUTHER: It was.

HOLMES: (MURMURS TO SELF) The murder of a dying man... (ALOUD, DELIGHTED) Ha! This is really excellent!

WATSON: I doubt whether Mr Proctor would have seen it that way, Holmes.

HOLMES: The victim is simply a factor in a problem, Watson. And this problem is distinctly out of the ordinary. I will endeavour to return the favour by bringing a little light into Dr Anstruther's darkness.

FX: HOLMES CLAPS HIS HANDS...

HOLMES: (...AND LAUGHS)

ANSTRUTHER: (LOW) Er, Watson, is he always..?

WATSON: I've become used to it.

FIRST COMMERCIAL

JONES:	"Tome", gentlemen. "T-O-M-E". It means a book. In fact, it means a *large* book.
HOLMES:	We're very well aware of what it means, I assure you, Inspector..?
JONES:	Jones, Mr Holmes, Peter Jones. I believe you know my brother, Athelney.
HOLMES:	Of course. Watson, you recall the murder at the assayer's firm of Hobbs and Shelley?
WATSON:	Of course, *now* I see the resemblance.
HOLMES:	Grateful though I am to hear proofs of the Yard's extensive vocabulary, Jones, what is the significance of the word "tome" in this particular instance?
JONES:	A message from beyond the grave, gentlemen.
WATSON:	Beyond the grave?
HOLMES:	Don't tell me that the force is going over to the spiritualists in an effort to decrease their number of unsolved cases?
WATSON:	I've heard there's a fellow called Lees who dabbles in such matters...
JONES:	Yes, very amusing. But I'll excuse your ignorance, gentlemen.
HOLMES:	Most considerate.
JONES:	Oh, I'll give you credit for a fertile imagination and a certain analytical talent, Mr Holmes, but we're dealing in the realm of fact here. And the fact is that the victim wrote something on his palm.
WATSON:	"Tome", no doubt.
JONES:	Correct, Doctor.
HOLMES:	Hardly a message from beyond the grave, Inspector.

JONES:	From the death-bed, then – quite literally.
HOLMES:	You're surely not suggesting that Willoughby Proctor wrote on his own palm as he was being murdered?
JONES:	Well-
WATSON:	And the murderer failed to notice?
JONES:	It-
HOLMES:	Why didn't he simply write the name of said murderer?
JONES:	(AGGRAVATED) Well, it obviously means something! Proctor thought it important enough to write on his palm!
WATSON:	Then why-
JONES:	The murderer probably didn't see it in the lamplight! (A BEAT) Satisfied?
HOLMES:	That's certainly plausible.
JONES:	(MILDLY SARCASTIC) Why, thank-you.
HOLMES:	I should like to examine this writing. The body is at the mortuary?
JONES:	It is, but the writing's been washed away by the Police Surgeon.
HOLMES:	(SUDDENLY ANGRY) Then how am I expected to conduct my investigation?
JONES:	I don't expect anything of you, Mr Holmes – you're not here at *my* request. But as it happens, I had the writing photographed...
HOLMES:	Ah!
JONES:	Your friend Lestrade told me he wouldn't be in the least bit surprised if you chose to interest yourself in this case.
FX:	JONES PRODUCES SOME PHOTOS

JONES:	And he suggested that if you did, you'd surely wish to examine these.
HOLMES:	Splendid, Inspector! If we can get you as well-trained as Lestrade, perhaps there's hope for the Yard yet.
WATSON:	(CLEARS HIS THROAT)
HOLMES:	Impolite?
WATSON:	Perhaps just a little, Holmes.
JONES:	You can see that it clearly says "Tome". "T-O-M-E", look.
WATSON:	There's always the possibility that we're looking at it the wrong way up, Inspector.
FX:	WATSON PICKS OUT A PHOTOGRAPH
WATSON:	Turn the photograph upside-down, and it might say... (READS, HESITANTLY) nothing legible.
JONES:	At least tome is a proper word.
HOLMES:	Have you noticed that the bottom stroke of the "E" is not quite straight?
JONES:	What of it?
HOLMES:	Oh, it may be nothing at all – or it may be a matter of the greatest importance.
JONES:	What is this, some parlour game, where we have to guess what you're thinking?
WATSON:	Holmes doesn't approve of guessing, Inspector.
JONES:	Doesn't he, now? Well, I *am* prepared to guess, Doctor – especially when my guess is likely to turn into a certainty. And my guess is that somewhere in this house, in one of Willoughby Proctor's books, we'll find a clue to the identity of his murderer.

HOLMES:	I do hope you intend to be careful, Jones – some of these volumes appear extremely old.
JONES:	Antiques, Mr Holmes. Miss Proctor tells me her late father was always buying things at auction.
WATSON:	These certainly aren't the items one would ordinarily expect to find in a Hampstead home, even one as grand as this.
HOLMES:	The books *are* exceedingly interesting...
FX:	HE PULLS ONE OFF THE SHELF
JONES:	Some of them from the library of an abbey sacked by Henry VII, I believe.
HOLMES:	Really? (TO WATSON) Look at this, Watson.
WATSON:	I'm afraid I don't read- whatever language this is written in.
HOLMES:	*The Memoirs of the Borgias.* It's a pity your friend Anstruther is our client and not this daughter – I'd ask for this in lieu of a fee.
JONES:	Perhaps you can mention it to her when you speak to her.
HOLMES:	Perhaps.
WATSON:	It might not be appropriate at this time, Holmes.
HOLMES:	(SOMEWHAT DISAPPOINTED) Oh. Well, if you think so, Watson.
ERNESTINE:	(SLIGHTLY OFF-MIC) Since you admire it so much, you're welcome to it, Mr Holmes.
JONES:	Miss Proctor!
ERNESTINE:	(SLIGHTLY OFF-MIC) Inspector Jones. I heard you address one of these gentlemen as Mr Holmes – Sherlock Holmes, I imagine. And the other must be Dr Watson.
WATSON:	A pleasure, Miss Proctor. And this gentleman is a relative, perhaps?

BRUNO:	(SLIGHTLY OFF-MIC) Merely a friend of the family, sir. Just hold on a second. (AS HE APPROACHES, TO ERNESTINE) Ernestine, m'dear, you might want to take care coming in here – some idiot's been dropping books all over the floor.
ERNESTINE:	(APPROACHING) I shall step carefully, Mr Bruno.
BRUNO:	I'm certain you will – I never met anyone so sure-footed.
HOLMES:	And you are, sir?
BRUNO:	Jack Bruno, Mr Holmes.
WATSON:	You've travelled quite some way, Mr Bruno, judging by your accent.
BRUNO:	I've lived in lots of places, but San Francisco is the place I call home these days, Doctor. Ever been there?
WATSON:	No.
HOLMES:	Once.
WATSON:	Really? I didn't know that.
HOLMES:	It was before your time, Watson.
ERNESTINE:	Mr Holmes, do you think it at all likely that you will find the man responsible for murdering my father?
HOLMES:	There are certainly difficulties, Miss Proctor, but I remain hopeful. In order to understand what has happened here, I think it necessary to understand the vic-
WATSON:	(COUGHS POINTEDLY)
HOLMES:	*Your father*. I perceive he was an enthusiastic collector.
ERNESTINE:	He wished to make up for his lack of culture and education by acquiring it wherever and whenever he could. Both the suit of armour to your left and that painting directly in front of you were salvaged from the fire at Arnsworth Castle seven years ago, and

225

	sold at auction shortly thereafter.
WATSON:	*Young Girl With a Gazelle* by Jean Baptiste Greuze if I'm not mistaken. And the armour...
FX:	WATSON LIFTS THE FACE-PLATE
BRUNO:	"To your left", "directly in front of you"! Ernestine, if I didn't have your word for it that you were truly blind, I'd never believe it!
FX:	FAR OFF-MIC (AND BARELY AUDIBLE), THE HEAVY FRONT DOOR OPENS AND SHUTS
ERNESTINE:	You're kind to say so, Mr Bruno, but I'm really only confident in my own home... I believe I just heard the boy return with the black wreath. Could you ensure that he hangs it on the front door, and then tell him he's dismissed for the time being?
BRUNO:	But then you won't have any staff here at all, my dear. How do you propose to- Of course. I was forgetting. You're a remarkable woman, Ernestine, and this is your home.
ERNESTINE:	For the time being. I don't know that I wish to live here for very much longer.
BRUNO:	I understand how you feel, my dear. Well, if you wish, I'll be happy to book you a room at the Northumberland Hotel. We can be neighbours – for about a day or so, anyhow.
ERNESTINE:	That's most kind, Mr Bruno.
HOLMES:	You're leaving Edelweiss Lodge, sir?
BRUNO:	It's for the best, I think. I was paying an old friend a visit, and- well, my friend is gone. But don't worry, gentlemen, I won't be leaving London *quite* yet. Just ask at the desk for my room number. (TO ERNESTINE) My dear... (HE KISSES HER CHEEK. DEPARTING) You'll see me again soon.
FX:	BRUNO OPENS THE DOOR AND LEAVES

WATSON:	Inspector, can you be certain Mr Bruno will be going to the Northumberland Hotel?
JONES:	Quite certain, Doctor – I had my sergeant confirm that he'd booked the room.
HOLMES:	Booking a room is not the same thing as occupying it, Inspector.
FX:	<u>FAR OFF-MIC (AND BARELY AUDIBLE), THE HEAVY FRONT DOOR OPENS AND SHUTS</u>
JONES:	A constable will be following him all the way to the hotel.
ERNESTINE:	You surely can't be saying that Mr Bruno is a suspect in my father's murder? They were friends for... for many years.
HOLMES:	I make it a habit never to discount any possibility, however improbable it may seem, until it has been thoroughly investigated.
WATSON:	And since it's likely the crime was committed by someone inside the house...
ERNESTINE:	Last night was an exceptionally warm one – might father have left his window open?
HOLMES:	Well, Inspector?
JONES:	(MOMENTARILY FLUMMOXED) Uh... yes, I believe it was. *Is*.
ERNESTINE:	Someone might have placed a ladder up against the window.
HOLMES:	Jones, have you examined the area under Mr Proctor's window for indentations?
JONES:	(LYING) I was going to do it... after I'd finished with the books.
HOLMES:	Of course.
JONES:	And the safe.

WATSON:	Safe?
JONES:	(REGAINING CONFIDENCE) Yes, Doctor, the safe. We're expecting the manufacturer to come down from Liverpool at some time today.
ERNESTINE:	Doesn't Mr Flint have the combination?
JONES:	Apparently not, Miss. (TO HOLMES & WATSON) Er, Thomas Flint is the family solicitor, gentlemen.
HOLMES:	So we gathered. *Thomas* Flint, you say?
WATSON:	What is it you expect to find in the safe, Inspector – a will, perhaps?
JONES:	Perhaps. It might give us some idea of who might want to kill Willoughby Proctor.
ERNESTINE:	I have no doubt that, apart from some minor bequests, I am the sole beneficiary. You're surely not suggesting that I'm responsible for my father's murder?
JONES:	By no means, Miss!
HOLMES:	Do you have any notion what else your father's safe might contain, Miss?
ERNESTINE:	Apart from a manuscript – he was working on his memoirs – I don't believe there was- (SUDDENLY DISTRACTED) Inspector, are any of your officers in the house?
JONES:	No, Miss Proctor – the last one left a few moments ago, following Mr Bruno. Why do you ask?
ERNESTINE:	Because I can hear footsteps in the room above us.
JONES:	Footsteps?
FX:	A FAINT CREAK
WATSON:	She's right!

228

HOLMES:	It seems you have an unexpected visitor. Miss Proctor. Is the room above by any chance-
WATSON:	My father's bedroom, yes.
HOLMES:	Jones, may I suggest that subtlety might be the better part of-
FX:	JONES RUSHES OUT AND, OFF-MIC, HEADS UPSTAIRS
JONES:	(OFF-MIC) Scotland Yard! You're under arrest!
HOLMES:	(SIGHS)
WATSON:	At least he's got his man cornered. If he's upstairs-
HOLMES:	If he's upstairs, then he no doubt used a ladder in order to effect an entry and may leave the same way.
FLINT:	(OFF-MIC CRIES OUT)
FX:	OFF-MIC, A BODY (AND A WOODEN LADDER) HIT THE GROUND
FLINT:	(OFF-MIC, SCREAMS)
HOLMES:	Of course, a ladder may not be entirely safe when used in haste. Watson, I believe your medical expertise is required.

SECOND COMMERCIAL

FLINT:	(EMITS EXPRESSIONS OF PAIN THROUGH GRITTED TEETH)
WATSON:	Better keep that leg elevated – this splint is a bit of a makeshift job, but it'll have to do for the moment.
FLINT:	I think it's broken!
WATSON:	It is.
JONES:	I'm most grateful to you for your stupidity, Mr Flint – without it, I might never have caught you.

HOLMES: This, then, is Thomas Flint, solicitor for the late Willoughby Proctor?

JONES: It is, Mr Holmes. (TO FLINT) Mr Flint, it'd save time if you made your confession now – I'll just get my notebook.

FLINT: I'm saying nothing! I want to be taken to a hospital!

JONES: And you shall, sir – just as soon as I've got my statement. (PAUSE) Nothing?

WATSON: Inspector, I really think he needs proper medical attention-

JONES: Very well, Flint, I'll start you off. You lied to me when you said you didn't know the combination of your client's safe, didn't you?

FLINT: I refuse to answer!

JONES: I found the safe open just now – this morning it was still locked.

FLINT: Cir- (A GASP OF PAIN) Circumstantial!

HOLMES: But suggestive, Mr Flint. Suggestive, nonetheless.

FX: <u>JONES PRODUCES A PIECE OF PAPER</u>

JONES: And this document in his pocket is all the evidence I need.

WATSON: Looks like a contract of some kind.

HOLMES: May I?

FX: <u>JONES HANDS THE CONTRACT TO HOLMES</u>

HOLMES: It is indeed – a contract of a most... unusual sort. In return for his assurance that he will propose to Miss Ernestine Proctor... the young lady's father agrees to allow himself to be murdered by Thomas Flint.

WATSON: Murdered?

HOLMES: Here you are, Inspector.

FX:	JONES SHAKES THE CONTRACT
JONES:	Mr Flint, do you deny that this is your handwriting?
FLINT:	If I admit to it, will you take me to hospital?
JONES:	Don't tell me – you've always wondered what it felt like to kill someone, eh? To have the power of life and death? Well, take my word for it, Flint, it's overrated. I should know – I've sent a dozen men to the gallows.
WATSON:	(LOW, DRY) Some of whom may actually have been guilty.
JONES:	What was that, Doctor?
HOLMES:	Watson was just making a rather interesting deduction about the writing on Proctor's palm.
JONES:	Was he now? (TO WATSON) Well, go on, then – let's hear it.
WATSON:	(FLUMMOXED) Well, er... the letters were T-O-M-E, yes?
JONES:	"Tome", of course.
WATSON:	Yes! Yes, "tome". But, ah...
HOLMES:	Watson was struck by my observation about the bottom stroke of the letter "E". May we see the photograph again, Jones?
JONES:	As you wish.
FX:	JONES PRODUCES THE PHOTOGRAPH
FLINT:	I don't see how any of this is helping my predicament.
JONES:	You brought your predicament on yourself when you fell off that ladder! (TO WATSON) Well, Doctor?
WATSON:	(HESITANTLY AT FIRST, BUT GROWING IN CONFIDENCE) Well... it seems to me that that final stroke may have been added later. The word isn't "tome" at all.

JONES:	So what is it? "Tomf"? That isn't a word. (BEAT) Is it?
WATSON:	It isn't, Inspector, no. I think that Willoughby Proctor wrote "Tom F" on his palm.
HOLMES:	I believe Watson may have hit upon something.
JONES:	(WITH A DAWNING REALIZATION) "Tom F"... short for Thomas Flint! That was what Proctor was trying to tell us! When Flint saw what he'd written, he added that extra line.
HOLMES:	Why?
JONES:	Why?
HOLMES:	Yes, Jones. Why?
JONES:	To throw us off the scent, of course!
HOLMES:	In an unnecessarily complicated fashion – wouldn't it have been far easier simply to erase the words on his victim's palm?
JONES:	Well... Perhaps it was written in indelible ink.
HOLMES:	Didn't you tell us the Police Surgeon had washed the words off? Clearly not indelible, then.
JONES:	What are you talking about? He's obviously guilty!
FX:	JONES SHAKES THE CONTRACT
JONES:	This proves it! Flint doesn't deny writing it up and signing it!
FLINT:	Why should I?
JONES:	Because it's practically a confession! I've sent a dozen men to the gallows, and you're number thirteen, Flint!
HOLMES:	Have you actually read this contract, Jones?
JONES:	I... skimmed it. Why?

HOLMES:	Watson?
WATSON:	Inspector, may I?
FX:	WATSON TAKES THE CONTRACT
WATSON:	Thank-you.
HOLMES:	Does anything strike you?
WATSON:	Er... Yes! The contract specifies the date and time Flint's murder of Proctor is to take place – ten o'clock on the 20th.
HOLMES:	Next Tuesday.
WATSON:	Furthermore, the contract states the way in which the crime is to be committed – by strangulation.
JONES:	Despicable! Aren't you disgusted with yourself, Flint?
FLINT:	(GRUNTS IN PAIN) Not particularly. All I did was write words on a piece of paper – those fellows in *The Strand* Magazine do it all the time.
JONES:	You plotted the death of Willoughby Proctor – now Willoughby Proctor is dead.
HOLMES:	In a manner entirely unlike the one agreed upon by the victim and his solicitor. I shouldn't hasten Mr Flint to the scaffold just yet, Inspector.
JONES:	What are you saying, Holmes?
FLINT:	He's saying that a good lawyer could tear your case to shreds, Jones – and I happen to be a good lawyer.
HOLMES:	Additionally, why did Flint have to resort to burglary to retrieve the contract this morning when he would surely have taken it from the safe *after* committing the murder?
WATSON:	He *did* know the combination, after all.

JONES:	(AGGRAVATED) Yes, good point, Dr Watson! (TO HOLMES) Alright, Mr clever-clogs detective – if Flint is innocent (and I can't see how he could be), why did Proctor write "Tom F" on his hand?
HOLMES:	Why do you insist that he did?
JONES:	I don't – Dr Watson here does!
WATSON:	I, uh, was merely making an observation.
HOLMES:	It's virtually impossible to write on one's palm in a style recognisable as one's own handwriting.
JONES:	Hang on, let me get a pen... (AS HE WRITES) T...O...M...F...
HOLMES:	Well, Inspector?
JONES:	Mr Flint, you're coming with me to the station.
FLINT:	*After* the hospital!
JONES:	Yes, all right, *after* the hospital, I'm placing you under arrest.
FLINT:	On what charge?
JONES:	Breaking and entering, to start with... followed by anything else I can think of. Now get up!
FX:	JONES MANHANDLES FLINT
HOLMES:	I have one question for you, Mr Flint – where was the contract you attempted to steal drawn up? In your office, no doubt?
FLINT:	Willoughby Proctor was a dying man, Holmes. All business was conducted in his home. Satisfied?
HOLMES:	Entirely.
MUSIC:	BRIDGE
FX:	INTERIOR OF A MOVING CAB

HOLMES:	Inspector Peter Jones isn't quite the imbecile his brother is. Not *quite*. But the family resemblance is undeniable – both men are tiresome and always predictable. (LONG, AWKWARD PAUSE) You're a quite invaluable helpmate, Watson – you have such a grand gift of silence.
WATSON:	You really can be quite insufferable at times, you know.
HOLMES:	So I've been advised. You're upset.
WATSON:	Excellent deduction, my dear Holmes.
HOLMES:	Because I put you in an awkward position with regard to the Inspector's precious "dying message".
WATSON:	By rights, I should punch you on the nose.
HOLMES:	By rights, you should. But I'd hardly call that characteristic behaviour. But you did come to the correct conclusion – eventually. Your average is rising.
WATSON:	That was almost a compliment, Holmes.
HOLMES:	Why, thank-you. I endeavour to give satisfaction. And in turn, I'm glad to see my lessons in observation haven't fallen upon deaf ears. You've been a diligent student, Watson, and have graduated with honours.
WATSON:	The question remains, *did* the killer enter via Willoughby Proctor's bedroom window as his daughter suggested?
HOLMES:	Unfortunately, the ground beneath the window was disturbed by Thomas Flint when attempting to steal the contract.
WATSON:	Then there's no way of being certain.
HOLMES:	Oh, I wouldn't go that far, Watson – I had a notion or two.
WATSON:	What on Earth was Proctor thinking, attempting to marry his only daughter off to the man he knew was going to murder him? I mean, I know he wanted to ensure that she would be cared for after his death, but..?

HOLMES:	Well, the contract merely stipulated that Thomas Flint propose to Miss Proctor. She was under no obligation to accept.
WATSON:	From the little I've seen of her, I'd say she had too much sense to even consider Flint's offer.
HOLMES:	I am not a wholehearted admirer of womankind, but I would certainly agree with you, Doctor. Ernestine Proctor appears to be a most remarkable young woman...
WATSON:	When you say remarkable, Holmes-
HOLMES:	Until a case is closed, I have a habit of looking at everyone with suspicion. Tell me, have you given any further thought to the message written on the dead man's palm?
WATSON:	After this morning's debacle, I've tried not to.
HOLMES:	If it wasn't written by the victim...
WATSON:	Then it must have been written by his murderer. Yes, yes.
HOLMES:	A murderer who planted not one, but two false clues, fully expecting the first to be discounted.
WATSON:	Perhaps he knew you'd be retained to investigate the crime.
HOLMES:	Or perhaps he gave Inspector Jones credit for more than he possesses. In any case, Watson, we're dealing with a rare intellect playing a sinister game to the finish.
WATSON:	It sounds to me as though the killer is toying with us.
HOLMES:	I believe so. And I, for one, find that most invigorating.
FX:	CAB BG OUT
MUSIC:	*DANSE MACABRE*

PART TWO CAST:

ANNOUNCER (DENIS BATEMAN)

HOLMES (JOHN PATRICK LOWRIE)

WATSON (LAWRENCE ALBERT)

INSPECTOR PETER JONES (STEVE MANNING)

DR RUPERT ANSTRUTHER (DAVID NATALE)

ERNESTINE PROCTOR (ANNA LISA CARLSON)

JACK BRUNO (JEFF STEITZER)

DIRECTED BY JOHN PATRICK LOWRIE

MUSIC:	*DANSE MACABRE* UP & UNDER
ANNOUNCER:	*The Further Adventures of Sherlock Holmes*! Featuring John Patrick Lowrie as Holmes, and Lawrence Albert as Dr Watson. Tonight: *The Mystery of Edelweiss Lodge, Part Two*.
WATSON:	Our investigation into the poisoning of Willoughby Proctor of Edelweiss Lodge was not proceeding well. It seemed at first that Proctor's lawyer, Thomas Flint, was the guilty party, but Holmes proved that the evidence against him had been falsified. Now we were visiting the Northumberland Hotel with the intention of interviewing Mr Jack Bruno, the only person apart from Proctor's blind daughter Ernestine to have been present on the night of the murder...
MUSIC:	OUT
BG:	SCATTERED POLITE CHATTER
BRUNO:	*Recollections of an Eventful Life*!
HOLMES:	(BEMUSED) Excuse me, Mr Bruno?
BRUNO:	This damn book!
FX:	HE SLAMS THE BOOK ON THE TABLE
WATSON:	The memoirs of Sir Ronald Ramsgate. You remember him, of course, Holmes?
HOLMES:	The theft of the Jaria Diamond. A seedy patchwork of discontent and hatred, I recall.
WATSON:	Does your book mention that incident?
BRUNO:	I haven't finished it, and I don't intend to! The fellow's got a damn nerve!
HOLMES:	He's done something to offend you, perhaps?
FX:	BRUNO FLICKS THROUGH THE BOOK, JABS AT ONE OF THE PAGES

BRUNO:	This! This! Ramsgate was as British as you, Mr Holmes, but he made his money out in Alaska, just like me. We shared many a drink, back in the early 50's, while we scrabbled through mud, searching for the glory dust. I called that man "friend", and this is how he repays me!
WATSON:	How?
BRUNO:	By writing about a certain "John Grover", who he describes as a claim jumper, a cheat and a liar!
HOLMES:	It would seem that this Grover has more cause to be offended than you, Mr Bruno.
BRUNO:	(GROWING LOUDER AS HE GROWS ANGRIER) John Grover *is* me! At least, that's the idea. Ramsgate has him doing and saying enough of the things *I* did to make that pretty plain to anyone who knew me back then! It's libellous! Well, I won't stand for it! I'm gonna send a cable to my lawyers in the States!
BG:	ONE OF THE GUESTS SAYS "SHHHH!"
WATSON:	I do apologise.
HOLMES:	If that's your intention, then I'm afraid you're destined to be disappointed, Mr Bruno.
BRUNO:	Huh?
HOLMES:	Watson, does the Northumberland keep a copy of *The Times* for its guests?
WATSON:	Ah... yes, just here.
FX:	WATSON PRODUCES THE NEWSPAPER
HOLMES:	If you happen to look through this, Mr Bruno, you'll find Sir Ronald Ramsgate's obituary.
WATSON:	Oh?
HOLMES:	The causes, I regret to say, were entirely natural – a trend that's

becoming far too widespread for my liking.

BRUNO: So the fella blackens my good name and gets off scot free?

WATSON: Well, to be strictly accurate, it's John Grover's good name.

HOLMES: Mr Bruno, we haven't come all this way to discuss the matter of your reputation.

BRUNO: Of course you haven't, Mr Holmes, of course. Forgive me – sometimes a fellow's just got to get these things off his chest. (CLEARS HIS THROAT) Now, what can I do to assist you gentlemen? Just name it.

HOLMES: Inspector Jones informs us that you were the one who discovered Willoughby Proctor's body.

BRUNO: That's right. Boy, he's quite something, that Inspector, huh? Yeah, I found the body – my friend. Willoughby hadn't appeared for breakfast, and, given his condition, Ernestine was naturally concerned. I knocked on his door, there was no answer, so I went in, and- Well, you know what I found. In a way, I'm glad.

WATSON: Glad?

BRUNO: I wouldn't have had Ernestine see him like that. (QUICKLY) Not *see*, I mean, uh, *discover*.

WATSON: And you knew instantly that it was murder?

BRUNO: I had no idea. I mean, I've seen dead men before, prospectors who died of exposure in Alaska, but... Seeing him lying there, I thought... going in your sleep, that's a good way to go. Peaceful.

WATSON: Then it wasn't until Dr Anstruther was called that you knew it was murder.

BRUNO: Actually, that was down to Ernestine. Even from the doorway, she said she could smell the cyanide, the stuff she used to use when she caught butterflies. I couldn't smell a damn thing.

HOLMES: The heightened senses of the blind, no doubt.

BRUNO:	(SLIGHTLY UNCONVINCED?) Sure.
HOLMES:	How were you associated with the late Mr Proctor?
BRUNO:	We were friends – I guess you could say we were also rivals.
WATSON:	Rivals in love?
BRUNO:	(CHUCKLES) Not the kind of love you mean, Dr Watson - love of England and English antiquities. Many times we'd engaged in bidding wars over some item or another. That's the danger of having deep pockets – you can afford to indulge yourself. Never a good thing in a grown man. Indulgence is for children and young maidens.
HOLMES:	And did your friend indulge his daughter?
BRUNO:	I wouldn't care to say, Mr Holmes. I haven't been in England for over a decade, and even though she could see back then, it's been such a long time, I doubt if Ernestine even remembers me. So I don't know whether it'd be fair to say that Willoughby spoiled her... But I know he considered himself responsible for her blindness.
WATSON:	How so?
BRUNO:	He was always eager to find a husband for Ernestine. When she was just nineteen, and the family were living out in Kent near his ironworks, Willoughby introduced her to a banker named Harold Saintsbury. He fell for her, but she didn't return his affections. One day, when she was out riding, she was thrown from her horse. The blow Ernestine took to the head...
HOLMES:	Resulted in her losing her sight.
BRUNO:	Yeah, I guess. Willoughby was convinced Saintsbury put a burr under the horse's saddle, caused the beast to throw her.
WATSON:	You mean he tried to kill her for rejecting him?
BRUNO:	I don't mean anything, Doctor – I'm just repeating what Willoughby told me a few days ago.

HOLMES:	Did he confront the man Saintsbury?
BRUNO:	He said not. Claimed the fellow vanished just after the accident. Fled out of guilt maybe, or fear or getting arrested.
WATSON:	Or perhaps some other fate befell him...
MUSIC:	BRIDGE
FX:	JONES' OFFICE AT SCOTLAND YARD
JONES:	So you think Willoughby Proctor did away with Saintsbury, then, Doctor?
WATSON:	As Holmes would say, it's a capital error to theorize without data-
HOLMES:	Do I really say that?
WATSON:	Repeatedly, Holmes. (TO JONES) But I really think the matter bears further investigation, Inspector.
JONES:	I can probably spare my sergeant, but I really think it's a waste of time, gentlemen. I'm quite confident I know who the murderer is.
HOLMES:	Then you don't consider the objections against Thomas Flint's guilt persuasive?
JONES:	Flint? Oh, Flint had nothing to do with Proctor's death, I'm quite convinced of that.
HOLMES:	(DRY) Really?
JONES:	As a matter of fact, I let him go a couple of hours ago.
WATSON:	I thought you intended to charge him with house-breaking!
JONES:	Miss Proctor called in to say she didn't wish charges to be pressed. Something about not wanting to cause even greater scandal.
WATSON:	She surely didn't come alone.

JONES:	No, she was in the company of some Doctor chappie.
WATSON:	Anstruther.
JONES:	But I don't doubt she could've made it to Scotland Yard on her own if she'd wanted to.
HOLMES:	Inspector Jones, if you've released Flint, who do you believe the murderer to be?
JONES:	Ernestine Proctor herself, of course.
WATSON:	What!
HOLMES:	On what grounds, pray?
JONES:	The will was much as Miss Proctor predicted – she inherits everything.
WATSON:	And could you explain to me how a blind woman would be capable of committing such a crime?
HOLMES:	I don't believe the Inspector is entirely convinced that she *is* blind, Watson.
JONES:	Quite right, Holmes. I was struck by Mr Bruno's observation that she was so confident in here movements, she might as well not be blind at all. That set me to thinking...
WATSON:	Why would anyone lie about such a thing?
JONES:	Who knows what goes on in the minds of women?
HOLMES:	We're at least of the same mind on *that* point, Jones. However, I imagine her condition was diagnosed following her accident.
JONES:	By Dr Anstruther, no doubt – and I got the impression that if he's not the young lady's sweetheart, he wishes he was. Who's to say he wasn't acting on her instructions, telling her father that she was blind when she could see as well as you or I.
HOLMES:	In order that, having lulled her father into a false sense of

security over a period of some years, she might poison him as he slept.

JONES: Precisely, Mr Holmes! The fiendishness of it makes me shiver.

WATSON: I think you may have a touch of 'flu, Inspector.

HOLMES: Surely the length of time over which the ruse would have to have been sustained seems a trifle- shall we say, excessive?

JONES: Revenge is a dish best served cold, so Johnny Foreigner says.

WATSON: Revenge for what, precisely? What wrong is Willoughby Proctor supposed to have done by his daughter?

JONES: (WHO DOESN'T KNOW) Well, uh... (INSPIRATION STRIKES) Introducing her to the man responsible for her accident! And later, attempting to marry her off to a man with murderous intentions – and a lawyer, to boot! Oh yes, I daresay that any day now, Dr Anstruther will announce that he's perfected some miracle cure for her blindness, and shortly thereafter, we'll see a wedding announcement in the better quality newspapers.

WATSON: (RESTRAINING HIS FURY) Inspector, you'll forgive me, but this is all utter rot!

JONES: Is it, though, Doctor?

WATSON: This is simply wild conjecture!

JONES: Don't be so quick to condemn it, Doctor. *Think* for a moment. Mr Holmes and I excel at that – you should try a spot of it, too.

HOLMES: (SUPPRESSES A LAUGH BY COUGHING) Forgive me – dust.

JONES: Who inherits everything? She does. Where was the murder committed? In her home. Who did the cyanide belong to?

WATSON: *To whom.*

JONES: Phrase the question any way you like, Doctor, the answer's still the same. And poison is a woman's weapon, of course.

HOLMES:	Your argument is quite compelling, Jones.
JONES:	Why, thank-you, Mr Holmes. I felt certain you'd appreciate it.
WATSON:	Except that it slanders my friend and neighbour, Dr Anstruther.
HOLMES:	You must not allow loyalty to your profession to prevent you from uncovering the truth, Watson, no matter how unpalatable it may be.
JONES:	Couldn't have said it better myself!
HOLMES:	However, I believe a certain amount of caution should be exercised at this... sensitive stage of the investigation.
JONES:	Oh?
WATSON:	I believe Watson here is acquainted with an oculist who has consulting rooms in Devonshire Place – may I suggest that Miss Proctor be referred to him before you make any accusations you might have cause to regret.
JONES:	A second opinion, you mean?
HOLMES:	I really think it might be for the best.
WATSON:	Sounds like an eminently sensible suggestion, Holmes. And if she should prove to actually *be* blind, your entire theory collapses like a house of cards.
JONES:	By no means, Doctor. Blind or not, all the evidence points to her.
WATSON:	Which brings us back to the question of how she was able to commit the murder at all.
JONES:	Because she knows every inch of Edelweiss Lodge. It seems to me that a blind woman might prowl around in the dark with as much confidence as she would during the day!
HOLMES:	Evidently the Inspector has anticipated every difficulty.
JONES:	One way or another, she's the murderer.

HOLMES:	If you insist.
JONES:	Never arrested a woman before, not for murder. But it seems that she'll be number thirteen in my collection.
WATSON:	Of hangings.
JONES:	Do you suppose they make exceptions for the blind? Well, doesn't matter. When I come to write my memoirs, I daresay, Miss Ernestine Proctor will merit a chapter all to herself.
HOLMES:	Speaking of memoirs, Inspector, have you taken the time to peruse the manuscript in the safe?
JONES:	What manuscript?
WATSON:	Didn't she say her father was writing his memoirs?
HOLMES:	Might there be something in there that might suggest a motive for his murder?
JONES:	You want a motive? I can give you one without even thinking.
HOLMES:	Of that I have no doubt, Inspector. Might I, in any case, be permitted to examine the manuscript?
JONES:	As a matter of fact, you won't, Mr Holmes. It wasn't in the safe.
WATSON:	Then where is it?
JONES:	(DISINTERESTED) I don't know. Maybe he decided it wasn't worth the effort and just chucked it on the fire.
WATSON:	Not in the height of Summer, surely.
HOLMES:	Did you examine the fireplaces in Edelweiss Lodge, Jones?
JONES:	What was the point? Who'd be mad enough to do a thing like that?
HOLMES:	I am, it seems. I can assure you that no fires have been lit in quite some time. Where, then, are Willoughby Proctor's memoir's?

JONES:	Who cares?
FX:	OUT

FIRST COMMERCIAL

ANSTRUTHER:	The impudence of the fellow! He deserves a punch on the nose!
HOLMES:	I find this tendency towards violence in our general practitioners most unsettling, Dr Anstruther.
ERNESTINE:	Nevertheless, Mr Holmes has persuaded the Inspector not to place me behind bars – at least for the time being, while I undergo this eye examination.
WATSON:	Holmes and I regret the inconvenience of that, Miss Proctor. I can assure you however, that Doyle is a thoroughly competent fellow.
ANSTRUTHER:	He'll be glad of the business, too. From what I hear, he's taken to writing cheap detective fiction to pass the time.
WATSON:	Oh, it's not quite so bad as all that. (TO HOLMES) Holmes, you must read some of it.
HOLMES:	You know my opinion of that particular field of literary endeavour, Watson.
ERNESTINE:	Then perhaps I may provide you with a volume you may appreciate, Mr Holmes.
FX:	SHE PRODUCES A WRAPPED PARCEL
HOLMES:	If, as its dimensions suggest, that package contains *The Memoirs of the Borgias*, then I cannot accept it, Miss Proctor.
ERNESTINE:	May I ask why not?
HOLMES:	Because I have yet to positively identify the person responsible for murdering your father.
ERNESTINE:	Then consider it a gift. I'm hardly in a position to begin a hobby

as a bibliophile, or to enjoy much of my father's collection. I'm giving the Greuze painting to Dr Anstruther.

ANSTRUTHER: There really is no need, Ernestine-

ERNESTINE: You've admired it many times, Rupert. And before his departure from Edelweiss Lodge, Mr Bruno requested the suit of armour from Arnsworth Castle. He and my father were engaged in a furious bidding war for it, apparently.

WATSON: It seems to me a somewhat inappropriate request, given what occurred only the day before.

ERNESTINE: One must make allowances for our brash American friends. And business matters demand his attention back in San Francisco, so he must set sail very soon.

HOLMES: Miss Proctor, what do you know of your father's memoirs?

ERNESTINE: Very little, Mr Holmes.

ANSTRUTHER: Save that in the weeks following my diagnosis, he approached the work with renewed vigour. Isn't that right, my dear?

ERNESTINE: Yes, he said that Rupert had forced him to face the harshest reality of all.

HOLMES: Oh?

ANSTRUTHER: The inevitability of one's own death, Mr Holmes.

HOLMES: Of course.

ERNESTINE: And as a result, he felt there was much he wished to say.

WATSON: A pity we don't know what that was.

ERNESTINE: You're quite welcome to read the manuscript if you think it'll be useful, Dr Watson. Isn't it in my father's safe?

HOLMES: Unfortunately not, Miss Proctor.

ERNESTINE:	How peculiar! Well, then... I can't imagine where it could be.
HOLMES:	Inspector Jones is similarly baffled, but perhaps that's less surprising. Incidentally, I've suggested to him that he should post a man outside your home at all times – to discourage you from fleeing the country, naturally.
ERNESTINE:	Naturally. Well, Rupert trusts Dr Watson, and Dr Watson trusts *you*... I shall abide by your wishes.
ANSTRUTHER:	What's to prevent Ernestine from missing her oculist's appointment and taking a cab straight to the docks?
WATSON:	(SLIGHTLY OFF-MIC) At a rough guess, I'd say the plain-clothes officer in the street below. Jenkins – good man.
ERNESTINE:	How strange to be the focus of so much attention – one hardly knows whether to be offended or flattered.
ANSTRUTHER:	Given that witless Inspector's notions, I'd hardly consider it a compliment. (DEPARTING) Come along, my dear – I'll hail us a cab.
FX:	<u>ANSTRUTHER OPENS THE DOOR</u>
ERNESTINE:	Mr Holmes, I'm troubled by something. And yet I'm unable to put my finger on it. I know only that something is very, very wrong.
HOLMES:	You' re most astute, Miss Proctor. And since you've followed my instructions thus far, I shall give you another – put it from your mind for the time being.
ERNESTINE:	You know who's responsible, then?
HOLMES:	I've sketched the outlines of a composition, but I need to fill in the detail. Without proof, Jones will pay no heed to my deductions. You must remain patient a little while longer.
ERNESTINE:	Can't you even give me an indication?
HOLMES:	Only that the truth is always darker and more complex than we

would have it. Good-day, Miss Proctor.

ERNESTINE: (DEPARTING) Mr Holmes.

FX: SHE AND ANSTRUTHER LEAVE

WATSON: "There was much he wished to say", Holmes. It sounds to me as though Proctor wished to confess to something.

HOLMES: And what might that have been?

WATSON: Well, without the manuscript – or some startling feat of deduction – there's no way of knowing for certain. But if I had to guess...

HOLMES: A habit I discourage.

WATSON: I should say it was the murder of Saintsbury, the man he considered responsible for his daughter's blindness. He still hasn't been found.

HOLMES: For the very good reason that no-one is looking for him.

WATSON: I take it you disagree, then.

HOLMES: On the contrary – that's just one of seven separate possibilities I consider likely. But there's work to be done before the final curtain can be brought down.

MD: OUT

SECOND COMMERCIAL

FX: A QUIET VICTORIAN STREET. HOLMES, WATSON AND JONES WALK BRISKLY

WATSON: A burglary? Here?

JONES: So Miss Proctor claims, Doctor. But I'm not entirely convinced someone *did* break into Edelweiss Lodge last night.

HOLMES: She seems convinced she heard something, Jones.

250

JONES: The constable didn't see anything. No, no, Miss Proctor *says* she
                    heard something because she knows I'm on to her. Blind she may
                    be, but I remain convinced she killed her own father.

FX: THEY GO UP A FEW STONE STEPS

WATSON: There are likelier suspects, surely.

JONES: If you mean that fellow Harold Saintsbury, he turned up working
                    for a branch of the Anglo-Hellenic Bank in Manchester.

FX: HE PULLS ON A BELL – IT RINGS INSIDE THE HOUSE

JONES: And an entire Masonic lodge is prepared to swear to his
                    whereabouts on the night of the murder.

FX: THE DOOR OPENS

BRUNO: It's about time! (SURPRISED) Inspector!

JONES: Mr Bruno? What are *you* doing here?

BRUNO: I'm sorry, I was expecting-

HOLMES: Workmen, coming to remove the suit of armour you were
                    promised. I sent them a telegram, saying they were no longer
                    required. May we come in?

FX: STREET BG OUT

HOLMES: Mr Bruno, you claimed Ernestine Proctor would be unable to
                    remember you since when you saw her last, she was but a child.

BRUNO: It's not a claim, Mr Holmes, it's the truth.

HOLMES: I disagree. I suggest she has no memory of you because, until a
                    few days ago, she'd had never met you before. And the reason
                    she'd never met you is because you do not exist.

BRUNO: (CHUCKLES) Dr Watson, you can tell him I exist, can't you?
                    Coming from you, he might tend to believe it.

WATSON:	Holmes, what exactly do you mean?
HOLMES:	Simply that there never was any such person as Jack Bruno.
BRUNO:	Never any such person? Aren't I standing right here?
ERNESTINE:	Mr Holmes, father told me that Jack Bruno was an old and dear friend!
BRUNO:	You see? Well, if you won't take Ernestine's word for it, I don't intend to jump through hoops just to prove I am who I say I am.
HOLMES:	I don't think that will be necessary. One simple question will suffice. If you had not been to Britain for more than a decade, as you told Dr Watson and myself, how is it possible that you were present at the auction of this* suit of armour, which occurred only seven years ago?
FX:	*HOLMES PATS THE ARMOUR
ERNESTINE:	(SUDDEN REALIZATION) That was it! That's what was troubling me!
BRUNO:	Seven years ago? Are you sure?
ERNESTINE:	*Quite* sure!
BRUNO:	Then... I guess I must be mistaken.
HOLMES:	A mistake has been made, certainly. And it's one that may cost you your liberty, and very probably your life.
JONES:	You mean... *he's* number thirteen?
HOLMES:	I was struck by the fact that the moment Dr Watson took an interest in the suit of armour, you were quick to change the subject, subtly casting doubt on Miss Proctor's blindness. Now, why should this suit be of such interest, and why should you be so anxious to acquire it?
BRUNO:	I just... like it. That's all.

WATSON:	One might hide something in it.
FX:	WATSON LIFTS THE FACE-PLATE
WATSON:	The face-plate reminds me of a letter-box. (MUFFLED AS HE LOOKS INSIDE) I don't see anything. Perhaps if we take it apart, piece by piece...
JONES:	Oh, for heaven's sake! (A FEROCIOUS GRUNT)
FX:	THE ARMOUR IS PUSHED OVER, AND FALLS TO PIECES
HOLMES:	Most effective, Inspector. And what have we here?
FX:	HE LIFTS THE MANUSCRIPT FROM THE WRECKAGE
HOLMES:	The missing manuscript, if I'm not mistaken. Now what could be so important...
FX:	HE FLIPS THROUGH THE PAGES
HOLMES:	Ah! This is interesting!
ERNESTINE:	What is it, Mr Holmes?
HOLMES:	It seems your father did indeed own a metalworks in Kent, but he purchased it in 1861 – with money earned during the previous decade in the illegal trade of ivory smuggling.
ERNESTINE:	Ivory smuggling?
HOLMES:	He and his associate, Timothy Longstreet, were responsible for the murders of their competitors, and of several individuals who opposed their transportation of ivory across Africa via caravan, and then from the shores of the Gold Coast to England.
ERNESTINE:	It's impossible!
HOLMES:	Regrettably not, Miss Proctor. It seems that at the end of his days, your father decided to confess his sins. He, of course, escaped the noose, but it places his former partner in an unenviable position.

JONES: I'd very much like to speak to this Timothy Longstreet.

HOLMES: Well, Inspector, the manuscript states that he's presently living a comfortable existence as a gentleman of property in the Yorkshire Dales...

WATSON: But Mr Bruno's desire to remove the suit of armour and the missing memoirs from Edelweiss Lodge suggests that he's far closer.

JONES: (FINALLY CATCHING ON) You mean he- he..?

HOLMES: I do, Inspector.

BRUNO: (IN AN ENGLISH ACCENT FROM NOW ON) I did my best to ensure this would all go smoothly, Holmes. Damn you, why did you have to spoil everything? Don't you realise how hard it was for me to have to do this to my best friend?

JONES: You call what you did to Proctor friendship, do you?

BRUNO: I call it self-preservation, Mr Jones. Willoughby didn't have anything else to live for, and when he wrote to me, told me he was writing a book about his life... I knew what I had to do.

HOLMES: And he suspected nothing when you asked to visit him in the guise of Jack Bruno of San Francisco?

BRUNO: No, I always use Bruno's name whenever I come South – I'm more cautious than my old partner ever was.

JONES: Much good it did you.

BRUNO: When did you know?

JONES: I suspected you all along-

BRUNO: (SCORNFUL) Not *you*! Holmes.

HOLMES: It was clear from the method used that the killer was to be found within the house – anyone entering via the bedroom window would surely have brought his own weapon. Additionally, the initial attempt to implicate Thomas Flint suggested someone who may have overheard their negotiations – negotiations which took place within Edelweiss Lodge.

BRUNO: I practically signed my name to it, didn't I?

HOLMES: Your eagerness to cast suspicion on everyone but yourself certainly didn't help your cause.

BRUNO: I regret that. (TO ERNESTINE) I owe you an apology in particular, Ernestine. I panicked, didn't know what to do. (PAUSE) Do you... forgive me?

ERNESTINE: Mr Bruno- *Mr Longstreet*... Perhaps I could know if you were truly sorry if I were to feel your face... May I?

BRUNO: Of course.

FX: SHE SLAPS HIM *VERY* HARD

BRUNO: Aah! I suppose that answers my question. (TO JONES) Inspector... I think I'd like to go now.

MUSIC: BRIDGE

FX: WATSON TURNS THE PAGES OF A BOOK

WATSON: Hmmm...

HOLMES: Interesting reading, Watson?

WATSON: Not interesting, but certainly enlightening, Holmes - *Recollections of an Eventful Life* by Sir Ronald Ramsgate, one of two sets of memoirs on this case.

HOLMES: Ah! And how does it strike you?

WATSON: After the first few chapters, far from eventful – unless you have a sound knowledge of our financial systems.

HOLMES: And there are many turf accountants who would attest to your lack of sound judgement in that area.

WATSON:	Most amusing, Holmes. However, it occurs to me that there are still one or two unanswered questions.
HOLMES:	The first being?
WATSON:	What was the purpose of Jack Bruno's fury over Sir Ronald's memoirs? He can't possibly have been portrayed in them, since he never truly existed.
HOLMES:	And you believe you've hit upon the solution?
WATSON:	I do. It all hinges upon the unseasonably warm weather.
HOLMES:	(INDULGING HIM) The weather? You astound me, Watson!
WATSON:	As you pointed out, Bruno, alias Longstreet, couldn't possibly burn Proctor's manuscript without creating the attention he was anxious to avoid - that's why he hid it in the suit of armour.
HOLMES:	Sound reasoning. Go on.
WATSON:	He couldn't be certain we wouldn't find it before he could dispose of it properly. It was essential, then, to create in our minds the certainty that Jack Bruno had no connection with Timothy Longstreet. His anger was directed at the description of the actions of a fellow named Grover.
HOLMES:	And when did these actions occur, Watson?
WATSON:	The early '50s - the same time Proctor and Longstreet were making their fortunes in ivory.
HOLMES:	Excellently done, Doctor! Isn't it rewarding to use the senses the good Lord gave us? I consider myself extremely fortunate to work with someone who inspires not by vacuum but by actual contribution. Yes, I've no doubt your deductions are correct.
WATSON:	Why do I get the feeling you'd already arrived at the same conclusion?
HOLMES:	You're far too hard on yourself, Watson. You're not to blame if you failed to observed the smudges of newspaper print on his

fingers, smudges which were then transferred to the pages of the book.

WATSON: Suggesting what?

HOLMES: That the idea came to him when he saw the Northumberland's copy of *The Times* – you recall it was close to hand when we interviewed him? He'd already come across Sir Ronald Ramsgate's obituary, read the details of his life, including his background and some mention of his recently-published autobiography. He then purchased a copy from the nearest bookshop, and had enough time to skim through it and claim that one of Sir Ronald's Texan acquaintances was a thin imitation of himself.

WATSON: Better to be a claim-jumper than a murderer. And with Sir Ronald conveniently deceased, there'd be no need to carry out his threat of legal action.

HOLMES: I said we were dealing with a rare intellect.

WATSON: Perhaps if he hadn't been so thoroughly ingenious, you wouldn't have caught him.

HOLMES: Possibly not. But the frailty of genius, Watson, needs an audience. Tell me, what was your second unanswered question?

WATSON: The second? Oh, yes! If Longstreet was expecting to receive the suit of armour as a gift, why on Earth did he attempt to break into Edelweiss Lodge last night?

HOLMES: He didn't, Watson – *I* did.

WATSON: What!

HOLMES: I've never been one to trust in the happy felicity of luck. I had to be certain where the manuscript was hidden and I had to know what was in it. You don't seriously suppose I put my finger on the relevant page in a matter of moments, did you? I knew where to find the incriminating evidence because I'd read it by candle-light the night before.

WATSON:	And replaced the manuscript when you were done.
HOLMES:	Precisely.
WATSON:	You never told me!
HOLMES:	My profession would be a drab and sordid one if I didn't sometimes set the scene to glorify the results. My methods may be irregular on occasion, but it's their effectiveness which is important.
WATSON:	How did you get past the officer guarding the house?
HOLMES:	I find your lack of confidence in my house-breaking skills most disheartening, Watson. Were it not for Miss Proctor's acute hearing, my presence that night would never have been suspected.
WATSON:	Ah, yes, Miss Proctor... The revelation concerning her father's past has shaken her terribly.
HOLMES:	I can uncover facts, but I cannot change them.
WATSON:	We can only hope that Dr Anstruther's obvious affection for her will soften the blow somewhat.
HOLMES:	"Hope" is not a practical use of my time and abilities.
WATSON:	You know, Holmes, Bruno could always claim you planted the evidence that implicated him.
HOLMES:	Indeed he could – if he had known about it. I think it best that the truth never dawns on him, don't you?
MUSIC:	*DANSE MACABRE*

The Classic Adventures of Sherlock Holmes –
A Study in Scarlet
(Original Airdate April 4, 2007)

It would make perfect sense for the first story featuring Sherlock Holmes to be the first in a series of adaptations recorded by Imagination Theater; in fact, it was the seventh. My fault. It had been my ambition to dramatise both *The Yellow Face* and *The Three Students*, two stories that had – to the best of my knowledge – only been attempted once before, in the BBC's Complete Canon project starring Clive Merrison and Michael Williams. As a matter of fact, I later discovered that there were two other versions of *The Three Students*: one recorded for the BBC in 1953 with Carleton Hobbs and Norman Shelley (and very likely wiped), the other – under the title *A Hollow Victory*, for some reason - for South African Radio in the 1980s. Imagination Theater recorded *The Yellow Face* in late 2005, and *The Three Students* early the next year. I suggested that it would be inaccurate to describe them as *The* Further *Adventures of Sherlock Holmes* (although Anthony Boucher and Denis Green sometimes included Canonical adaptations in their *New Adventures* series for Rathbone and Bruce), so the title *The Classic Adventures of Sherlock Holmes* was decided upon for such episodes. Even then, four more episodes passed before I got around to dramatising the first novel, which I found fit fairly well into an hour-long slot, with only one important element missing – the Mormon flashback that takes up most of the second half of the book.

"It don't much matter to you why I hated these men," says Jefferson Hope after his capture, and he's quite right; but for the sake of avoiding confusion, the killer is only seeking vengeance for his beloved Lucy, with no mention of her father. It seems that as many adaptations omit the Mormon sequence as include it. To have put it into the Imagination Theater version would have meant spreading the story over two hour-long episodes, the second of which hardly features Holmes and Watson at all.

In the novel, it's a period of some weeks of lodging together before Watson became aware of Holmes' profession, and the two embarked upon their first joint investigation. In order to keep the plot moving at a good pace, I changed the time-frame so that Holmes should receive a request for assistance from Scotland Yard on the very day they move in together. The BBC's 2010 television series *Sherlock* took the same approach, so I suppose I must have been on the right track. Incidentally, the Friday before *Sherlock* first aired, I was invited to appear on BBC 2's *Newsnight* programme alongside writer/producer Steven Moffat. The request was swiftly withdrawn once it was discovered that I didn't live particularly close to *Newsnight*'s London studios and would have to be put up in an hotel overnight (it's not much of an anecdote, I admit, but there it is).

I'd decided to begin the episode almost at the exact moment of the first meeting between our heroes, but it was felt that hard-core fans would never forgive us if we omitted the scene at the Criterion Bar between Watson and Stamford, where Holmes' name first comes up. This volume contains my original version of the script, minus those additional lines. Brevity also demanded the removal from the script of Madame Charpentier and his daughter (their testimony is related by Inspector Gregson), and the sequence in which Holmes tests Hope's poison on a sickly dog. In an attempt to please nit-pickers (such as myself) I added a throwaway line where Watson mistakenly calls their landlady "Mrs Turner" - a reference to the much-debated line from *A Scandal in Bohemia*.

One question raised by commentators ever since the story's publication is why Jefferson Hope should come to Baker Street at the climax, apparently believing that he is simply picking up a fare – surely he must have seen it in the newspaper advertisement regarding the ring, which Holmes placed in order to trap him. Bert Coules' 1989 BBC radio dramatisation states that Hope was well aware he was walking (well, riding) into a trap, but that he went anyway, having accepted his fate. Most versions ignore the question entirely, and I was somewhat vague on the matter also, suggesting that Wiggins, one of the Irregulars, led Hope to Holmes' address. There are still objections to this, so it isn't really explored in any great detail.

CAST

ANNOUNCER (DENNIS BATEMAN)

HOLMES (JOHN PATRICK LOWRIE)

WATSON (LAWRENCE ALBERT)

GREGSON (JOHN MURRAY)

LESTRADE (RICK MAY)

STAMFORD (DAVID NATALE)

MESSENGER (DENNIS BATEMAN)

CONSTABLE RANCE (DENNIS BATEMAN)

"MRS SAWYER" (JOHN ARMSTRONG)

JEFFERSON HOPE (JOHN ARMSTRONG)

ENOCH J DREBBER (DENNIS BATEMAN)

DIRECTED BY LAWRENCE ALBERT

FX:	OPENING SEQUENCE, BIG BEN
ANNOUNCER:	*The Classic Adventures of Sherlock Holmes* by Sir Arthur Conan Doyle, featuring John Patrick Lowrie as Holmes, and Lawrence Albert as Dr Watson. Tonight: *A Study in Scarlet*.
MUSIC	*DANSE MACABRE* UP AND UNDER
WATSON:	My name is Dr John H Watson, and I would like to tell you the story of my first meeting with Sherlock Holmes. My military career came to an abrupt end following the outbreak of the Second Afghan War. Wounded, and with my health irretrievably ruined, I returned to London, that great cesspool into which all the loungers and idlers of the Empire are irresistibly drained. With neither kith nor kin in England, I was as free as air - or as free as an army pension of eleven shillings and sixpence a day will permit a man to be. But a chance encounter with Stamford, one of my old colleagues at St Bartholemew's Hospital, changed all that…
MUSIC:	OUT
FX:	WATSON & STAMFORD'S FOOSTSTEPS
STAMFORD:	Now remember, Watson, you mustn't blame me if you don't get along with him.
WATSON:	If we don't get on, it'll be easy to part company. You know, Stamford, it seems to me you've some reason for washing your hands of the matter. What is it you're not telling me about this Sherlock Holmes chap?
STAMFORD:	I don't know much of anything about him; I'm not even sure he's a medical student. He's either performing experiments in the hospital laboratory from morning till night, or else avoids the place for weeks.
WATSON:	What sort of experiments?
STAMFORD:	He says he's trying to find a reagent that's precipitated by haemoglobin, and by nothing else.

WATSON:	Well, I'm sure that's… very useful.
STAMFORD:	He seems to have a passion for definite and exact knowledge.
WATSON:	Quite right, too.
STAMFORD:	Yes, but when it comes to beating the corpses in the dissecting-rooms with a stick to verify how far bruises are produced after death, it's going a bit far, don't you think?
WATSON:	Good Lord!
STAMFORD:	So as I say, if you don't get on with him, don't blame me. Ah, you're in luck. It seems he's here after all.
FX:	THEY PUSH OPEN A DOOR
HOLMES:	(APPROACHING) Stamford, I've found it! I have found it!
STAMFORD:	Dr Watson, Mr Sherlock Holmes.
WATSON:	Pleased to make your acquaintance.
HOLMES:	How do you do? You've been in Afghanistan, I perceive.
WATSON:	How on Earth did you know that?
HOLMES:	(IGNORING HIM) Stamford, this is the most important medico-legal discovery for years! If this test had been in existence earlier, Von Bischoff would have been hanged for that murder at Frankfurt last year. Then there was Mason of Bradford, and the notorious Muller, and Lefevre of Montpellier, and Samson of New Orleans. I could name a score of cases in which it would have been decisive. Why did they escape the noose? Because there was no reliable test for blood corpuscles more than a few hours old. But now - we have the Sherlock Holmes Test!
WATSON:	(DURING HOLMES' SPEECH) Er, excuse me… How did you… er… excuse me… I say… How could you tell…
STAMFORD:	We came on business, Holmes. I was Watson's dresser when he was a surgeon here. He tells me he's looking for comfortable

rooms at a reasonable price, and I remembered you saying you could get no one to go halves with you on that suite in Baker Street, so I thought I'd better bring the two of you together.

HOLMES: I see. (TO WATSON) Doctor, are you bothered by the smell of strong tobacco?

WATSON: No, I smoke an Arcadia mix myself.

HOLMES: I generally have chemicals about, and occasionally do experiments. Would that annoy you?

WATSON: By no means. I'd prefer to lodge with someone of studious and quiet habits, in fact. You see, after the war… well, my nerves are a little shaken.

HOLMES: You wouldn't mind if I played the violin?

WATSON: (BEMUSED) No, go right ahead.

HOLMES: No, not *now*. I mean at Baker Street.

WATSON: Whether the music is good or bad depends on the player, I always say.

HOLMES: Well, that's settled then. The rooms will suit you down to the ground, I'm sure. If you're agreeable, we can move in tomorrow.

WATSON: What's the house number?

HOLMES: 221b.

WATSON: (THOUGHTFULLY) 221b Baker Street… Let's take a look.

STAMFORD: See, Watson? Didn't I say you two would get on famously?

FX: HOLMES IS PUSHING A LARGE BOX INTO THE ROOM

HOLMES: This is the last box, Watson.

WATSON: I'm glad to hear it. What's in this one?

HOLMES:	Chemical apparatus. (HE GIVES A GRUNT AS...)
FX:	...HE RIPS THE LID FROM THE CRATE
WATSON:	Need a hand?
HOLMES:	Thank-you. But please be careful, I use a great many poisons in my work.
WATSON:	I've been meaning to ask you about that, Holmes. What exactly – (SUDDENLY DISTRACTED) Is that a syringe?
HOLMES:	(CAGEY) Er… It's all right, I'll take care of that. You were, er, saying, Watson?
WATSON:	I was about to ask… what exactly *is* your work?
HOLMES:	A fair question. I am a consulting detective.
WATSON:	Consulting detective? I've never heard of such a thing.
HOLMES:	It's not likely that you should, given that I'm the only one in the world. You see, I have a turn both for observation and deduction, and I depend upon them for my bread and cheese. People come to me when they're in trouble. I listen to their story, they listen to my comments, and I pocket my fee.
WATSON:	You mean that without leaving this room you can unravel some knot which other men can make nothing of?
HOLMES:	Now and again a case turns up where I have to bustle about and see things with my own eyes. Observation with me is second nature. For instance, you were surprised when I told you, on our first meeting, that you'd come from Afghanistan.
WATSON:	I was.
HOLMES:	The train of reasoning ran this way: "Here is a medical type, but with the air of a military man. Clearly an army doctor. He's just come from the tropics, for his face is dark, but his wrists are fair. His haggard face shows he's undergone hardship and sickness. His left arm has been injured. He holds it in a stiff and unnatural

265

manner. Where in the tropics could an English army doctor have seen much hardship and got his arm wounded? Clearly in Afghanistan." The whole train of thought didn't occupy a second.

WATSON: It sounds simple enough when you explain it. As a matter of fact, I was wounded at the Battle of Maiwand – took a bullet in the shoulder. It shattered the bone and grazed the subclavian artery.

HOLMES: The Battle of Maiwand occurred last July, did it not?

WATSON: Yes. When I was recuperating in the base hospital at Peshawar, I contracted enteric fever.

HOLMES: Ah, the curse of our Indian possessions.

WATSON: For months my life was despaired of, and when at last I came 'round a medical board decided I should be sent back to England. Then I bumped into Stamford at the Criterion Bar, and – well, here we are.

HOLMES: You've had a rough time of it, Watson.

WATSON: Perhaps while I recuperate, I'll have the opportunity of studying your methods.

HOLMES: I very much doubt it, I'm afraid. There are no great crimes and no great criminals these days. No man lives or has ever lived who has brought the same amount of study and natural talent to the detection of crime as I have done.

WATSON: If you do say so yourself.

HOLMES: And what's the result? There's no crime to detect, or, at most, some bungling villainy with a motive so transparent even a Scotland Yarder can see through it.

WATSON: Well, have you ever thought of- I wonder what that fellow's looking for?

HOLMES: What fellow?

WATSON: Down in the street.

266

HOLMES:	Oh, you mean the retired sergeant of Marines. It appears he's coming here.
FX:	DOORBELL RINGS IN BG
WATSON:	Now you know I can't possibly verify that.
HOLMES:	Well, we'll know soon enough. Perhaps the envelope has was carrying was for one of us.
FX:	KNOCK AT THE DOOR
HOLMES:	Come in!
FX:	DOOR OPENS
MESSENGER:	Message for a Mr Sherlock Holmes.
HOLMES:	Thank-you.
FX:	HOLMES OPENS IT
HOLMES:	Listen to this, Watson: "My dear Mr Holmes, There's been a bad business during the night at 3, Lauriston Gardens, off the Brixton Road. Our man on the beat saw a light there about two in the morning, and as the house was an empty one, suspected something was amiss. He found the door open, and in the front room discovered the body of a well-dressed gentleman. There are marks of blood in the room, but there is no wound upon his person. If you can come round to the house any time before twelve, you will find me there. Yours faithfully, Inspector Tobias Gregson". No reply, thank-you.
MESSENGER:	Very good, sir.
WATSON:	Excuse me, my man. May I ask what your trade might be?
MESSENGER:	Commissionaire, sir. Uniform away for repairs.
WATSON:	(GLEEFULLY) *Commissionaire*, Holmes; *not* a Marine Sergeant.

MESSENGER:	It's funny you should say that, sir. I *was* a sergeant - Royal Marine Light Infantry.
WATSON:	I see. Here you are, Sergeant.
MESSENGER:	Oh, thank-you very much, sir. Good day to you.
FX:	HE LEAVES
WATSON:	How in the world did you deduce that?
HOLMES:	Blue anchor tattooed on the back of his hand, military carriage and regulation side-whiskers, air of command - obviously a retired marine sergeant.
WATSON:	Incredible!
HOLMES:	Elementary, my dear, er… my dear fellow.
WATSON:	Do you want me to order you a cab?
HOLMES:	Why?
WATSON:	The telegram – the murder!
HOLMES:	Oh, what does it matter to me? Supposing I unravel the whole matter, you can be sure Inspector Gregson will pocket all the credit.
WATSON:	But he begs you to help him.
HOLMES:	Because he knows I'm his superior, but he'd cut his tongue out before admitting it to any third person.
WATSON:	Holmes, what were you just saying about great crimes? This is the chance you were waiting for.
HOLMES:	I suppose. I might have a laugh at Gregson if I nothing else. Very well, get your hat.
WATSON:	I beg your pardon?

HOLMES:	Well, if you have nothing better to do, you might as well come along.

FIRST COMMERCIAL

FX:	LIGHT STREET BG
GREGSON:	Ah, Mr Holmes! Good of you to come.
HOLMES:	My pleasure, Gregson. This is Dr Watson, my… associate.
WATSON:	Inspector Gregson.
GREGSON:	Gone into partnership, eh? Excellent! Three heads are better than two. I've had everything left untouched.
HOLMES:	Except the path. A herd of buffalo couldn't have caused greater mess.
GREGSON:	I've had so much to do inside the house, Mr Holmes. I relied on Lestrade to look after it.
HOLMES:	With two such men as yourself and Lestrade upon the ground there won't be much us to find out. Did either of you come here in a cab?
GREGSON:	No, Mr Holmes.
HOLMES:	I see. Well, let's go and look at the room.
GREGSON:	This way, gentlemen.
FX:	GREGSON CLOSES THE DOOR. STREET BG OUT. THEY WALK DOWN A PASSAGE.
WATSON:	Holmes? Who's Lestrade?
HOLMES:	(LOW) Inspectors Gregson and Lestrade are the pick of a bad lot, Watson. They have their knives into one another. There'll be some fun if they're both on the scent.
FX:	OUT

269

GREGSON:	Lestrade, Mr Holmes has arrived. And this is his new colleague, Dr Watson.
LESTRADE:	This case will make a stir, gentlemen. It beats anything I've seen, and I'm no chicken.
WATSON:	Are you quite sure there's no wound on the body, Inspector? There's blood all over the place.
LESTRADE:	Positive!
HOLMES:	Fascinating. May we examine the body, Lestrade?
GREGSON:	Go ahead.
WATSON:	Has he been moved at all?
GREGSON:	No more than was necessary for the purpose of our examination.
HOLMES:	Forty-three or forty-four years of age, wouldn't you say, Watson?
WATSON:	About that, yes. See how his lower limbs are interlocked. The death struggle must have been a grievous one. And a horrible contortion of the features... I've seen death in many forms, Holmes, but nothing like this. What killed this man?
HOLMES:	Patent leather boots.
WATSON:	What!
HOLMES:	I was just looking at the man's shoes. I'm so sorry, Watson, what were you saying?
WATSON:	Oh, nothing.
HOLMES:	Gentlemen – there's something under the body. I can just – reach it. There!
WATSON:	It's a woman's wedding ring!
LESTRADE:	There's been a woman here!
HOLMES:	I wonder... Anything in his pockets, Gregson?

GREGSON:	I made a note of it- Oh yes! A gold watch with gold Albert chain, gold ring with masonic device, Russian leather cardcase, with cards of Enoch J Drebber of Cleveland, corresponding with the EJD upon the linen. Loose money to the extent of seven pounds thirteen. And two letters - one addressed to E J Drebber and one to Joseph Stangerson, addressed to the American Exchange - to be left 'til called for.
LESTRADE:	According to the letters, Drebber and his secretary Stangerson are both from the Guion Steamship Company, and they were about to return to New York.
WATSON:	So how did Drebber end up dead in a blood-soaked room?
HOLMES:	Have you made any inquiries to Cleveland?
GREGSON:	We telegraphed this morning, detailing the circumstances, and said we'd be glad of any information which could help us.
HOLMES:	Is that all? Will you not telegraph again?
GREGSON:	I've said all I have to say, Mr Holmes. You know as much as we do now.
LESTRADE:	As a matter of fact, Mr Gregson, while you were waiting for Mr Holmes, I made a discovery of the highest importance. Over here. See, this is the darkest corner of the room, but when that candle on the mantelpiece was lit, it would have been the brightest.
FX:	LESTRADE LIGHTS THE MATCH
LESTRADE:	Now look at that!
WATSON:	Great Scott! "R-A-C-H-E" – written in blood!
GREGSON:	(UNIMPRESSED) All right, what does it mean now that you've found it?
LESTRADE:	It means the writer was going to put the female name Rachel, but was disturbed before he or she had time to finish. You mark my words, when this case is cleared up, you'll find that a woman

271

named Rachel has something to do with it.

GREGSON: This complicates matters. Heaven knows, they were complicated enough before.

HOLMES: You're sure it doesn't simplify them? Come come, Gregson, there's nothing to be learned by staring at the ring!

LESTRADE: It's all very well for you to criticize, Mr Holmes, but the old hound is the best, when all's said and done.

HOLMES: Lestrade, I do beg your pardon. You certainly have the credit of being the first of us to find this and, as you say, it bears every mark of having been written by the other participant in last night's mystery. Gregson, I should like to speak to the constable who found the body.

GREGSON: John Rance. He's off duty now. You'll find him at 46, Audley Court, Kennington Park Gate.

HOLMES: Very well. If you'll let me know how your investigations progress, I'll be happy to give you any little help I can. Good evening to you.

GREGSON: Mr Holmes! No advice?

HOLMES: You're doing so well now it'd be a pity for anyone to interfere. I'll tell you… *one* thing which may help you in the case. (RAPIDLY) There has been murder done, and the murderer was a man. He was more than six feet high, was in the prime of life, had small feet for his height, wore coarse, square-toed boots and smoked a Trichinopoly cigar. He came here with his victim in a four-wheeled cab, which was drawn by a horse with three old shoes and one new one on his off foreleg. In all probability the murderer had a florid face, and the fingernails of his right hand were remarkably long. (A BEAT) These are only a few indications, but they may assist you.

LESTRADE: If this man was murdered, how was it done?

HOLMES: Poison. By the way, Lestrade, don't waste your time looking for Miss Rachel – 'Rache' is the German for 'revenge'. Come along,

Doctor.

MUSIC: HUMOROUS STING

FX: CAB BG

WATSON: You amaze me, Holmes. Surely you're not as sure as you pretend to be of all those particulars you gave.

HOLMES: There's no room for a mistake. They say that genius is an infinite capacity for taking pains. It's a very bad definition, but it does apply to detective work.

WATSON: Well, my head's in a whirl. The more one thinks of it the more mysterious it grows. What were these two men doing in an empty house? What's become of the cabman who drove them? How could one man compel another to take poison? Where did the blood come from?

HOLMES: You sum up the difficulties of the situation very succinctly, Watson.

WATSON: I've barely started, Holmes! What was the object of the murderer, if robbery had no part in it? How came the woman's ring there? Above all, why should the second man write the word "Rache" on the wall? I can't see any possible way of reconciling all these facts.

HOLMES: I'll tell you one more thing, then. The murderer and his victim Drebber came in the same cab, and they walked down the pathway together as friendly as possible - arm-in-arm, in all probability. When they got inside, they walked up and down the room - or rather, Drebber stood still while the murderer walked up and down. And as he walked he grew more and more excited. That's shown by the increased length of his strides. He worked himself up into a fury, then the tragedy occurred. Now I've told you all I know myself. And even though my mind's entirely made up upon the case, we may as well learn all that is to be learned from Constable Rance.

FX: OUT

RANCE:	I'll tell it you from the beginning, gents. About two o'clock, I thought I'd take a look and see that all was right down the Brixton Road, when suddenly the glint of a light caught my eye in the window of Number 3, Lauriston Gardens. Now, I knew that house was empty on account of him that owns them won't have the drains fixed, though the very last tenant died of typhoid fever. All was quiet inside, so I went into the room where the light was a-burnin'. There was a candle flickering on the mantelpiece… and by its light I saw-
HOLMES:	We know what you saw. You walked round the room several times, knelt down by the body, walked through and tried the kitchen door, then-
RANCE:	'Ere, 'ere! Where was you hid to see all that? It seems to me that you knows a deal more than you should!
HOLMES:	Calm yourself, Constable; I am one of the hounds, not the wolf - Inspector Gregson or Lestrade will answer for that. What did you do next?
RANCE:	I walked back to the gate to see if I could see Constable Murcher's lantern, but there wasn't no sign of him.
WATSON:	There was no-one in the street?
RANCE:	As far as anybody that could be of any good goes. I've seen many a drunk chap in my time, but never anyone so crying drunk as that cove. He was at the gate, a-leanin' up ag'in the railings, and a-singin' at the pitch of his lungs. He couldn't stand, far less help.
HOLMES:	What sort of man was he?
RANCE:	He was an uncommon drunk sort of man! He'd've found himself in the station if we hadn't been so took up. Tall chap, florid face.
HOLMES:	What became of him?
RANCE:	We'd enough to do without looking after him. I'll wager he found his way home all right.

FX:	<u>CAB BG</u>
HOLMES:	The blundering fool! Just to think of his having such an incomparable bit of good luck, and not taking advantage of it.
WATSON:	It's true that this drunkard might be the second party in this mystery, but why should he come back to the house?
HOLMES:	The ring, man, the ring! If we have no other way of catching him, we can always bait our line with the ring. I shall have him - I'll lay you two to one that I have him. What's the matter, Watson? You're not looking quite yourself. This Brixton Road affair has upset you.
WATSON:	To tell the truth, Holmes, it has. I ought to be more case-hardened after my Afghan experiences. I saw my own comrades hacked to pieces at Maiwand without losing my nerve.
HOLMES:	But there is a mystery about this which stimulates the imagination; and where there is no imagination there is no horror.
FX:	<u>CAB BG OUT. BACK AT BAKER STREET, WATSON TURNS THE PAGE OF A NEWSPAPER.</u>
WATSON:	(READING) "Found in the Brixton Road this morning: a plain gold wedding ring, in the roadway between the White Hart Tavern and Holland Grove. Apply… *Dr Watson*, 221B Baker Street, between eight and nine."
HOLMES:	I had that advertisement placed in every London paper. Excuse my using your name, old fellow.
WATSON:	That's quite all right. But supposing anyone applies? I have no ring.
HOLMES:	Oh, yes, you have. Here. It's almost a facsimile.
WATSON:	And who do you expect will answer this advertisement?
HOLMES:	Why, the murderer, of course. He'd rather risk anything than lose the ring. I imagine he dropped it while stooping over Drebber's

body.

WATSON: And when he returned to the house, he found the police already
               in possession, and had to pretend to be drunk.

HOLMES: Well done, Watson. On thinking the matter over, it must have
               occurred to him that it was possible that he'd lost the ring in the
               road *after* leaving the house. What would he do?

WATSON: Look out for the evening papers in the hope of seeing it among
               the articles found. His eye, of course, would light upon this.

HOLMES: Why should he fear a trap? There'd be no reason why the finding
               of the ring should be connected with the murder.

FX: A RING OF THE BELL DOWNSTAIRS

WATSON: Holmes, it's eight o'clock *now*.

HOLMES: Have you a weapon?

WATSON: My old service revolver and a few cartridges.

HOLMES: Splendid. It's as well to be ready for anything.

FX: A KNOCK AT THE DOOR

WATSON: (CLEARS HIS THROAT) Come in!

FX: DOOR OPENS

MRS SAWYER: Dr Watson?

WATSON: Yes, my… good woman?

MRS SAWYER: It's your advertisement as has brought me, sir: a gold wedding
               ring in the Brixton Road. It belongs to my girl Sally, as was
               married only this time twelve-month. Her husband is steward
               aboard a Union boat, and what he'd say if he comes 'ome and
               found her without her ring is more than I can think. She lost it on
               her way back from the circus last night.

WATSON:	Is- *this* the ring?
MRS SAWYER:	The Lord be thanked! Sally will be a glad woman this night.
WATSON:	And, er, what may your address be?
MRS SAWYER:	13 Duncan Street, Houndsditch. A weary way from here.
HOLMES:	The Brixton Road does not lie between any circus and Houndsditch.
MRS SAWYER:	The gentleman asked for *my* address, sir. Sally lives in lodgings at 3 Mayfield Place, Peckham.
WATSON:	And your name is?
MRS SAWYER:	My name is Sawyer - hers is Dennis, which Tom Dennis married her - and a smart, clean lad, too, as long as he's at sea, and no steward in the company more thought of; but when on shore, what with the women and the drink…
WATSON:	Quite. Well, here is your ring, madam. It clearly belongs to your daughter, and I'm glad to be able to restore it to the rightful owner.
MRS SAWYER:	Thank-you an 'undred times, sir. Goodnight to you both.
FX:	SHE LEAVES. HOLMES BEGINS TO BUSTLE
HOLMES:	She must be an accomplice – I'll follow her. Wait up for me, Watson!
FX:	HE OPENS THE DOOR & SLAMS IT SHUT
MUSIC:	STING

SECOND COMMERCIAL

WATSON:	You perched on *the back* of her cab?
HOLMES:	It's an art which every detective should be an expert at, Watson. The old crone told the driver to take her to 13 Duncan Street,

Houndsditch. This begins to look genuine, I thought. Well, away we rattled, and never drew rein until we reached the street in question. I hopped off before we came to the door, and strolled down the street. I saw the cab pull up, the driver jump down, open the door and stand expectantly. When I reached him, he was groping about frantically in the empty cab, and giving vent to the finest assorted collection of oaths I ever listened to.

WATSON: You don't mean to say that tottering, feeble old woman was able to jump from the cab while it was in motion?

HOLMES: Old woman be damned! *We* were the old women to be so taken in. It must have been a young man, and an active one, too, besides being an incomparable actor. It shows that the fellow we're after isn't as lonely as I imagined, but has friends who are ready to risk something for him. (CHUCKLES) I wouldn't have the Scotland Yarders know it for the world.

MUSIC: BRIDGE

FX: WATSON TURNS THE PAGE OF HIS NEWSPAPER

WATSON: The *Daily Telegraph* is blaming political refugees for the crime.

HOLMES: Balderdash!

WATSON: Well, the writing on the wall *did* point to a German.

HOLMES: A real German, Watson, invariably prints in the Latin character, so that we may safely say that this was not written by one, but by a clumsy imitator who overdid his part. It was simply a ruse to divert inquiry into a wrong channel by suggesting Socialism and secret societies.

WATSON: "We are glad to learn that Mr Lestrade and Mr Gregson of Scotland Yard are both engaged upon the case, and it is confidently anticipated that these well-known officers will speedily throw light upon the matter."

HOLMES: Ha! Didn't I tell you that whatever happens, Lestrade and Gregson would be certain to score?

WATSON:	Surely that depends on how it turns out.
HOLMES:	Oh, bless you, it doesn't matter in the least. If the man is caught, it will be on account of their exertions; if he escapes, it will be in spite of them.
FX:	THE DOORBELL RINGS IN BG
WATSON:	Anything interesting in that telegram you received?
HOLMES:	Very little, save for the name of the murderer.
WATSON:	Pity. WHAT!?
FX:	A KNOCK AT THE DOOR
HOLMES:	Now we're going to hear some news with a vengeance! (CALLS) Come in, Gregson!
FX:	GREGSON ENTERS
GREGSON:	Congratulate me, gentlemen! I've made the whole thing as clear as day!
WATSON:	You mean you're on the right track, Inspector?
GREGSON:	The right track! Why, we have the man under lock and key, Doctor.
HOLMES:	And his name is?
GREGSON:	Arthur Charpentier, sub-lieutenant in Her Majesty's navy.
HOLMES:	Ah! Take a seat, Gregson, and try one of these cigars. We're anxious to know how you managed it. Will you have some whisky and water?
FX:	HOLMES PREPARES A DRINK
GREGSON:	I don't mind if I do. (SIGHS) The tremendous exertions I've gone through during the last day or two have worn me out. Not so much bodily exertions, you understand, as the strain upon the

mind. You'll appreciate that, Mr Holmes – we're both brainworkers. Thank-you. (DRINKS)

HOLMES: You do me too much honour. Let us hear how you arrived at this most gratifying result.

GREGSON: (CHUCKLING) The fun of it is that Lestrade, who thinks himself so smart, has gone off upon the wrong track altogether. He's after the secretary Stangerson, who had no more to do with the crime than the babe unborn! Now, the first difficulty was the finding of this American's antecedents. You probably won't remember, but there was a hat beside the dead man.

HOLMES: By John Underwood and Sons, 129 Camberwell Road.

GREGSON: Oh. I had no idea that you noticed that. Have you been there?

HOLMES: No.

GREGSON: Ah. You should never neglect a chance, Mr Holmes, no matter how small it may seem.

HOLMES: To a great mind, nothing is small.

GREGSON: Erm, quite. Well, I went to Underwood, and asked him to look over his books. He'd sent the hat to a Mr Drebber, residing at Charpentier's Boarding Establishment, Torquay Terrace. Thus I got his address.

HOLMES: Smart - very smart!

GREGSON: When I called upon Madame Charpentier, I found her very pale and distressed. She was looking red about the eyes and her lips trembled as I spoke to her. That didn't escape my notice. You know the feeling, Mr Holmes, when you come upon the right scent - a kind of thrill in your nerves. Well, I fixed her with my eye in a way I've always found effective with women, and through careful questioning, I was soon able to get at the truth.

WATSON: Which was?

GREGSON: Drebber and Stangerson had been staying at that establishment for nearly three weeks. Stangerson was a quiet, reserved man, but his employer was coarse in his habits and brutish in his ways. The very night of his arrival he became very much the worse for drink, and after twelve o'clock in the day he could hardly ever be said to be sober.

WATSON: Why didn't the landlady give them notice? Surely she could get rid of her boarders when she wished.

GREGSON: They were paying a pound a day each, Doctor, and this is the slack season. The lady is a widow, and her son in the navy has cost her much.

HOLMES: The money must have been a sore temptation.

GREGSON: Exactly. But eventually, she did give Drebber notice to leave. You see, his manners towards the maidservants were disgustingly free and familiar, and he speedily assumed the same attitude towards Madame Charpentier's daughter, Alice. On one occasion he actually seized her in his arms and embraced her - an outrage which caused his own secretary to reproach him for his unmanly conduct.

HOLMES: And at what o'clock did they leave the boarding house?

GREGSON: Eight. Madame Charpentier heard Stangerson say there were two trains - one at 9:15 and one at 11, and they planned to catch the first. But they evidently missed it, because Drebber returned to the house less than an hour later, and very much the worse for drink. He then proceeded to propose that Alice Charpentier should fly with him.

WATSON: Good gracious!

GREGSON: He said...* let me see... oh, yes! "You are of age and there is no law to stop you. I have money enough and to spare. Never mind the old girl, but come along with me straight away. You shall live like a princess." Well, the girl was so frightened that she shrunk away from him, but he caught her by the wrist and endeavoured to draw her towards the door. At which point, Madame Charpentier's son Arthur came into the room. He's on leave at present, did I forget to mention that?

FX:	*FLIPS THROUGH NOTEBOOK
HOLMES:	You did, Inspector, but I gathered it all the same.
GREGSON:	Well, there's a scuffle, then Drebber's out of the house with young Arthur in pursuit… carrying an oak cudgel in his hand. Madame Charpentier can't say what time her son returned home – he has his own latchkey, but he hadn't returned when she went to bed at eleven. I traced the Lieutenant to a nearby alehouse. When I touched him on the shoulder and warned him to come quietly, he answered us as bold as brass… hang on…* "I suppose you're arresting me for the death of that scoundrel Drebber". I'd said nothing about it, so that his alluding to it had a most suspicious aspect.
FX:	*TURNS ANOTHER PAGE IN NOTEBOOK
HOLMES:	So what is your theory, Gregson?
GREGSON:	In my opinion, he followed Drebber as far as the Brixton Road. When there, a fresh altercation arose between them, in the course of which Drebber received a blow from the stick, in the pit of the stomach perhaps, which killed him without leaving any mark. The night was so wet that no one was about, so Charpentier dragged the body of his victim into the empty house. As to the candle, and the blood, and the writing on the wall, and the ring, they may all be so many tricks to throw the police on to the wrong scent.
WATSON:	But Inspector, what abou-
HOLMES:	Well done! Really, Gregson, you're coming along. We shall make something of you yet.
GREGSON:	I flatter myself that I managed it rather neatly.* Charpentier claims he chased Drebber, but the American jumped into a cab in order to get away from him. On his way home he met an old shipmate, and took a long walk with him. On being asked where this shipmate lived, he was unable to give any satisfactory reply. The whole case fits together uncommonly well. What amuses me is to think of Lestrade, he's on completely the wrong scent.
FX:	*DOORBELL RINGS IN BG. AT THE END OF GREGSON'S

HOLMES:	Good morning, Lestrade!
GREGSON:	Lestrade!
LESTRADE:	This is a most extraordinary case, Mr Holmes. A most incomprehensible affair.
GREGSON:	Ah, you find it so, do you? I thought it might prove too much for you.
WATSON:	Inspector, have you managed to find the secretary, Stangerson?
LESTRADE:	Mr Joseph Stangerson was murdered at Halliday's Private Hotel about six o'clock this morning.
HOLMES:	The plot thickens.
LESTRADE:	It was already thick enough for my liking.
GREGSON:	Lestrade, are you sure of this piece of intelligence?
LESTRADE:	I've just come from the room. I was the first to discover the body.
HOLMES:	Poisoned, no doubt.
LESTRADE:	Stabbed, Mr Holmes. A milk boy on his way to the dairy saw the murderer. As he walked down the lane at the back of the hotel, he saw a man descend from a ladder propped against one of the windows of the second floor. He came down so openly the boy imagined him to be some carpenter or joiner at work in the hotel.
HOLMES:	A description, Lestrade!
LESTRADE:	He was a tall man with a reddish face, and he was dressed in a long, brownish coat.
WATSON:	Holmes! The man with the florid face again!
LESTRADE:	He must have stayed in the room some little time after the murder - I found bloodstained water in the basin, where he

washed his hands.

HOLMES: Did you find nothing in the room which could furnish a clue to the murderer?

LESTRADE: A purse with eighty-odd pounds in it. Whatever the motives of these extraordinary crimes, it isn't robbery. A telegram, dated from Cleveland a month ago, and containing the words, "JH is in Europe"… and a small chip ointment box containing a couple of pills.

HOLMES: (A TRIUMPHANT SIGH) The last link! My case is complete! Lestrade, could you lay your hand upon those pills?

LESTRADE: I've got them here. I was taking them to the station. But I'm bound to say that I don't attach any importance to them.

HOLMES: Thank-you. I have now in my hands all the threads which have formed such a tangle. There are, of course, details to be filled in, but I'm as certain of all the main facts, from the time Drebber parted from Stangerson at the station, up to the discovery of the body of the latter, as if I'd seen them with my own eyes. Dr Watson, are these ordinary pills?

WATSON: Let me see. No, certainly not. From their lightness and transparency, I should imagine they're soluble in water.

HOLMES: Precisely so. Now, gentlemen, if you'll give me an hour of your time, I expect to be able to tell you the precise nature of these pills.

MUSIC: BRIDGE

FX: HOLMES IS TINKERING WITH HIS CHEMISTRY SET. PERHAPS SOMETHING IS BUBBLING

LESTRADE: (MUTTERS) How much longer..?

GREGSON: Well, Mr Holmes?

HOLMES: Fascinating! Of the two pills in that box, one is a quick-acting poison, and the other entirely harmless. Of course, I ought to have known that before ever I saw the box at all.

GREGSON: Now look here, Mr Holmes, we're all ready to acknowledge that you're a smart man, but we want something more than mere theory and preaching now. It's a case of taking the murderer. You've thrown out hints here, and hints there, but the time has come when we have a right to ask you straight: Can you name the man who did it?

HOLMES: I can.

LESTRADE &
GREGSON: (BEGIN TO PROTEST)

HOLMES: The mere knowing of his name is a small thing, however, compared with the power of laying our hands upon him. If he had the slightest suspicion, he'd change his name, and vanish in an instant among the four million inhabitants of this great city. Without meaning to hurt either of your feelings, I'm bound to say that I consider this man to be more than a match for the official force.

WATSON: I have to agree with Inspector Gregson, Holmes - any delay in arresting the assassin might give him time to perpetrate some fresh atrocity.

HOLMES: There will be no more murders.

FX: YET AGAIN, THE FRONT DOOR BELL IN BG

GREGSON: You expecting another visitor, Mr Holmes?

WATSON: Perhaps it's someone to see the landlady, Mrs Turner.

HOLMES: Mrs *Hudson*, Watson. I say, Lestrade, why don't you introduce this pattern of handcuffs at Scotland Yard? See how beautifully the spring works.

FX: HOLMES HOLDS UP A PAIR OF HANDCUFFS

LESTRADE: The old pattern's good enough, if we can only find the man to put 'em on!

FX:	A KNOCK AT THE DOOR
HOLMES:	Come!
FX:	DOOR OPENS
HOPE:	(POOR COCKNEY ACCENT) Someone ordered a cab?
HOLMES:	Over here, my man. Just give me a hand with these boxes. Give the fellow some room, Doctor.
HOPE:	Sure. Is it the buckle?
FX:	THE HANDCUFFS SNAP SHUT
HOPE:	(REAL ACCENT) What the hell-?
HOLMES:	Gentlemen! Allow me introduce you to Mr Jefferson Hope, the murderer of Enoch Drebber and Joseph Stangerson!
MUSIC:	STING

THIRD COMMERCIAL

FX:	HOLMES, WATSON & GREGSON WALK DOWN AN ECHOEY CORRIDOR
GREGSON:	You'll appreciate this is against strict regulations, gentlemen, but you've provided so much assistance, Mr Holmes, I thought it only right that you should be here for the questioning.
HOLMES:	Most kind, Gregson.
WATSON:	Will Inspector Lestrade be joining us?
GREGSON:	He's got his work cut out for him, trying to find a new home for the murderer's horse. A cabman! Who'd've believed it?
FX:	THEY STOP. GREGSON UNLOCKS A CELL DOOR. THEY ENTER, AND CLOSE IT BEHIND THEM
HOPE:	Oh, it's you.

GREGSON: Jefferson Hope, you're to be put before the magistrates in the course of the week. In the meantime, have you anything you wish to say? I must warn you that your words will be taken down, and may be used against you.

HOPE: I've got a good deal to say.

GREGSON: Think about saving some of it for your trial.

HOPE: I may never *be* tried. Nah, it's not suicide I'm thinking of. You – you're a doctor, right?

WATSON: That's correct.

HOPE: Then put your hand here, on my chest. Feel that?

WATSON: Good Lord! You have an aortic aneurism!

HOPE: That's what they call it. I got it from over-exposure and under-feeding among the Salt Lake Mountains. I went to a doctor last week, and he told me it's bound to burst before many days pass. But I've done my work now, and I don't care how soon I go, but I'd like to leave some account of the business behind me. I don't want to be remembered as a common cutthroat. I'm on the brink of the grave, and I'm not likely to lie to you.

GREGSON: Do you consider, Doctor, that there is an immediate danger?

WATSON: Most certainly there is.

GREGSON: In that case, Mr Hope, it is clearly my duty, in the interests of justice, to take your statement.

HOPE: Every word I'm about to say is the absolute truth, and how you use it is of no consequence to me. It don't much matter to you why I hated these men; it's enough that they were guilty of the death of another human being - a girl named Lucy Ferrier. After the lapse of time that's passed since their crime, it was impossible for me to secure a conviction against them in any court. But I knew of their guilt, and I determined that I should be judge, jury, and executioner all rolled into one. You'd have done the same, if you have any manhood in you, if you had been in

287

my place.

GREGSON: That's a very bold assumption, Hope.

HOPE: That girl I spoke of was to have married me twenty years ago. She was forced into marrying Drebber, and broke her heart over it. I took the marriage ring from her dead finger, and I vowed that his dying eyes should rest upon that very ring, and that his last thoughts should be of the crime for which he was being punished. I carried it about with me, and I followed him and his accomplice over two continents until I caught them.

HOLMES: The accomplice was Stangerson, the secretary.

HOPE: That's right. Well, they were rich and I was poor, so it was no easy matter for me to follow them. When I got to London my pocket was about empty, and I found I had to turn my hand to something for my living. Driving and riding are as natural to me as walking, so I applied at a cab owner's office, and soon got employment. It was some time before I found out where my two gentlemen were living, but once I found them I knew I had them at my mercy. Go where they would about London, I was always at their heels. They were very cunning, though, for they'd never go out alone, and never after nightfall. They must have thought that there was some chance of their being followed.

WATSON: The telegram – "JH is in Europe".

HOPE: For two weeks I drove behind them every day, and never once saw them separate. Drebber was drunk half the time, but Stangerson wouldn't be caught napping. At last, one evening I was driving up and down Torquay Terrace, when I saw a cab drive up to their boarding house. Presently some luggage was brought out, and after a time Drebber and Stangerson followed it, and drove off. I whipped up my horse and kept within sight of them. At Euston Station they got out, and I left a boy to hold my horse, and followed them on to the platform. I heard them ask for the Liverpool train, and the guard said one had just gone and there wouldn't be another for some hours.

GREGSON: You see, I was right – they *did* miss their train!
HOLMES: Congratulations, Gregson. Do go on, Mr Hope.

HOPE:	Drebber said he had a little business of his own, and they arranged to meet at Halliday's Private Hotel. The moment for which I'd waited so long had come at last. Together they could protect each other, but singly they were at my mercy. Drebber went into a liquor shop, and when he came out, he was pretty drunk. There was a hansom just in front of me, and he hailed it. I followed it so close the nose of my horse was within a yard of his driver all the way.
HOLMES:	All the way *back* to Torquay Terrace.
HOPE:	That's right! He entered the boarding house, and his hansom drove away. I waited for a quarter of an hour, when suddenly there came a noise like people struggling inside the house. Next moment the door was flung open and Drebber ran out, chased by a young fellow I'd never seen before.
FX:	LIGHT STREET BG. DREBBER APPROACHES AT A RUN.
DREBBER:	(AS HE RUNS) Driver! You there! Take me to Halliday's Private Hotel – and don't stop!
FX:	HE SLAMS THE CAB DOOR SHUT – THE HORSE SETS OFF. STREET BG OUT.
HOPE:	When I had him fairly inside my cab, my heart jumped so with joy that I feared my aneurism might go wrong. I drove along slowly, weighing in my own mind what it was best to do. It chanced that some days before a gentleman who had been engaged in looking over some houses in the Brixton Road had dropped the key of one of them in my carriage.
HOLMES:	So you had access to at least one spot in London where you could be free from interruption.
HOPE:	It was nearer one than twelve, and a wild, bleak night, blowing hard and raining in torrents. Dismal as it was outside, I was glad within - so glad that I could have shouted out from pure exultation. If any of you gentlemen have ever pined for a thing, and longed for it during twenty long years, and then suddenly found it within your reach, you'd understand my feelings. I lit a cigar, and puffed at it to steady my nerves, but my hands were

trembling, and my temples throbbing with excitement. As I drove, I could see sweet Lucy looking at me out of the darkness and smiling at me, just as plain as I see you all in this room.

FX:	<u>DRIVING RAIN - A DOG YELPS IN BG. HOPE OPENS CAB DOOR.</u>
DREBBER:	(SNORES)
HOPE:	(BAD COCKNEY) Wake up, Guv'nor. Wake up.
DREBBER:	(WAKENS, STILL DRUNK) Are we there?
HOPE:	Halliday's Private Hotel, sir. Just like you asked. Here, let me give you a hand. (HE GRUNTS AS HE LIFTS DREBBER UP)
FX:	<u>RAIN OUT. INSIDE THE HOUSE, DREBBER AND HOPE WALK UNCERTAINLY. ECHO ON FX AND VOICES.</u>
HOPE:	Here we are, Mr Drebber.
DREBBER:	It's infernally dark!
HOPE:	We'll soon have a light.
FX:	<u>HE STRIKES A MATCH</u>
DREBBER:	How- how did you know my name? Did I tell you my name?
HOPE:	(REAL ACCENT) Now, Enoch Drebber - who am I?
DREBBER:	N-no! No! (BABBLES IN TERROR)
HOPE:	I've hunted you from Salt Lake City to St Petersburg, and you've always escaped me! Now, at last your wanderings have come to an end! What do you think of Lucy Ferrier now? Punishment has been slow in coming, but it's overtaken you at last.
DREBBER:	I didn't kill her! I didn't kill her!
HOPE:	You broke her innocent heart! From that day on, she was as good as dead!

DREBBER:	Would you… *murder* me?
HOPE:	There'll be no murder. Let the high God judge between us. There are two pills in this box.
FX:	HE OPENS THE PILLBOX
HOPE:	Choose and eat. There's death in one and life in the other.
DREBBER: HOPE:	You're mad! I said eat!
DREBBER:	(STRUGGLES, BUT IS FORCED TO SWALLOW)
HOPE:	Now I'll take the other. (HE SWALLOWS) Let's see if there's justice upon the earth, or if we're ruled by chance.
(PAUSE)	
DREBBER:	(BEGINS TO LAUGH) Nothing's happening! It's you! You've got it! (HIS LAUGH GROWS LOUDER AND MORE HYSTERICAL – FINALLY, IT IS A LAUGH OF SHEER TERROR, WHICH HALTS ABRUPTLY)
FX:	DREBBER FALLS TO THE GROUND, DEAD
GREGSON:	Good Lord.
HOPE:	The pulses in my temples beat like sledgehammers, and I believe I would have had a fit of some sort if the blood hadn't gushed from my nose. I don't know what put it into my head to write "Rache" on the wall with it - maybe some mischievous idea of setting the police on the wrong track. The night was still pretty wild when I walked back to my cab - nobody was about.
HOLMES:	At what point did you realise you'd lost your fiancée's ring?
HOPE:	When I put my hand into the pocket in which I usually kept it. It was the only memento that I had of my Lucy. So I drove back. I was ready to dare anything rather than lose the ring. I left my cab in a side street, but when I arrived at the house, I walked right into the arms of a police officer.

WATSON:	Constable Rance. But you managed to disarm his suspicions by pretending to be hopelessly drunk.
GREGSON:	I shall have a word with Constable Rance!
HOLMES:	So much for Enoch Drebber. But Stangerson was a different matter. When you confronted him in his hotel room, he refused to take the pill you offered him.
HOPE:	He flew at my throat. In self-defence I stabbed him to the heart. It would have been the same in any case, for Providence would never have allowed his guilty hand to pick out anything but the poison. You may consider me to be a murderer; but I hold that I'm just as much an officer of justice as you are.
GREGSON:	Hmph!
HOPE:	Well, I went on cabbing it for a day or so, until I could save enough to take me back to America. I was standing in the yard when a ragged youngster appeared, said my cab was wanted, and led me to this address.
HOLMES:	That would be Wiggins, one of my Baker Street Irregulars – I gave him your description. There's more work to be got out of one of those little beggars than out of a dozen of the official force. No offence, Gregson.
HOPE:	Next thing I knew, this gentleman had the bracelets on my wrists. That's the whole of my story, and it's as well, for I'm about done up.
HOLMES:	One question more, please, Mr Hope: Who was your accomplice who came for the ring which I advertised?
HOPE:	Well now, sir, I can tell my own secrets but I don't get other folk into trouble. I saw your advertisement, thought it might be a plant. My friend volunteered to go and see. I think you'll own he did it smartly.
WATSON:	Not a doubt of that.
HOPE:	Don't take it too much to heart, Mr Holmes. The way you kept on

	my trail was a caution. If there's a vacant place for a chief of the police, I reckon you're the man for it.
GREGSON:	Steady on, Mr Hope.
<u>MUSIC:</u>	<u>BRIDGE</u>
WATSON:	(READING) "The public have lost a sensational treat through the sudden death of Jefferson Hope, who was suspected of the murder of Mr Enoch Drebber and Mr Joseph Stangerson. The details of the case will probably be never known now, though we are informed that the crime was the result of an old standing romantic feud. It is an open secret that the credit of this smart capture belongs entirely to the well-known Scotland Yard officials, Messrs Lestrade and Gregson!"
<u>FX:</u>	<u>HE PUTS DOWN THE NEWSPAPER</u>
HOLMES:	Didn't I tell you so, Watson? It's heads I win and tails you lose. Never mind. I wouldn't have missed this investigation for anything. Simple as it was, there were several most instructive points about it.
WATSON:	Simple!
HOLMES:	Well, really, it can hardly be described as otherwise.
WATSON:	It may seem simple to *you*, Holmes, but I'm as much in the dark as before! Within minutes of entering that house on Lauriston Gardens, you were able to describe Hope's age, his height, his florid face – even his preferred brand of cigar and the fact that he had long fingernails. Now how did you deduce all that?
HOLMES:	I'm not sure I should tell you. A conjurer gets no credit once he's explained his trick and if I show you too much of my method of working, you'll come to the conclusion that I'm a very ordinary individual after all.
WATSON:	I'll never do that! You've brought detection as near an exact science as it'll ever be brought in this world.
HOLMES:	Thank-you, old chap. Very well – the footprints on the path told

me that the nocturnal visitors were two in number, one wearing square-toed boots and the other, to judge from the small and elegant impression, fashionably dressed. On entering the house, my well-booted man lay before me. Square-toes, then, had done the murder. Having sniffed the dead man's lips I detected a slightly sour smell, and came to the conclusion that he'd had poison forced upon him. Now, the height of a man, in nine cases out of ten, can be told from the length of his stride. I had this fellow's stride on the clay outside the house and the dust within. Then I had a way of checking my calculation. When a man writes on a wall, his instinct leads him to write above the level of his own eyes. That writing was just over six feet from the ground. The plaster was slightly scratched, which wouldn't have been the case if his nails had been trimmed.

WATSON: And his age? The prime of life, you said.

HOLMES: There was a puddle measuring four and a half feet on the garden walk, which Square-toes had hopped over. If a man can stride such a distance without the smallest effort, he can't be in his declining years. As for the cigar, I gathered up some dark and flaky ash from the floor. I flatter myself that I can distinguish at a glance the ash of any known brand either of cigar or tobacco.

WATSON: Astonishing! What about the florid face?

HOLMES: Since there were no signs of a struggle, the blood which covered the floor must have burst from the murderer's nose in his excitement. The track of blood coincided with the track of his feet. What was the motive, if not robbery? The discovery of the ring settled that question. Clearly the murderer had used it to remind his victim of some dead or absent woman.

WATSON: So you telegraphed to Cleveland.

HOLMES: To the head of the police, limiting my enquiry to the circumstances connected with the marriage of Enoch Drebber. The reply said that Drebber had applied for the protection of the law against an old rival in love, named Jefferson Hope. I now knew the name of the murderer; all that remained was to lay my hands on him.

WATSON:	No small task! How long was it before you realised Hope was working as a cabdriver?
HOLMES:	Oh, I knew that before I knew anything else.
WATSON:	Impossible!
HOLMES:	By no means. The very first thing I observed on arriving at Lauriston Gardens was that a cab had made two ruts with its wheels close to the curb. We'd had no rain for a week until the night of the murder, so the cab must have been there *after* the rain began, and since it wasn't there at any time during the morning it follows that it must have brought those two individuals to the house.
WATSON:	But Hope might have been another passenger.
HOLMES:	(SIGHS) The marks in the road showed that the horse had wandered on in a way which would have been impossible had there been anyone in charge of it. Where could the driver be, except inside the house? It's absurd to suppose that any sane man would carry out a deliberate crime under the very eyes of a third person, who was sure to betray him. And supposing one man wished to dog another through London, what better means could he adopt than to turn cabdriver?
FX:	WATSON APPLAUDS
WATSON:	(LAUGHING) Wonderful, Holmes! Your merits should be publicly recognized. You should publish an account of the case. And if you won't, I will!
HOLMES:	Do as you wish, old fellow. But I warn you now – I can't imagine that the public would be particularly interested in the adventures of Sherlock Holmes and Dr Watson.
FX:	A FEW PRACTICE SCRAPES ON HIS VIOLIN
HOLMES:	And I have you to thank for it all. I might not have gone but for you, and so have missed the finest study I ever came across: a study in scarlet.

MUSIC:	HE BEGINS TO PLAY
HOLMES:	There's the scarlet thread of murder running through the colourless skein of life, and our duty is to unravel it, and isolate it, and expose every inch of it.
WATSON:	(TO SELF) A study in scarlet? Not a bad title…
MUSIC:	CHANGES TO *DANSE MACABRE*

The Classic Adventures of Sherlock Holmes –
The Return of Sherlock Holmes
(Original Airdate March 29, 2009)

I wish I could recall precisely when it occurred to me that these two pivotal stories should be melded together in this fashion; I simply remember Lawrence Albert's excitement when, during a Transatlantic telephone conversation, I explained that the episode should begin with the murder of Ronald Adair from *The Empty House*, then flash back to the events of *The Final Problem* (as related by Watson to Inspector Lestrade) and the apparent death of Sherlock Holmes, before returning to the resurrection story. I suspect my motivation was the belief that most people were familiar with the Reichenbach drama, and those that weren't knew too well the conventions of so many dramas where the hero supposedly dies, only to reappear in the final act. This approach creates its own problems, however, since Watson's flashback contains *another* flashback, Holmes' recollection of his first meeting with Moriarty. Conan Doyle was adept at doing this, of course, with *The Musgrave Ritual* containing perhaps the most masterly example. Here, it was a question of adding an effect to the voices in the confrontation scene to suggest to the listener that we are delving even further back in time. This, I hasten to add, was the producer's idea, not mine, and it serves the episode perfectly. As I said, every new script is a learning experience, and this was something else to add to my memory banks for later use, should the need ever arise.

Note that the Holmes-Moriarty scene contains a direct reference to the events of *The Valley of Fear*, which the original did not and could not, since Conan Doyle hadn't thought of that story yet. I wonder whether the Douglas case represents the time when Holmes crossed the Professor's path, the time Holmes incommoded him, the time Holmes seriously inconvenienced him, or the time Moriarty found himself absolutely hampered in his plans by Holmes. Perhaps it doesn't relate to any of them.

It had never occurred to me that this episode should be called anything other than *The Final Problem and The Empty House*, until it was pointed out to me that this was an unnecessarily cumbersome title, and ought to be changed. I chose *The Return of Sherlock Holmes* – the collection in which the second story appears – because I doubted anyone would be at all surprised when the elderly bookseller removes his disguise revealing that he was, in fact, our hero all along. Long after the episode aired, I was looking at illustrator Sidney Paget's depiction of the struggle between Holmes and Moriarty, and noted that it was entitled *The Death of Sherlock Holmes*. To this day, I wonder if, despite the fact that it is factually inaccurate, it wouldn't have served the episode better. Well, live and learn.

The original draft of Act Two began with Lestrade reading the "it is with a heavy heart..." speech aloud from an old copy of *The Strand*, but Watson actor Lawrence Albert requested that he deliver these famous lines – and who can blame him?

There's a mention of the Meerschaum, the pipe with which Sherlock Holmes is most frequently associated, despite the fact that he never smokes one in the Canon. In fact, the Meerschaum was used by American stage actor William Gillette, who found it easier to deliver his lines though a curly-stemmed pipe. As a sly joke, I suggested that Watson had bought one for Holmes, but didn't get the chance to give it to him before his "death". Despite this, I've never made mention of him using it in any post-*Empty House* episodes. I rely upon you, the listener, to imagine that Holmes always has it to hand from now on.

CAST:

ANNOUNCER (DENNIS BATEMAN)

HOLMES (JOHN PATRICK LOWRIE)

WATSON (LAWRENCE ALBERT)

LESTRADE (RICK MAY)

MORIARTY (RICHARD ZIMAN)

PETER STEILER (DENNIS BATEMAN)

BOY (DENNIS BATEMAN)

COLONEL SEBASTIAN MORAN (STEVE MANNING)

DIRECTED BY JOHN PATRICK LOWRIE

MUSIC:	SAD UNDERCURRENT
WATSON:	It was in the spring of the year 1894 that all London was interested, and the fashionable world dismayed, by the murder of the Honourable Ronald Adair under most unusual circumstances. Surely, this inexplicable affair demanded the attentions of the first criminal agent in Europe, whose intellect which would have been fascinated by the strangeness of the murder. But that mind could never solve this or any other crime... for Sherlock Holmes was dead.
MUSIC:	CHANGES TO *DANSE MACABRE*, UP AND UNDER
ANNOUNCER:	*The Classic Adventures of Sherlock Holmes* by Sir Arthur Conan Doyle, featuring John Patrick Lowrie as Holmes and Lawrence Albert as Dr Watson. Tonight: *The Return of Sherlock Holmes.*
MUSIC:	OUT
FX:	BUSY LONDON STREET
BG:	LOTS OF CHATTER FROM ONLOOKERS
WATSON:	(NARRATING) It can be imagined that my close friendship with Sherlock Holmes had interested me deeply in crime, and that after his death I never failed to read with care the various problems which came before the public. I even attempted more than once for my own private satisfaction to employ his methods in their solution, though with indifferent success. There was none, however, which appealed to me like the tragedy of Ronald Adair.
LESTRADE:	(APPROACHING) Dr Watson! Doctor!
WATSON:	Inspector Lestrade! It's been years!
LESTRADE:	Too many, Doctor. How've you been?
WATSON:	Oh... well... you know.
LESTRADE:	I heard about your wife, Doctor. I'm sorry.

WATSON:	Thank-you, Lestrade. I appreciate it.
LESTRADE:	What are you doing on Park Lane? Do your medical rounds usually take you this far afield?
WATSON:	Well, I always take a special interest in London's more sensational crimes – old times, you know.
LESTRADE:	His death is a loss to the community, Doctor. This one would have appealed to him. I was just on my way back to the Yard, as a matter of fact. And you?
WATSON:	(BLEAKLY) Home.
LESTRADE:	Well, I'm sure it won't matter if I go a little out of my way – Adair won't be any less dead. That's to say... if you're in the mood for company?
WATSON:	That would be splendid, Lestrade, splendid.
LESTRADE:	Excellent! Come along, then.
WATSON:	Oof!
FX:	A COLLISION OF TWO BODIES. A PILE OF BOOKS FALLS TO THE GROUND
HOLMES:	(AS THE ELDERLY BOOKSELLER) Watch where you're going!
WATSON:	I- I'm most terribly sorry.
HOLMES:	You clumsy oaf! These are first editions.
WATSON:	I *did* say I was sorry. Here, let me help you.
FX:	WATSON AND "THE BOOKSELLER" PICK UP A FEW BOOKS
HOLMES:	I can do it, I can do it!
LESTRADE:	Just leave him to it, Dr Watson. (CALLS OUT) Cab!

301

BG:	OUT

FX:	FADE THRU TO INTERIOR OF MOVING CAB

LESTRADE: So, how much do you know about the case?

WATSON: Only what I read in the *Times*. They're calling it "The Park Lane Mystery". The Honourable Ronald Adair is – or should I say *was* - second son of the Earl of Maynooth, Governor of one of the Australian Colonies. Why the rest of the family returned to England, I don't know.

LESTRADE: Adair's mother had to undergo an operation for cataracts. She, her son, and her daughter Hilda were living together at number 427, Park Lane.

WATSON: Ronald moved in the best society, and, so far as is known, had no enemies, and no particular vices. Correct?

LESTRADE: Quite correct. He'd been engaged to Miss Edith Woodley, of Carstairs, but the engagement had been broken off by mutual consent some months before.

WATSON: Ah! Any resentment?

LESTRADE: No sign of it, no. And the rest the of the fellow's life moved in a narrow and conventional circle, his habits were quiet, his nature unemotional.

WATSON: And yet someone murdered him.

LESTRADE: Between the hours of ten and eleven-twenty on the night of March 30th – and in a most strange and unexpected form.

WATSON: Your audience is transfixed, Inspector. Please continue.

LESTRADE: After dinner on the day of his death, Adair played cards at the Bagatelle Club, along with a Mr Murray, Sir John Hardy, and Colonel Sebastian Moran.

WATSON: And did Adair lose heavily?

LESTRADE:	No more than five pounds.
WATSON:	And his fortune was a considerable one, so such a loss couldn't affect him in any way.
LESTRADE:	My enquiries show that he was a cautious player, and usually ended up a winner. In partnership with Colonel Moran, he won four hundred and twenty pounds in a sitting some weeks before from Godfrey Milner and Lord Balmoral.
WATSON:	Lord Balmoral, eh? He's the father of Lord Robert St Simon – you remember the case of the Noble Bachelor?
LESTRADE:	It all keeps coming back to Mr Holmes, eh? Anyway, on the evening of the crime, Adair returned from the club exactly at ten. His mother and sister were out spending the evening with a relation. The servant says she heard him enter the front room on the second floor. She'd lit a fire there, and opened the window to let out the smoke. At eleven-twenty, Lady Maynooth and her daughter returned home. They wanted to say good-night to Ronald, but the door was locked on the inside, and he didn't answer their knocking. Help was obtained and the door was forced. The unfortunate young man was found lying near the table, dead.
WATSON:	He was attacked?
FX:	LESTRADE FISHES FOR SOMETHING IN AN ENVELOPE
LESTRADE:	Not attacked, no. I've got something in this envelope... the coroner removed it from the body. Recognise it?
WATSON:	Indeed I do, Lestrade – it's an expanding revolver bullet. It's mushroomed out... the wound it inflicted must have caused instantaneous death.
LESTRADE:	His head *was* horribly mutilated.
WATSON:	Great Scott.
LESTRADE:	On the table lay- uh, let me see...
FX:	LESTRADE CHECKS HIS NOTEBOOK

LESTRADE:	Oh yes, two bank-notes for ten pounds each and seventeen pounds ten in silver and gold, arranged in little piles of varying amount. There were also some figures on a sheet of paper with the names of some club friends opposite them.
WATSON:	Perhaps he was endeavouring to make out his losses or winnings at cards before his death. Settling accounts. Might his death have been suicide?
LESTRADE:	No weapon of any sort was found in the room, Doctor. No-one heard the sound of a shot, and I can't find any reason *why* Adair should have fastened the door on the inside.
WATSON:	If it *was* murder, perhaps the murderer locked the door, and escaped by the open window.
LESTRADE:	Sorry, Mr Ho- I mean, *Dr Watson*... The drop's at least twenty feet, and there's a bed of crocuses in full bloom beneath. No sign of disturbance in the flowers or the earth, no marks on the narrow strip of grass which separates the house from the road. And no man could have climbed up to the window without leaving traces.
WATSON:	And nor could anyone inflict so deadly a wound with a revolver from *outside* the house.
LESTRADE:	And yet we have a dead man - *and* this revolver bullet. And things are even more complicated, since young Adair wasn't known to have any enemy.
WATSON:	Clearly you can rule out robbery, since the murderer made no attempt to remove the money in the room.
LESTRADE:	What would our old friend have done, I wonder?
FX:	THE CAB COMES TO A STOP. STREET BG HEARD CLEARLY.
WATSON:	Well, here we are. This is my surgery... my home.
LESTRADE:	Anyone waiting for you, Doctor?

WATSON:	No-one.
LESTRADE:	Well, perhaps I could just step inside for a moment? Take a spot of tea, perhaps?
WATSON:	Of course. Forgive me, Inspector. Where are my manners?
FX:	STREET BG OUT. IN WATSON'S HOME, LESTRADE PICKS UP AN ITEM AND REPLACES IT.
LESTRADE:	These pipes, Doctor? They were all his?
WATSON:	All except the Meerschaum. I was going to give it to him as a gift, but...
LESTRADE:	How long has it been now?
WATSON:	Almost three years ago. He was sitting just where you're sitting, when it began. Forgive me, Lestrade, you must have heard all this before.
LESTRADE:	Actually, Doctor, I never knew all the details. The Moriarty business was Inspector Patterson's case.
WATSON:	(UNSETTLED) Moriarty...
FX:	ECHO ON HOLMES' DIALOGUE
HOLMES:	He is the Napoleon of crime, Watson. He is the organizer of half that is evil and of nearly all that is undetected in this great city.
FX:	ECHO OUT
LESTRADE:	Doctor?
WATSON:	Hm? Oh, so sorry, Inspector, I was just- Yes, it was during the early spring of '91... I saw in the papers that Holmes had been engaged by the French government on a matter of supreme importance. I gathered from his letters that his stay in France was likely to be a long one, so, you can imagine my surprise when I saw him walk into my consulting-room upon the evening of April 24th. It struck me that he was looking even paler and

thinner than usual.

HOLMES:	I must apologize for calling so late, Doctor. And I must further beg you to be so unconventional as to allow me to leave your house presently by scrambling over your back garden wall.
WATSON:	Holmes, you look dreadful!
HOLMES:	Yes, I've been using myself up rather too freely of late. Forgive me, Watson, Have you any objection to my closing your shutters?
WATSON:	The shutters?
FX:	HOLMES CLOSES AND BOLTS THE SHUTTERS
WATSON:	You're afraid of something?
HOLMES:	Air-guns.
WATSON:	Air-guns?
HOLMES:	One particular, air-gun, in fact, of a unique design, constructed by Von Herder of Germany.
WATSON:	Holmes, what on earth is going on?
HOLMES:	I assure you, Watson, my plight is quite genuine. I think you know me well enough, to understand I'm by no means a nervous man. At the same time, it is stupidity rather than courage to refuse to recognize danger when it's close upon you. Might I trouble you for a match?
FX:	HOLMES STRIKES A MATCH
HOLMES:	Is *Mrs* Watson in?
WATSON:	She's away on a visit.
HOLMES:	(EXHALES SMOKE) Indeed! Then it makes it the easier for me to propose that you should come away with me for a week to the Continent.

WATSON:	Where?
HOLMES:	Oh, anywhere. It's all the same to me.
WATSON:	Holmes, this isn't like you. What's it all about?
HOLMES:	Have you ever heard of Professor James Moriarty?
WATSON:	Never.
HOLMES:	There's the wonder of the thing! The man pervades London, the Western World even, and no one has heard of him. That's what puts him on a pinnacle in the records of crime. I tell you, Watson, in all seriousness, that if I could free society of him, I should feel that my own career had reached its summit. For years past I've continually been conscious of some power behind the malefactor, some deep organizing power which forever stands in the way of the law, and throws its shield over the wrong-doer. Again and again in cases of the most varying sorts I've felt the presence of this force. I've endeavoured to break through the veil which shrouded it, and at last the time came when I seized my thread and followed it, until it led me, after a thousand cunning windings, to ex-Professor Moriarty of mathematical celebrity.
WATSON:	Holmes, this... this idea of a "criminal mastermind"... you seem so certain, but-
HOLMES:	(LOSING PATIENCE) He's the Napoleon of crime, Watson! He is the organizer of half that is evil and of nearly all that is undetected in this great city. He's a genius, a philosopher, an abstract thinker. He sits motionless, like a spider in the centre of its web, but that web has a thousand radiations, and he knows well every quiver of each of them. Oh, his agents may be caught, but he... he is never so much as suspected. This was the organization which I deduced, Watson, and which I devoted my whole energy to exposing.
WATSON:	And is that how you acquired that hand injury? May I see?
HOLMES:	As you see, it's not an airy nothing. On the contrary, it's solid enough for a man to break his hand over. But I've woven my net round Moriarty, and now it's ready to close. In three days - on

Monday next - the Professor, with all the principal members of his gang, will be in the hands of the police. Then will come the greatest criminal trial of the century, the clearing up of over forty mysteries, and the rope for all of them. If I could have done this without his knowledge, all would have been well. But he was too wily for that. This morning, I was sitting in my room in Baker Street, when the door opened and Professor Moriarty stood before me.

WATSON: The man himself!

HOLMES: My nerves are fairly proof, Watson, but I must confess to a start when I saw the very man who'd been so much in my thoughts standing there on my thresh-hold. (IMITATING MORIATY) "You have less frontal development that I...

FX: FADE IN BAKER STREET BG

MORIARTY: ...than I should have expected, Mr Holmes. It is a very dangerous habit to finger loaded firearms in the pocket of one's dressing-gown.

HOLMES: My apologies.

FX: HOLMES PLACES THE GUN ON A TABLE

MORIARTY: You evidently don't now me.

HOLMES: On the contrary, I think it is fairly evident that I do. I can spare you five minutes if you have anything to say.

MORIARTY: All I have to say has already crossed your mind.

HOLMES: Then my answer has crossed yours.

MORIARTY: You stand fast?

HOLMES: Absolutely. I will not rest until you are hanged for the murder of John Douglas.

MORIARTY: May I consult my notebook?

HOLMES:	By all means – but slowly. I should hate to have to pick up my revolver.
FX:	<u>MORIARTY TURNS OVER THE PAGES OF HIS SMALL NOTEBOOK</u>
MORIARTY:	You crossed my patch on the 4th of January. On the 23rd, you incommoded me; by the middle of February I was seriously inconvenienced by you; at the end of March I was absolutely hampered in my plans; and now, at the close of April, I find myself placed in such a position through your continual persecution that I am in positive danger of losing my liberty. The situation is becoming an impossible one.
HOLMES:	Have you any suggestion to make?
MORIARTY:	You must drop it, Mr Holmes. You really must, you know. A man of your intelligence will surely see that there can be but one outcome to this affair. It has been an intellectual treat to see the way in which you have grappled with this affair, and I say, unaffectedly, that it would be a grief to me to be forced to take any extreme measure. I assure you that it really would.
HOLMES:	Danger is part of my trade.
MORIARTY:	It is not danger, but inevitable destruction. You stand in the way not merely of an individual, but of a mighty organization, the full extent of which you, with all your cleverness, have been unable to realize. You must stand clear, Mr Holmes, or be trodden under foot. If you are instrumental in any way in bringing about my destruction, you will not be alive to enjoy your satisfaction.
HOLMES:	And we shall walk through the gates of eternity, hand in hand.
MORIARTY:	What a pretty picture that would make.
HOLMES:	Yes, wouldn't it. Do you know, I really think it might be worth it. I'm afraid that in the pleasure of this conversation I am neglecting business of importance which awaits me elsewhere.
MORIARTY:	Well, well. It seems a pity, but I've done what I could. I know every move of your game. It has been a duel between you and

me, Mr Holmes. You hope to place me in the dock. I tell you I will never stand in the dock. You hope to beat me. I tell you that you will never beat me. If you are clever enough to bring destruction upon me, rest assured that I shall do as much to you.

HOLMES: You have paid me several compliments, *Mr* Moriarty (THE "MISTER" IS INTENDED TO STING). Let me pay you one in return when I say that if I were assured of the former eventuality I would, in the interests of the public, cheerfully accept the latter.

FX: MORIARTY OPENS THE DOOR

MORIARTY: I can promise you the one...

FX: BAKER STREET BG OUT

HOLMES: ..."But not the other". That, Watson, was my singular interview with Professor Moriarty. I confess that it left an unpleasant effect upon my mind.

WATSON: Judging by your wounds, it seems this Moriarty isn't a man who lets the grass grow under his feet.

HOLMES: I was nearly run over on my way to Oxford Street this afternoon. I sprang for the foot-path and saved myself by the fraction of a second. Then, as I walked down Vere Street a brick came down from the roof of Marshall and Snelgrove's, and shattered to fragments at my feet. I spent the day at my brother Mycroft's rooms in Pall Mall, but on my way to see you, I was attacked by a rough with a bludgeon.

WATSON: You must spend the night here.

HOLMES: You might find me a dangerous guest. I'm therefore compelled to ask your permission to leave the house by some less conspicuous exit than the front door. But I have my plans laid, and all will be well. Matters have gone so far now that they can move without my help as far as the arrest goes, though my presence is necessary for a conviction.

WATSON: Hence this notion of a trip to the Continent. Well, the practice is quiet, and I have an accommodating neighbour. I should be glad to come.

HOLMES: Very well, we start tomorrow morning. These are your instructions, and I beg, my dear Watson, that you will obey them to the letter, for you are now playing a double-handed game with me against the cleverest rogue and the most powerful syndicate of criminals in Europe. Now listen!

MUSIC: <u>THRILLING UNDERCURRENT</u>

HOLMES: (NARRATING) You will despatch whatever luggage you intend to take by a trusty messenger unaddressed to Victoria tonight.

FX: <u>BUSY LONDON STREET BG</u>

HOLMES: (NARRATING) In the morning you will hail a hansom, taking neither the first nor the second which may present itself.

WATSON: (OFF-MIC) Cabbie! Cabbie, I say!

FX: <u>SPEEDING CAB</u>

HOLMES: (NARRATING) Into this hansom you will jump, and you will drive to the Strand end of the Lowther Arcade.

FX: <u>CAB OUT. AS PER DIALOG, WATSON RUNS FOR HIS LIFE</u>

WATSON: (PANTS AS HE RUNS)

HOLMES: (NARRATING, OVER RUNNING) The instant your cab stops, dash through the Arcade, timing yourself to reach the other side at a quarter-past nine. You will find a small brougham waiting close to the curb, driven by a fellow with a heavy black cloak tipped at the collar with red.

FX: <u>RUNNING OUT</u>

HOLMES: Into this you will step, and you will reach Victoria in time for the Continental express. The second first-class carriage from the front will be reserved for us.

MUSIC: <u>OUT</u>

FX:	A BUSY RAILWAY STATION
WATSON:	(SIGHS. THEN, TO HIMSELF) Holmes, where *are* you? (ALOUD) Excuse me, Porter, I don't suppose you've seen a tall man, with a nose like- no, I don't suppose you would have.
FX:	A WHISTLE BLOWS
WATSON:	(TO SELF) It's time. Holmes, please don't say Moriarty got to you after all.
FX:	WATSON OPENS THE DOOR TO THE TRAIN
WATSON:	(TO SELF) I've always followed your instructions to the letter – second first-class carriage from the front... and may God forgive me if I'm making a mistake.
FX:	WATSON CLOSES THE DOOR, CUTTING OUT THE RAILWAY BG
WATSON:	Er... excuse me, Padre, but I'm afraid this carriage is engaged.
HOLMES:	(AS THE GENIAL ELDERLY ITALIAN PRIEST, DRONES ON IN BARELY COMPREHENSIBLE ITALIAN)
WATSON:	(LOUDLY, AS IF THAT WILL HELP) I said, this carriage is reserved.
HOLMES:	(MORE ITALIAN MUMBLINGS)
WATSON:	Forgive me, but I don't speak- whatever language it is you're speaking!
HOLMES:	(AS HIMSELF) My dear Watson, won't you even condescend to say good morning?
WATSON:	(RELIEVED) Holmes! Good grief, you startled me!
FX:	THE TRAIN BEGINS TO PULL OUT
HOLMES:	Every precaution is still necessary, which is why I adopted this disguise. I have reason to think they're hot upon our trail. Look,

look, there's Moriarty himself.

MORIARTY: (FAINTLY, MUFFLED BY THE DOOR AND THE SOUND OF
                 THE TRAIN) Hooolmes!

HOLMES: I think he wants the guard to stop the train – too late, alas. (A
                 SIGH OF RELIEF) You see, Watson, with all our precautions,
                 we've cut it rather fine. They've evidently been watching you.
                 You couldn't have made any slip in coming?

WATSON: I did exactly what you advised.

HOLMES: Did you recognize your coachman?

WATSON: No.

HOLMES: It was my brother.

WATSON: Mycroft!

HOLMES: It's an advantage to get about in such a case without taking a
                 mercenary into your confidence. Have you seen the morning
                 paper?

WATSON: The morning paper? No.

HOLMES: You haven't seen about Baker Street, then?

WATSON: What about Baker Street?

HOLMES: They set fire to our rooms last night.

WATSON: Mrs Hudson-

HOLMES: Is safe, Watson. No great harm was done.

WATSON: Good grief. At least we've shaken Moriarty off now.

HOLMES: My dear Watson, the Professor is quite on the same intellectual
                 plane as myself. He has a magnificent brain – I should like to
                 present it, pickled in alcohol, to the London Medical Society.
                 You do not imagine that if I were the pursuer I should allow

313

myself to be baffled by so slight an obstacle. Why, then, should you think so meanly of him?

WATSON: What will he do?

HOLMES: What I should do - engage a special.

WATSON: Which will be too late.

HOLMES: By no means. This train stops at Canterbury - there's always at least a quarter of an hour's delay at the boat. He'll catch us there.

WATSON: Holmes, this is intolerable! One would think *we* were the criminals. We should have him arrested on his arrival.

HOLMES: It would be to ruin the work of three months. We'd get the big fish, but the smaller would dart right and left out of the net. On Monday we'll have them all. No, an arrest is inadmissible.

WATSON: What, then?

HOLMES: We get out at Canterbury. Then we make a cross-country journey to Newhaven, and so over to Dieppe. Moriarty will again do what I should do. He'll get on to Paris, mark down our luggage, and wait for two days at the depot. In the meantime, we shall treat ourselves to a couple of carpet-bags, encourage the manufacturers of the countries through which we travel, and make our way at our leisure into Switzerland, via Luxembourg and Basle.

FX: BRING UP SOUND OF TRAIN, THEN OUT

FIRST COMMERCIAL

MUSIC: UNDERCURRENT

WATSON: (READING) "It is with a heavy heart that I take up my pen to write these the last words in which I shall ever record the singular gifts by which my friend Mr Sherlock Holmes was distinguished."

MUSIC: STOPS ABRUPTLY

314

FX:	WATSON CLOSES THE MAGAZINE
LESTRADE:	That's a wonderful way of putting it. I wish I had your gift for words, Doctor.
WATSON:	I almost couldn't bring myself to write it, Lestrade. But then *Colonel* Moriarty attempted to defend his brother's memory in print... and I just had to let the truth be known.
LESTRADE:	I could never bring myself to read this issue of the *Strand* at the time. All I know is what you've told me so far.
WATSON:	Well, we alighted from the train at Canterbury as Holmes planned, only to find that we'd have to wait an hour before we could get a train to Newhaven.
MD:	IT'S A COUNTRY RAILWAY STATION, SO NATURE SOUNDS, BUT HOLMES & WATSON'S FOOTSTEPS ON CONCRETE
HOLMES:	How are you bearing up, Watson?
WATSON:	I was just wondering where our luggage is by now.
HOLMES:	Watson, look.
FX:	IN THE FAR BG, A TRAIN IS APPROACHING
HOLMES:	Already, you see.
WATSON:	Holmes, we have to hide somewhere. Over here!
FX:	THE TRAIN PASSES, THEN FADES INTO THE DISTANCE
HOLMES:	There *are* limits to our friend's intelligence.
WATSON:	I wonder what he would have done if he had overtaken us?
HOLMES:	Killed me. Or possibly both of us. Now, should we take a premature lunch here, or run our chance of starving before we reach the buffet at Newhaven?
FX:	RAILWAY STATION OUT

MUSIC:	UNDERCURRENT
WATSON:	(NARRATING) We made our way to Brussels that night and spent two days there, moving on the third day as far as Strasbourg. On the Monday morning Holmes had telegraphed to the London police, and in the evening we found a reply waiting for us at our hotel.
HOLMES:	He's escaped.
WATSON:	Moriarty?
HOLMES:	I think you'd better return to England, Watson. This man's occupation is gone. He is lost if he returns to London. If I read his character right, he'll devote his whole energies to revenging himself upon me. He said as much in our short interview, and I fancy that he meant it. I should certainly recommend you to return to your practice.
WATSON:	I'm an old campaigner, Holmes... as well as an old friend. I'm hardly likely to abandon you now.
HOLMES:	(AFTER A PAUSE) Very well, then. But I warn you - you will find me a dangerous companion now.
WATSON:	(NARRATING) That night we resumed our journey and were well on our way to Geneva. For a charming week, we wandered up the Valley of the Rhone, and then by way of Interlaken, to Meiringen. It was a lovely trip, the dainty green of the spring below, the virgin white of the winter above; but it was clear to me that never for one instant did Holmes forget the shadow which lay across him. I could tell by his quick glancing eyes and his sharp scrutiny of every face that passed us, that he was well convinced that, walk where we would, we could not walk ourselves clear of the danger which was dogging our footsteps. Once, as we walked along the border of the melancholy Daubensee...
MUSIC:	OUT
FX:	OUTDOOR BG

HOLMES:	I think that I may go so far as to say, Watson, that I have not lived wholly in vain. If my record were closed tonight I could survey it with equanimity. The air of London is the sweeter for my presence. In over a thousand cases, I'm not aware that I have ever used my powers upon the wrong side.
WATSON:	I should certainly say not!
HOLMES:	But of late... I've been tempted to look into the problems furnished by nature rather than those more superficial ones for which our artificial state of society is responsible.
WATSON:	By nature?
HOLMES:	Oh, we have much to learn from the bees, old fellow. Your memoirs will draw to an end, Watson, upon the day that I crown my career by the capture or extinction of the most dangerous and capable criminal in Europe.
WATSON:	Holmes, surely you're not thinking of retiring?
HOLMES:	If I could be assured that society was freed from Professor Moriarty, I'd cheerfully bring my own career to a-
FX:	A ROCKFALL, SOME DISTANCE AWAY
HOLMES:	Watson, look out!
FX:	A LARGE ROCK LANDS NEARBY
WATSON:	Holmes, are you all right? Do you see anything?
HOLMES:	No. (A PAUSE. THEN, A WEAK ATTEMPT TO BRUSH IT OFF) I'm sure it's nothing to worry about.
WATSON:	"Nothing to worry about"? We were nearly flattened!
HOLMES:	Oh yes, my guide book says such fall of stones are common in the spring-time in this spot. In a way we're quite lucky – the complete tourist experience.
FX:	OUTDOOR BG OUT

MUSIC: UNDERCURRENT

WATSON: (NARRATING) It was on the 3rd of May that we reached the little village of Meiringen, where we put up at the Englischer Hof. Our landlord was Peter Steiler the elder.

MUSIC: OUT

FX: BUSY DINING ROOM

STEILER: If you are heading for Rosenlaui, gentlemen, you must on no account to miss the falls of Reichenbach.

HOLMES: Reichenbach, eh?

STEILER: At this time of year, the torrent will be swollen by the melting snow. It plunges into a tremendous abyss, and the spray rolls up like the smoke from a burning house.

WATSON: Your English is excellent, Herr Steiler.

STEILER: I served for three years as waiter at the Grosvenor Hotel in London, Herr Doctor.

HOLMES: What do you say, Watson? A slight detour to Reichenbach Falls?

WATSON: I don't see why not.

STEILER: Be aware, though, the path has been cut half-way round the fall to afford a complete view - it ends abruptly, so you must return the way you came.

HOLMES: Unless you were to throw yourself into the chasm, of course.

STEILER: Please don't do that, Herr Holmes – I would never forgive myself. And you haven't paid your bill.

BG: OUT

FX: THE FALLS ROAR

HOLMES: Quite a spectacle, eh, Watson?

WATSON:	Incredible! Steiler didn't do it justice! It's immense! A fearful place. Don't look down, old chap, it could turn a man giddy.
HOLMES:	I believe my nerves can stand it, Doctor.
WATSON:	I wish I could say the same.
BOY:	(IN BG, APPROACHING) Doctor! Dr Watson!
HOLMES:	What's this?
WATSON:	Seems to be for me. Just wait a moment, Holmes.
FX:	WATSON WALKS DOWN THE PATH
WATSON:	Yes, what is it? A message for me?
FX:	AFTER A MOMENT, WATSON RETURNS TO HOLMES
HOLMES:	A medical emergency?
WATSON:	Yes. It's a note from Herr Steiler – it seems an English lady staying in the hotel is in the last stage of consumption.
HOLMES:	I saw no English lady.
WATSON:	She arrived just after we set out for the Falls, apparently. Steiler says the lady absolutely refuses to see a Swiss physician.
HOLMES:	Watson, you must go.
WATSON:	Holmes, if you're still in danger...
HOLMES:	The appeal cannot be ignored, old fellow. You can't refuse the request of a fellow-countrywoman dying in a strange land. I'll stay here at the Falls for a while, then walk over to Rosenlaui.
WATSON:	Very well. I'll join you there in the evening. Goodbye, Holmes.
FX:	WATSON DEPARTS
HOLMES:	Goodbye, Watson. (PAUSE) Goodbye.

FX:	FADE FALLS INTO COUNTRY BG. WATSON WALKS RAPIDLY TOWARDS MIC.
WATSON:	(APPROACHING) I trust she's no worse, Herr Steiler.
STEILER:	(BAFFLED) *Who* is no worse, Doctor?
FX:	WATSON STOPS ABRUPTLY, PULLS OUT THE NOTE
WATSON:	You didn't write this? There is no sick Englishwoman in the hotel?
STEILER:	Nein. But it has the hotel mark upon it! Ha, it must have been written by the Englishman who came in after you had gone. He said-
FX:	WATSON HURRIES AWAY AT A MAD DASH
STEILER:	Dr Watson!
FX:	FADE THRU TO THE FALLS
WATSON:	(NARRATING) It was two hours before I found myself at the fall of Reichenbach once more. The sight of Holmes' Alpine-stock, leaning against a rock, turned me cold and sick. He had not gone to Rosenlaui. He had remained on that narrow path, with sheer wall on one side and sheer drop on the other, until his enemy had overtaken him.
MUSIC:	UNDERCURRENT
WATSON:	(NARRATING) It was, alas, only too easy to read what had occurred from the marks in the soft, blackish. Two lines of footmarks were clearly marked along the farther end of the path, both leading away from me. There were none returning.
WATSON:	(CALLS OUT, OFF-MIC) Holmes! Hoolmes!
WATSON:	(NARRATING) But it was destined that I should after all have a last word of greeting from my friend and comrade. Next to the Alpine-stock, I found the silver cigarette-case which Holmes used to carry. As I took it up, a small square of paper fluttered to

the ground.

THE FALLS FADES AWAY DURING HOLMES' SPEECH

HOLMES: My dear Watson, I write these few lines through the courtesy of Professor Moriarty, who awaits my convenience for the final discussion of those questions which lie between us. He has been giving me a sketch of the methods by which he avoided the English police and kept himself informed of our movements. They certainly confirm the very high opinion which I formed of his abilities. I am pleased to think that I shall be able to free society from any further effects of his presence, though I fear that it is at a cost which will give pain to my friends, and especially, my dear Watson, to you. I have already explained to you, however, that my career had in any case reached its crisis, and that no possible conclusion to it could be more congenial to me than this. Indeed, if I may make a full confession to you, I was quite convinced that the letter from Meiringen was a hoax, and I allowed you to depart on that errand under the persuasion that some development of this sort would follow. I made every disposition of my property before leaving England, and handed it to my brother Mycroft. Pray give my greetings to Mrs Watson, and believe me to be, my dear fellow, very sincerely yours, Sherlock Holmes.

MUSIC: OUT

LESTRADE: The local police were summoned, of course?

WATSON: Of course, Lestrade. And their conclusions matched my own - that a personal contest between the two men ended, as it could hardly fail to end in such a situation, in their reeling over the Reichenbach Falls, locked in each other's arms.

LESTRADE: There was no funeral for either man – the bodies were never recovered?

WATSON: No. No, it was absolutely hopeless. There, deep down in that dreadful cauldron of swirling water and seething foam, will lie for all time the most dangerous criminal and the foremost champion of the law.

LESTRADE:	(AFTER AN AWKWARD PAUSE) Well, Doctor, I suppose I must, er, be getting back to the Yard. There'll be wondering what's happened to me.
WATSON:	Yes, I apologise for keeping you from your duties, Inspector.
LESTRADE:	Not at all, Doctor, not at all. I've rather enjoyed talking about old times. (HESITANTLY) Er, I was just wondering... Mr Holmes' old pipes...
WATSON:	I'm sure he would have wanted you to have one, Lestrade.
LESTRADE:	I wouldn't mind... Thank-you, Dr Watson.
WATSON:	The black clay? You've picked a very old one.
LESTRADE:	(DEFENSIVELY) It's the one I want.
FX:	LESTRADE OPENS THE DOOR
LESTRADE:	(FONDLY) It's the one I remember best. He really was quite extraordinary, wasn't he?
WATSON:	He was the best and the wisest man whom I have ever known.
LESTRADE:	Yes. Well, I'm sorry to say, the Adair case won't wait any longer. Although, confidentially, our old friend would probably have cleared it up in half an hour. Goodbye, Doc- oof!
HOLMES:	(AS THE ELDERLY BOOKSELLER) Please be careful, young man.
LESTRADE:	Visitor for you, Dr Watson.
WATSON:	Call again, Lestrade.
FX:	DOOR CLOSES
WATSON:	Please, take a seat, sir. My maid should have told you I'm not seeing any patients today, but if it's an emergency- Do I know you?

HOLMES:	*Do* you, Doctor?
WATSON:	Yes... Yes, you're the bookseller I bumped into this morning in Park Lane!
HOLMES:	You're surprised to see me.
WATSON:	I confess that I am.
HOLMES:	Well, I've a conscience, sir, and wished to tell you that if I was a bit gruff in my manner there wasn't any harm meant, and that I'm much obliged to you for picking up my books. It just so happened that I heard you give your address to the cab driver, and I thought to myself, I'll just go and see that kind gentleman.
WATSON:	You make too much of a trifle. May I ask how you knew who I was?
HOLMES:	Well, sir, if it isn't too great a liberty, I'm a neighbour of yours. You'll find my little bookshop at the corner of Church Street, and very happy to see you, I'm sure. Maybe you collect yourself, sir...
FX:	AS HE TALKS, HE PLACES THE BOOKS ON THE TABLE
HOLMES:	Here's *British Birds*, Catullus... *The Holy War* - a bargain every one of them.
WATSON:	Well, I don't really need-
HOLMES:	With five volumes you could just fill that gap on that second shelf. It looks untidy, does it not, sir?
WATSON:	Where? (SLIGHTLY OFF-MIC) I don't see- (CLOSE TO MIC AGAIN, GASPS)
HOLMES:	(AS HIMSELF) Watson, would you have any objection to my smoking a cigarette in your consulting room?
WATSON:	(STUNNED) Holmes! Ho-
FX:	WATSON HITS THE FLOOR IN A DEAD FAINT

HOLMES:	My dear Watson! I had no idea you'd be so affected!

SECOND COMMERCIAL

WATSON:	(GROANS)
HOLMES:	Watson... Watson... I owe you a thousand apologies, old fellow.
WATSON:	Holmes! Is it- Is it really you?
HOLMES:	Let me help you up.
WATSON:	Thank-you. You're not a spirit, anyhow!
HOLMES:	(LAUGHS)
WATSON:	I can hardly believe my eyes! Good heavens... to think that you - you of all men... My dear chap, I'm- I'm overjoyed to see you. Sit down, please, and tell me how you succeeded in climbing out of that awful abyss?
HOLMES:	I had no serious difficulty in getting out of it, Watson, for the very simple reason that I was never in it.
WATSON:	You... you were never in it?
HOLMES:	No, I was never in it. (A SATISFIED SIGH) I'm glad to stretch myself. It's no joke when a tall man has to take a foot off his stature for several hours on end.
WATSON:	(IMPATIENTLY) Holmes!
HOLMES:	Are you sure you're really fit to discuss things, Watson? I've given you a serious shock by my unnecessarily dramatic reappearance.
WATSON:	I'm all right, but please, Holmes! You were never in that chasm, you said?
HOLMES:	Oh, I had little doubt I'd come to the end of my career when I perceived the somewhat sinister figure of the late Professor Moriarty standing upon the narrow pathway which led to safety.

I obtained his courteous permission to write the short note which you afterwards received. Moriarty knew the game was up, and was only anxious to revenge himself upon me.

FX: WE'RE BACK AT THE FALLS. HOLMES AND MORIARTY TRADE BLOWS, JUST AS THEY DID IN *THE MORIARTY RESURRECTION*

HOLMES: (NARRATING, OVER THE FIGHT) We tottered together upon the brink of the fall. I have some knowledge, however, of baritsu, or the Japanese system of wrestling, which has more than once been very useful to me. I slipped through his grip, and he with a horrible scream kicked madly for a few seconds and clawed the air with both his hands. But for all his efforts, he couldn't get his balance, and over he went.

MORIARTY: (SCREAMS AS FALLS)

FX: IN THE FAR, FAR DISTANCE, MORIARTY'S BODY STRIKES A ROCK WITH A SICKENING CRUNCH, THEN HITS THE WATER WITH A BARELY-AUDIBLE SPLASH. REICHENBACH FALLS OUT

HOLMES: The instant the Professor disappeared, it struck me what a really extraordinarily lucky chance Fate had placed in my way.

WATSON: What?

HOLMES: I knew that Moriarty was not the only man who had sworn my death. But if all the world was convinced that I was dead these men would lay themselves open, and sooner or later I could destroy them. I'd thought this all out before Professor Moriarty had reached the bottom of the Reichenbach Fall.

WATSON: But- but the tracks! I saw them with my own eyes! Two went down the path and none returned!

HOLMES: Ah, yes. I examined the rocky wall behind me. A few small footholds presented themselves, and there was some indication of a ledge. It seemed to me best that I should risk the climb.

WATSON: You might have reversed your boots!

HOLMES:	I might - but the sight of three sets of tracks in one direction would certainly have suggested a deception.
FX:	FADE FALLS BACK IN. HOLMES CLAMBERS UP THE SLIPPERY ROCKS.
HOLMES:	(GRUNTS AND GASPS AS HE CLIMBS)
HOLMES:	(NARRATING, OVER FALLS AND HIS OWN EXERTIONS IN FLASHBACK) I am not a fanciful person, Watson, but I give you my word that I seemed to hear Moriarty's voice screaming at me out of the abyss.
MORIARTY:	(SOMEHOW, CRIES OF "HOLMES!" ARE BLENDED WITH THE ROAR OF THE FALLS IN SUCH A WAY THAT THE LISTENER CAN'T BE CERTAIN WHETHER THEY'RE ACTUALLY HEARING IT – I'M ASKING A LOT, I KNOW)
HOLMES:	(NARRATING) More than once, as tufts of grass came out in my hand or my foot slipped in the wet notches of the rock, I thought I was lost. But I struggled upwards, and at last I reached a ledge several feet deep and covered with soft green moss, where I could lie unseen in the most perfect comfort.
FX:	AS PER DIALOG, HOLMES COLLAPSES ON THE GRASS
HOLMES:	(GASPS)
WATSON:	(FAR OFF-MIC) Holmes! Hoolmes!
HOLMES:	(CALLS OUT) Wa- (CAN'T BRING HIMSELF TO SAY IT. THEN, IN A WHISPER) Watson...
HOLMES:	(NARRATING) There I was stretched when you, my dear Watson, and the Swiss police were investigating in the most sympathetic and inefficient manner the circumstances of my death. At last, when you had all formed your inevitable and totally erroneous conclusions, you departed for the hotel and I was left alone. I imagined I'd reached the end of my adventures, but there were surprises still in store for me.
FX:	A SHOT PINGS OFF THE ROCKS

326

HOLMES:	(NARRATING) Moriarty had not been alone. A confederate - and one glance had told me how dangerous a man that confederate was - had kept guard while the Professor had attacked me. He'd witnessed his employer's death and had waited, endeavouring to succeed where his comrade had failed. Scrambling down onto the path was a hundred times more difficult than getting up, but I had no time to think of the danger...
FX:	HOLMES IS WORKING HIS WAY ALONG THE ROCKS AGAIN, BUT AT A MORE FRANTIC PACE THIS TIME
HOLMES:	(HIS GRUNTS AND GROANS ARE TINGED WITH DISTRESS)
FX:	ANOTHER SHOT! HOLMES LOSES HIS GRIP AND...
HOLMES:	(CRIES OUT, BUT THE CRY IS CUT SHORT AS...)
FX:	HOLMES HITS THE PATH BELOW
HOLMES:	Oof!
FX:	FADE OUT FALLS
HOLMES:	It was by the blessing of God I that landed, torn and bleeding, upon the path. I took to my heels, did ten miles over the mountains in the darkness, and a week later I found myself in Florence with the certainty that no one in the world knew what had become of me.
WATSON:	And what *did* become of you? Where have you been all this time?
HOLMES:	I travelled for two years in Tibet, and amused myself by visiting Lhassa and spending some days with the head Lama. You may have read of the remarkable explorations of a Norwegian named Sigerson, but I'm sure that it never occurred to you that you were receiving news of your friend. I then passed through Persia, looked in at Mecca, and paid a short but interesting visit to the Khalifa at Khartoum, the results of which I've communicated to the Foreign Office. I then spent some months researching coal-

tar derivatives in a laboratory at Montpelier. All this time, I had only one confidant - my brother Mycroft.

WATSON: (OUTRAGED) Mycroft!

HOLMES: It was from him I obtained the money I needed.

WATSON: Holmes - *Mycroft!*

HOLMES: I owe you many apologies, my dear Watson, but it was all-important that it should be thought I was dead, and it's quite certain that you would not have written so convincing an account of my unhappy end had you not yourself thought that it was true.

WATSON: (BEGRUDGINGLY) Possibly...

HOLMES: Several times during the last three years, I've taken up my pen to write to you, but always I feared lest your affectionate regard for me should tempt you to some indiscretion which would betray my secret. I wished I'd been here to offer you support following the death of your wife.

WATSON: How did you- Of course, Mycroft. It was good of him to attend the funeral. He didn't even know Mary...

HOLMES: Work is the best antidote for sorrow, my dear Watson. And I have a piece of work tonight which, if we can bring it to a successful conclusion, will in itself justify a man's life on this planet.

WATSON: (STILL SULLEN) Go on...

HOLMES: You'll see and hear enough before morning. We have three years of the past to discuss. When I read of this very remarkable Park Lane Mystery, I came over at once to London, called in my own person at Baker Street, threw Mrs Hudson into violent hysterics, and found that Mycroft had repaired my rooms and preserved my papers. So it was, my dear Watson, that at two o'clock today I found myself in my old arm-chair in my own old room, and only wishing that I could have seen my old friend Watson in the other chair which he has so often adorned.

WATSON: Holmes I've never been more elated... or more furious in my life.

	I thought never to see you again.
HOLMES:	Yes, I know. But here we are, together again – Sherlock Holmes and faithful, reliable Dr Watson! And, if I may ask for your co-operation, we have a hard and dangerous night's work in front of us. Will you come with me tonight? (PAUSE) Watson?
WATSON:	When you like and where you like.
HOLMES:	(LAUGHS) Splendid! Just like the old days. Are those my pipes?
WATSON:	Yes.
HOLMES:	It's been too long since I had a decent smoke. Where the devil's my black clay? Oh, never mind.
MUSIC:	BRIDGE
FX:	A QUIET LONDON STREET
WATSON:	Holmes, what is this place?
HOLMES:	Shh!
FX:	HOLMES TURNS A KEY IN A LOCK. A DOOR OPENS.
HOLMES:	Come inside.
FX:	THEY ENTER. HOLMES CLOSES THE DOOR BEHIND THEM. STREET BG OUT.
WATSON:	This place is completely deserted.
HOLMES:	Still I urge caution. Upstairs, if you please. Watch out for the fourth stair from the bottom – it creaks.
FX:	THEY GO UP THE STAIRS
HOLMES:	Now – look out of the window. Do you know where we are?
WATSON:	Surely that's Baker Street!

HOLMES:	Exactly. We're in Camden House, opposite our own old quarters.
WATSON:	But why?
HOLMES:	Because it commands so excellent a view of that picturesque pile. Might I trouble you, my dear Watson, to draw a little nearer to the window, taking every precaution not to show yourself, and then to look at our rooms?
MUSIC:	SINISTER UNDERCURRENT
WATSON:	Great Scott!
HOLMES:	Well?
WATSON:	Holmes – it's you!
HOLMES:	I'm glad to see my three years of absence have entirely taken away my power to surprise you. I trust that age doth not wither nor custom stale my infinite variety. It really is rather like me, is it not?
WATSON:	It's marvellous! I'd be prepared to swear that dummy *was* you.
HOLMES:	The credit is due to Monsieur Oscar Meunier, of Grenoble, who spent some days in doing the moulding. The rest I arranged myself during my visit to Baker Street this afternoon.
WATSON:	But why?
HOLMES:	Because, my dear Watson, I had the strongest possible reason for wishing certain people to think I'm in my rooms when I'm really elsewhere.
WATSON:	You thought the rooms were being watched?
HOLMES:	No, I *knew* they were being watched.
WATSON:	By whom?
HOLMES:	By my old enemy, Watson,whose leader lies in the Reichenbach Falls. Only he knew I was still alive. Sooner or later, he believed

I'd come back to my rooms. I recognised his sentinel this
morning - a harmless enough fellow, Parker by name.

WATSON: The garrotter?

HOLMES: You remember! I care nothing for him, but I care a great deal for
the much more formidable person behind him, the bosom friend
of Moriarty, the most cunning and dangerous criminal in
London. That is the man who is after me tonight, Watson, and
that is the man who is quite unaware that *we* are after *him*.

MUSIC: OUT

WATSON: Holmes... the dummy has moved!

HOLMES: Of course it's moved! Am I such a farcical bungler, Watson, that
I should erect an obvious dummy and expect that some of the
sharpest men in Europe would be deceived by it?

WATSON: But how-

HOLMES: Mrs Hudson is under instructions to make some change in the
figure every quarter of an hour. She works it from the front so
that her shadow may never be-

FX: FROM FAR OFF, THE DOOR TO THE STREET OPENS

HOLMES: Ah!

FX: MORAN COMES UP THE STAIRS

HOLMES: (IN A WHISPER) Not a sound, Watson.

FX: MORAN ARRIVES, PLACES A CASE ON THE FLOOR. HE
OPENS THE WINDOW. FAINT STREET BG. MORAN
OPENS THE CASE AND BEGINS ASSEMBLING HIS RIFLE.

MORAN: (A LONG EXHALATION)

FX: THE FIRES THE AIR-RIFLE. ACROSS THE STREET, THE
WINDOW SHATTERS.

331

MORAN:	Goodbye, Mr Holmes.
HOLMES:	Good evening, Colonel Moran!
MORAN:	What the-
HOLMES:	"Journeys end in lovers' meetings," as the old play says. I don't think I've had the pleasure of seeing you since you favoured me with those attentions as I lay on the ledge above the Reichenbach Fall.
MORAN:	(ROARS)
HOLMES:	Watson, grab him!
FX:	A STRUGGLE COMMENCES
MORAN:	Let go of me, damn you!
HOLMES:	Time to call for assistance, I think.
FX:	HE BLOWS ON A POLICE WHISTLE. RUNNING FOOTSTEPS IN THE STREET, FOLLOWED BY THE DOOR DOWNSTAIRS BEING FLUNG OPEN.
LESTRADE:	(OFF-MIC) Upstairs, men!
HOLMES:	The forces of law and order, Colonel. I think it would be wise to admit defeat.
FX:	THE STRUGGLE CONCLUDES
LESTRADE:	Oh my Sunday helmet! It really *is* you, Mr Holmes!
HOLMES:	Good evening, Lestrade.
LESTRADE:	And Dr Watson...
WATSON:	(WINDED AFTER THE STRUGGLE) Lestrade.
LESTRADE:	Who've you got there, then?

MORAN:	You fiend! You cunning fiend!
HOLMES:	This, Lestrade, is Colonel Sebastian Moran, once of Her Majesty's Indian Army, and the best heavy game shot our Eastern Empire has ever produced. (TO LESTRADE) I believe I'm correct, Colonel, in saying that your bag of tigers still remains unrivalled?
MORAN:	Damn you!
HOLMES:	I wonder that my very simple stratagem could deceive an old shikari like you. Have you never tethered a young kid under a tree, lain above it with your rifle, and waited for the bait to bring up your tiger? This empty house is my tree and *you* are my tiger.
MORAN:	You may or may not have just cause for arresting me, Mr... Lestrade, was it? But there can be no reason why I should submit to the gibes of this person. If I'm in the hands of the law let things be done in a legal way.
LESTRADE:	Fair enough, I suppose. Have you anything further to say before we go, Colonel?
MORAN:	Only to ask what charge you intend to prefer?
LESTRADE:	What charge, sir? Why, of course, the attempted murder of Mr Sherlock Holmes, of course!
HOLMES:	Not so, Lestrade. I do not propose to appear in the matter at all. To you, and to you only, belongs the credit of the remarkable arrest which you have effected. Yes, Lestrade, I congratulate you! You've got him.
LESTRADE:	Got him? Got who?
WATSON:	"Got *whom*", Inspector. (TO HOLMES) Who *has* he got, Holmes?
LESTRADE:	The man that the whole force has been seeking in vain - the murderer of the Honourable Ronald Adair.
WATSON:	Adair? Moran killed Adair?

LESTRADE: How? Dr Watson and I were agreed that the crime was almost impossible.

HOLMES: Because you imagined that the crime was committed with a revolver, and no such weapon could fire accurately over so great a distance. But in fact, the Colonel used *this*-

FX: <u>HOLMES PICKS UP THE RIFLE AND GIVES IT TO LESTRADE</u>

HOLMES: Take good care of it, Lestrade, it's the only one of its kind in the world.

LESTRADE: You can trust us to look after it, Mr Holmes. (THOUGHTFULLY) Looks like an air rifle.

HOLMES: An admirable and unique weapon - noiseless and of tremendous power. Von Herder, the blind German mechanic, constructed it to the order of the late Professor Moriarty. I've been aware of its existence for years, though I never had the opportunity of handling it. I commend very specially to your attention, Lestrade, the bullets.

FX: <u>LESTRADE OPENS THE BOLT</u>

LESTRADE: Expanding revolver bullets!

HOLMES: And it was with an expanding bullet, fired from this specially-adapted an air-gun, that he was able to shoot Adair through the open window of the second-floor front of No 427, Park Lane. *That* is the charge, Lestrade.

MORAN: Moriarty was too easy on you. I should've shot you down the second you became a nuisance.

LESTRADE: Be sure to mention that at the trial, Colonel. Let's be going. (TO HOLMES) It's good to have you back in London, Mr Holmes.

HOLMES: I thought you might benefit from a little unofficial help. Three undetected murders in one year – it won't do, Lestrade. But you handled the Molesey Mystery with less than your usual- you handled it fairly well.

LESTRADE:	Thank-you, sir.
HOLMES:	Oh, and Lestrade..?
LESTRADE:	Yes, Mr Holmes?
HOLMES:	You can keep the pipe.
LESTRADE:	(AFTER A BEAT) Right.
MUSIC:	STING

THIRD COMMERCIAL

FX:	HOLMES THROWS OPEN A DOOR
HOLMES:	Well?
WATSON:	Well, apart from the bullet-hole in the window and the fragments of shattered bust all over the floor... Baker Street seems just as it was, Holmes.
HOLMES:	Hopefully, you can endure the draught. Help yourself to a cigar, if you require warmth.
WATSON:	(CHUCKLES) If anything, it's slightly tidier than I remember.
HOLMES:	Blame that on Mrs Hudson. I shall soon restore it to its original state.
WATSON:	The old chemical corner... your scrap-books and books of reference...
HOLMES:	Moriarty would've been glad to see them burned.
WATSON:	So would many a London criminal! Your violin...
FX:	WATSON PLUCKS AT THE VIOLIN STRINGS
HOLMES:	...The pipe rack-

HOLMES:	Empty at present, alas.
WATSON:	I'll bring them round in the morning. Look at this – even the old Persian slipper, and- yes, filled with tobacco! And- ah! Here it is!
HOLMES:	What?
WATSON:	*This* - it passed right through the dummy's head and flattened itself on the wall.
HOLMES:	A soft revolver bullet. There's genius in that, for who would expect to find such a thing fired from an air-gun. And now, Watson, let me see you in your old chair once more, for there are several points I should like to discuss with you.
FX:	WATSON SITS...
WATSON:	(...WITH A SATISFIED SIGH)
HOLMES:	The old shikari's nerves have not lost their steadiness nor his eyes their keenness. Plumb in the middle of the back of the head and smack through the brain. Colonel Moran was the best shot in India, and I expect there are few better in London. Have you heard the name?
WATSON:	Lestrade mentioned that poor Adair played cards with Moran at the Bagatelle Club on the day of his murder. Beyond that, I know nothing of the fellow.
HOLMES:	Well, well, such is fame! Let me just give me down my index of biographies...
FX:	HOLMES PULLS A BOOK FROM THE SHELF AND BEGINS FLIPPING THROUGH IT
HOLMES:	My collection of M's is a fine one. Moriarty himself is enough to make any letter illustrious, of course... and here is Morgan the poisoner, and Merridew of abominable memory, and Mathews, who knocked out my left canine in the waiting-room at Charing Cross, and, finally, our friend of tonight. If you please, Watson.
FX:	HE DROPS THE BOOK IN WATSON'S LAP

WATSON: (READS) "Moran, Sebastian Aloysius, Colonel. Formerly 1st Bengalore Pioneers. Born London, 1840. Son of Sir Augustus Moran, C.B., British Minister to Persia. Educated Eton and Oxford. Served in Jowaki Campaign, Afghan Campaign, Sherpur, Cabul... Address: Conduit Street. Clubs: The Anglo-Indian, the Tankerville, the Bagatelle Card Club.

HOLMES: And here?

FX: HOLMES TURNS OVER THE PAGE

WATSON: (READS) "The second most dangerous man in London."

FX: WATSON CLOSES THE BOOK

WATSON: This is astonishing! The man's career is that of an honourable soldier.

HOLMES: Up to a certain point he did well. He was always a man of iron nerve, and the story is still told in India how he crawled down a drain after a wounded man-eating tiger. But there are some trees, Watson, which grow to a certain height and then suddenly develop some unsightly eccentricity. You see it often in humans. I have a theory that the individual represents in his development the whole procession of his ancestors, and a sudden turn to good or evil stands for some strong influence which came into the line of his pedigree. The person becomes, as it were, the epitome of the history of his own family.

WATSON: Sounds rather fanciful, Holmes.

HOLMES: Well, I don't insist upon it. Whatever the cause, Colonel Moran began to go wrong. Without any open scandal, he made India too hot to hold him. He retired, came to London, and again acquired an evil name.

WATSON: At which point he was sought out by Moriarty, no doubt.

HOLMES: He was chief of the staff within Moriarty's organization. The Professor supplied him liberally with money and used him only in one or two very high-class jobs which no ordinary criminal could have undertaken. You may have some recollection of the

337

death of Mrs Stewart, of Lauder, in 1887.

WATSON: (STRUGGLES TO RECOLLECT) Eighty... seven?

HOLMES: No? Well, I'm sure Moran was at the bottom of it - but nothing could be proved. So cleverly was the Colonel concealed that even when the Moriarty gang was broken up we couldn't incriminate him. You remember when I called upon you in your rooms, how I put up the shutters for fear of air-guns? I knew exactly what I was doing, for I knew of the existence of that remarkable gun, and I knew also that one of the best shots in the world would be behind it. When we were in Switzerland he followed us with Moriarty.

WATSON: Then it was he who gave you that evil five minutes on the Reichenbach ledge.

HOLMES: So long as Moran was free my life would really not have been worth living. Night and day the shadow would have been over me, and sooner or later his chance must have come.

WATSON: So you read the English papers, I expect, on the lookout for any chance of laying the Colonel by the heels.

HOLMES: I could do nothing else. But I knew that sooner or later I should get him.

WATSON: Then came the death of the Honourable Ronald Adair.

HOLMES: And my chance had come at last!

WATSON: But how did you know Moran had done it?

HOLMES: Watson, Watson! Knowing what I knew, was it not certain? He played cards with the lad, he followed him home from the club, he shot him through the open window. There was not a doubt of it. The bullets alone are enough to put his head in a noose. I came over from France at once. I was seen by Parker the sentinel, who would, I knew, direct the Colonel's attention to my presence. He couldn't fail to connect my sudden return with his crime, and I was sure he'd make an attempt to get me out of the way at once, and bring round his murderous weapon for that purpose. Now, my dear Watson, does anything remain for me to explain?

WATSON: Yes. You haven't made it clear what Moran's motive was in murdering the Honourable Ronald Adair.

HOLMES: Ah! Well there, my friend, we come into those realms of conjecture where the most logical mind may be at fault. Each may form his own hypothesis upon the present evidence, and yours is as likely to be correct as mine.

WATSON: As it happens, Holmes, I *have* formed one.

HOLMES: Excellent! Then I should be pleased to hear it.

WATSON: Lestrade told me that Colonel Moran and young Adair had won a considerable amount of money at cards from Godfrey Milner and Lord Balmoral. Moran undoubtedly played foul.

HOLMES: Undoubtedly.

WATSON: I believe that on the day of the murder, Adair discovered Moran was cheating. Very likely he'd spoken to him privately, threatened to expose him unless he voluntarily resigned his membership of the club and promised not to play cards again.

HOLMES: It's unlikely that a youngster like Adair would make a hideous scandal by exposing a well-known man so much older than himself, I agree.

WATSON: The exclusion from his clubs would mean ruin to Moran, who no doubt lived by his ill-gotten card gains. (HE'S WORKING IT OUT AS HE SPEAKS) So he murdered Adair, who – *yes*! I remember now, Lestrade found piles of notes and coins in Adair's office, and a sheet of paper with the names of his fellow card-players on it. Adair was endeavouring to work out how much money he should return to them! He couldn't profit by his partner's foul play.

FX: AS HOLMES TALKS, WATSON POURS TWO GLASSES FROM A DECANTER

HOLMES: And he locked the door lest his mother and sister should surprise him and insist upon knowing what he was doing with these names and coins. I have no doubt you've hit upon the truth, Doctor. Meanwhile, come what may, Colonel Moran will trouble us no more, the famous air-gun of Von Herder will embellish the Scotland Yard Museum...

WATSON: And once again Mr Sherlock Holmes is free to devote himself to those interesting little problems which the complex life of London so plentifully presents. To you, Holmes.

HOLMES: To *us*, Watson.

FX: THEY CLINK GLASSES

MUSIC: *DANSE MACABRE*

Also from MX Publishing

Close To Holmes

A Look at the Connections Between Historical London, Sherlock Holmes and Sir Arthur Conan Doyle.

Eliminate The Impossible

An Examination of the World of Sherlock Holmes on Page and Screen.

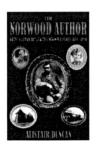

The Norwood Author

Arthur Conan Doyle and the Norwood Years (1891 - 1894) – Winner of the 2011 Howlett Literary Award (Sherlock Holmes book of the year)

In Search of Dr Watson

Wonderful biography of Dr. Watson from expert Molly Carr – 2nd edition fully updated.

www.mxpublishing.com

Arthur Conan Doyle, Sherlock Holmes and Devon

A Complete Tour Guide and Companion.

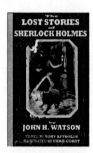

The Lost Stories of Sherlock Holmes

Eight more stories from the pen of John H Watson – compiled by Tony Reynolds.

Watsons Afghan Adventure

Fascinating biography of Watson's time in Afghanistan from US Army veteran Kieran McMullen.

Shadowfall

Sherlock Holmes, ancient relics and demons and mystic characters. A supernatural Holmes pastiche.

www.mxpublishing.com

Official Papers of The Hound of
The Baskervilles

Very unusual collection of the
original police papers from The
Hound case.

The Sign of Fear

The first adventure of the 'female
Sherlock Holmes'. A delightful fun
adventure with your favourite
supporting Holmes characters.

A Study in Crimson

The second adventure of the 'female
Sherlock Holmes' with a host of sub-
plots and new characters joining
Watson and Fanshaw

The Chronology of Arthur Conan
Doyle

The definitive chronology used by
historians and libraries worldwide.

Also From MX Publishing

Aside Arthur Conan Doyle

A collection of twenty stories from ACD's close friend Bertram Fletcher Robinson.

Bertram Fletcher Robinson

The comprehensive biography of the assistant plot producer of The Hound of The Baskervilles

Wheels of Anarchy

Reprint and introduction to Max Pemberton's thriller from 100 years ago. One of the first spy thrillers of its kind.

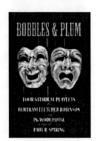

Bobbles and Plum

Four playlets from PG Wodehouse 'lost' for over 100 years – found and reprinted with an excellent commentary

www.mxpublishing.com

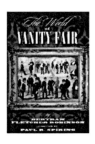

The World of Vanity Fair

A specialist full-colour reproduction of key articles from Bertram Fletcher Robinson containing of colour caricatures from the early 1900s.

Tras Las He huellas de Arthur Conan Doyle (in Spanish)

Un viaje ilustrado por Devon.

The Outstanding Mysteries of Sherlock Holmes

With thirteen Homes stories and illustrations Kelly re-creates the gas-lit, fog-enshrouded world of Victorian London

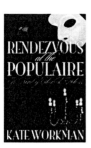

Rendezvous at The Populaire

Sherlock Holmes has retired, injured from an encounter with Moriarty. He's tempted out of retirement for an epic battle with the Phantom of the opera.

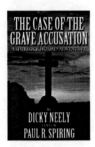
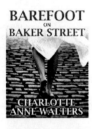

An Entirely New Country

Covers Arthur Conan Doyle's years at Undershaw where he wrote Hound of The Baskervilles. Foreword by Mark Gatiss (BBC's Sherlock).

Shadowblood

Sequel to Shadowfall, Holmes and Watson tackle blood magic, the vilest form of sorcery.

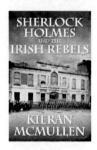

Sherlock Holmes and The Irish Rebels

It is early 1916 and the world is at war. Sherlock Holmes is well into his spy persona as Altamont.

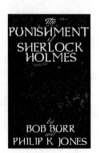

The Punishment of Sherlock Holmes

"deliberately and successfully funny"

The Sherlock Holmes Society of London

www.mxpublishing.com

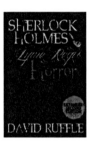

Lightning Source UK Ltd.
Milton Keynes UK
UKOW040059110212

187005UK00001BD/13/P